TERENCE
PHORMIO

TERENCE

PHORMIO

Edited by

R.H. MARTIN

Professor Emeritus in Latin
University of Leeds

Bristol Classical Press

This edition published in 2002 by
Bristol Classical Press
an imprint of
Gerald Duckworth & Co. Ltd.
61 Frith Street, London W1D 3JL
Tel: 020 7434 4242
Fax: 020 7434 4420
inquiries@duckworth-publishers.co.uk
www.ducknet.co.uk

First published in 1959
by Methuen & Co. Ltd.

A catalogue record for this book is available
from the British Library

ISBN 1 85399 633 5

Printed in Great Britain by
Booksprint

Cover illustration: Father, son and slave masks from a
marble relief found at Pompeii (drawing by Christine Hall)

Preface

Terence, once among the first Latin authors to be read in our Grammar Schools, has been unjustly neglected of late, and no commentary of any of his plays has been published in England for nearly half a century. The lively action and well-constructed plot of the *Phormio* make it worth reading for its own sake; moreover, though it lacks the subtlety of the *Adelphoe*, it is more representative of, and a better introduction to, the genre to which it belongs.

In the commentary my aim has been first to give straightforward explanation, but where points of controversy or of general interest arise, I have tried to add further helpful material. The student who comes to Terence for the first time may find the essential simplicity of Terence's Latin obscured by the initial strangeness of his colloquial idiom. For this reason I have explained in some detail, at their first occurrence, words and phrases that constantly recur, and I have allowed myself, especially in the earlier part of the commentary, more freedom to quote cross-references than would be normal in an edition of this kind. Textual questions lie outside the scope of this edition, but I have printed at the foot of each page all the instances, except those involving minor questions of punctuation and spelling, where the Oxford Text of Kauer and Lindsay has a reading different from mine.

Of printed editions I have got most help from that of Dziatzko-Hauler (Teubner: Leipzig, 1913), but since the work is out of print and in a foreign language, few references to it appear in my notes. I gratefully acknowledge the help I have had from friends and scholars, from Professor W. A. Laidlaw on questions of metre and prosody, from my colleagues Professor E. J. Wood for his comments on the Introductory Sections and Mr E. L. Harrison for his careful reading of the proofs, and from the General Editor of this series, Professor W. S. Maguinness, whose help has gone far beyond that of general criticism and encouragement. But my greatest debt is to Professor G. B. A. Fletcher of King's College, Newcastle upon Tyne; there is scarcely a page of the commentary that has not profited from his suggestions, and it would be quite impossible for me to mark in detail the improvements I owe to him. For any faults or shortcomings that remain the responsibility is mine alone.

R. H. M.

Leeds

Contents

Introduction

PLOTS AND CHARACTERS IN THE
FABULA PALLIATA

The extant plays of Roman Comedy, twenty by Plautus (d. 184 B.C.) and six by Terence, are all examples of the *fabula palliata*, translations and adaptations of Greek originals, so called because the actors wore Greek dress including the *pallium* or Greek cloak (*ἱμάτιον*). The Greek models that the authors of the *palliata* used were plays not of the Old Comedy of the fifth century B.C., but of the New Comedy[1] (of the later fourth and third century), whose most famous exponent was Menander (342/1–291/0.B.C.). New Comedy and, after it, the *palliata* make much use of stock themes and characters. Although the plays of Plautus and Terence can be enjoyed without knowledge of these stock elements, some acquaintance with them will increase appreciation of the plays. This is particularly true in the case of Terence, much of whose excellence lies in the slight and subtle alterations he makes to these traditional characters and themes.

According to Ovid (Trist. II 369):

'Every play of lively Menander has love as its theme.'[2]

If this statement is applied not only to Menander, but to the New Comedy and the *fabula palliata* in general, it can be said to convey an important half-truth. In all Terence's plays and in the majority of Plautus' the action of the play centres on the love affair of an

---

[1] 'There is no clear evidence of the use of Middle Comedy by the Romans' (Duckworth, *The Nature of Roman Comedy*, p. 24).
[2] fabula iucundi nulla est sine amore Menandri.

adulescens. But since there were few occasions in Greece when a young unmarried woman of free birth might appear outside, and since the action of these plays takes place out of doors, the relationship between the young lovers cannot play an active part in the play. Instead, the comedy evolves from the fact that the young man's love affair is threatened by some external complication, and the interest of the play lies not in the love affair itself, but in the manner in which the obstacles to its success are overcome. Among the most frequent obstacles in the path of the young lovers are parental disapproval, the existence of a rival for the hand of the young woman, and shortage of the money needed to buy her from a *leno*.[1]

An essential element in the plot of almost all *fabulae palliatae* is Misunderstanding—the failure of one or more of the characters to understand the true facts of the situation. The misunderstanding[2] may be of facts or of identity or of both; it may either arise accidentally or be deliberately contrived by one character or group of characters to deceive another character or group; where deliberate deception forms an important part of the play, the play may more specifically be described as a comedy of intrigue. As an example of a play in which the misunderstanding has arisen accidentally may be cited the *Hecyra* of Terence. All the characters are well-intentioned towards each other, but fail to find a solution to the central problem—Pamphilus' estrangement from his wife—till their misapprehensions are removed by the discovery that the father of Philumena's child is Pamphilus himself. Plautus' *Mostellaria* will serve as an example of the comedy of intrigue at its simplest. Tranio, the *seruus callidus*, carries out a series of deceptions upon the *senex*, Theopropides, so that his young master, Philolaches, can enjoy the company of his mistress,

---

[1] For the meaning of this and other Latin words describing types of character, see p. 3 f.

[2] *Epitasis* (the part of a play wherein the plot thickens) *incrementum processusque turbarum ac totius, ut ita dixerim, nodus erroris* (Euanthius *de fabula* IV. 5).

Philematium, without interruption. Frequently the themes of error and deception are combined in the same play; so, for instance, in the *Phormio* ignorance of Phanium's parentage and the deception of the *senes* both contribute to the development of the plot.

There are two notable features, each of which is common to all but one of Terence's plays. The first feature is that all the plays except the *Hecyra* have double plots, involving the love affairs of two *adulescentes*. Secondly, a determining factor in the action of all plays except the *Eunuchus* is the relationship between the *adulescens* who is in love and his father, whose opposition the son fears; thus the problems that the characters of these plays are concerned with are essentially matters affecting the family circle. It is important that the broad resemblances between the plays should be understood, lest a preoccupation with the resemblances should obscure the no less important differences between them. The following elements of plot are found in all Terence's plays except the *Hecyra*.

'Two young men, often brothers, are engaged in love affairs. One of them loves a courtesan, the other wishes to marry a young woman, who is either poor but freeborn, or ostensibly a courtesan. The father opposes his son's marriage or even wants him instead to marry the daughter of a friend or relation. The young woman turns out to be freeborn or the daughter in question, and all ends well.'

The characters who appear in the New Comedy and the *fabula palliata* are representatives of types rather than individuals. The most commonly recurring characters are those who most frequently become involved in the love affair that provides the subject matter for so many plays—members of the family of the *adulescens*, his rival (often a *miles gloriosus*), the *leno* who owns the girl he loves.

The character of the young lovers is not often clearly defined. The young men (ADVLESCENTES) are always of free birth and of respectable family. They are quick to give way to despair when any obstacle or threat to their love affair arises, and they rarely take an active part in the attempts to surmount the difficulties that confront them. On occasions they do try to give help to a friend who is suffering from similar love trouble.

The young women they love may, like the *adulescentes*, be Athenian citizens (VIRGINES, MVLIERES), or they may be courtesans (MERETRICES). Mention has already been made of the rarity with which freeborn young unmarried women could be portrayed on the stage; as a result, if the plot demands the appearance of the lady-love, she is almost always a courtesan. A common feature of New Comedy is that a young woman lives the life of a courtesan, having been exposed or kidnapped in her youth. When, in the course of the play, it is discovered that she is of freeborn Athenian parentage, the way for her marriage to a freeborn youth is open. In such cases, though she has been trained professionally as a courtesan, the playwright always makes it clear that she is still a virgin, or, if she has been seduced, her seducer is the man who eventually marries her. The practising professional courtesan, however, is normally completely mercenary in her outlook. Donatus commends Terence for his innovation in the *Hecyra* in making Bacchis a *bona meretrix*. It should be added that by their own standards the behaviour of the young men in these matters is entirely moral. Association with a courtesan never leads to marriage, and all freeborn unmarried women are chaste. The assumption is that in due course the young men will settle down and lead respectable married lives.

Since the *adulescens* rarely takes steps to help himself, in those plays where deception is necessary to advance his cause the task is assigned to a lieutenant, usually a slave of the young man's household. Such a slave, to whom the epithet *callidus* is often given (SERVVS CALLIDVS), schemes and acts on behalf of the *adulescens* with a remarkable disregard for the possible consequences to himself; he talks freely of the punishment his conduct is likely to earn for him, but does not let the prospect deter him from undertaking the intrigue. Much less frequently the slave remains loyal to his old master against the intriguing party; he is then portrayed as dull, stupid, and easy to deceive.

The SENEX of Roman Comedy usually belongs to one of three types. (1) Occasionally he may be a neighbour of the *adulescens*, and lend his assistance to the intrigue necessary for the furtherance of the love affair (e.g. Periplectomenus in Plautus' *Miles Gloriosus*). (2) In a number of cases the *senex* tries to share in his son's amorous escapades: in such cases the father usually succeeds only in making himself ridiculous, for 'there's no fool like an old fool'. (3) The *senex* is, as in the preceding type, the father of the young man whose love affair forms the point around which the play moves, but though his general attitude to his son may vary between the extremes of lenience and severity, as far as the love affair of the play is concerned, he disapproves of his son's conduct. In a comedy of errors the discovery of the true facts of the situation effects a reconciliation between father and son: in a comedy of intrigue the father may be the victim of the deception practised by the son's lieutenant. It is interesting to note the difference between Plautus and Terence in their treatment of the *senex*. Terence does not use either of the first two types [unless Chremes in the *Hautontimorumenos* is a partial example of type (1)], and, whereas Plautus will push the role of father as dupe to its uttermost limit of farce, the Terentian father, even though he may at times act foolishly, never altogether forfeits his own self-respect and his son's filial obedience.

The wife of the *senex* (MATRONA), when she figures in the play, is often an *uxor dotata*, a woman who, controlling the purse strings, dominates her household and her husband. Not infrequently she is prepared to be lenient towards her son when her husband wishes to assert his parental authority. The antipathy between husband and wife can be exaggerated till it reaches farcical limits, as in the following passage from Plautus (*Trinummus* 51–6):

CA. How's your wife? Well?
ME. Far too well.
CA. I'm delighted she's alive and well.
ME. Just like you to delight in my misfortune.
CA. I only want my friends to be in the same boat as I am.
ME. Why? How's *your* wife?
CA. Immortal. She'll live for ever.

Here again, as in the case of the *senex*, Plautus' farcical treatment of the *matrona* is quite foreign to Terence.

Of the other female roles only that of the nurse (NVTRIX) is of much importance to the plot. Like the *seruus*, she is completely devoted to her mistress (who is usually the girl whom the *adulescens* loves), but she does not (at least, in Terence) initiate comic action or intrigue. Frequently her function in the plot is to assist in the ἀναγνώρισις (recognition), which in so many cases makes a happy ending to the play possible.

Outside the family circle there are three frequently recurring roles, those of *miles gloriosus*, *leno*, and *parasitus*. All are rich in comic possibilities; the first two are often the dupes of the intrigue carried out by the agent of the *adulescens*—the *miles* when he is the rival of the young man, the *leno* when the penniless *adulescens* is in love with one of his charges.

The motto of the PARASITVS (parasite, sponger, hanger-on) is 'anywhere for a free meal'. He will endure any indignity or humiliation in the hope of an invitation to dinner. His monomania is an easy target for ridicule. Very rarely the parasite is a man of resource (e.g. in the name parts of Plautus' *Curculio* and

Terence's *Phormio*). In this case his function is very like that of the *seruus callidus*. The complex figure of Phormio is discussed in the next section.

The MILES GLORIOSVS (boastful soldier, braggart warrior) is pompous, swaggering, ever ready to relate military exploits which he never performed, and equally ready to believe that every young lady who sees him falls madly in love with him. His inflated bombast simply asks to be pricked with a pin, and usually is.

The LENO is often regarded as a pimp or pander; more accurately he is a slave dealer who owns attractive female slaves, and sells them or hires them out. His chief trait is his greed for money; he feels no compunction in breaking his word, if a more lucrative offer is made for one of his charges. He is a social outcast and the legitimate object of every kind of abuse and physical indignity. The *leno* appears only in two plays of Terence (*Phormio* and *Adelphoe*). It is worth noting that, though he is abused and, in the *Adelphoe*, manhandled, he is not, as often happens in Plautus, swindled out of the money that is due to him.

THE PLOT AND CHARACTERS OF
THE *PHORMIO*

During the absence abroad of Demipho and Chremes, two Athenian brothers, their two sons, Antipho and Phaedria, have been entrusted to the tutelage of Geta, a slave of Demipho. Geta, finding that his attempts to hold the two *adulescentes* in check bring him more kicks than halfpence, has decided to let the young men have their own way. He relates how Phaedria has become enamoured of a *citharistria* who lives nearby, while Antipho has fallen in love with a freeborn but penniless orphan (Phanium). Realizing that his father will never consent to his marriage with a dowerless orphan, Antipho has let a friendly parasite, Phormio, bring an action of *epidikasia*[1] against him.

[1] Cf. note on lines 125–6.

Phormio alleges that Antipho is Phanium's nearest relation and thus obliged by Athenian law to marry her. Needless to say, Antipho makes no attempt to refute Phormio's allegation and is compelled to marry Phanium. All this, we learn from Geta, has taken place before the action of the play begins. So far all has gone well, but Demipho's return from Cilicia is now imminent; the certainty that he will disapprove of Antipho's marriage makes Antipho and Geta, who has aided and abetted him, view the prospect of the old man's return with considerable apprehension.

After Antipho and Phaedria have appeared and each lamented his own misfortune, Geta enters post-haste with the news of Demipho's approach. Antipho is unable to steel himself to face his father and flees, leaving Phaedria and Geta to plead his cause. They fail to pacify Demipho but manage to persuade him that the chief blame rests on Phormio. Demipho sends Geta to fetch the parasite. Phormio now appears for the first time; he taunts Demipho and challenges him to try to get the court's verdict reversed. Demipho, after receiving conflicting advice from three lawyers he has brought along to help him, decides to await the return of his brother Chremes. He goes off to the harbour to find out if there is any news of him.

..While Demipho is away, Antipho returns and is reassured by Geta that his cause has been stoutly upheld during his absence. The plot now takes an important new turn. Phaedria appears with the *leno* Dorio. It transpires that Dorio, tired of waiting for Phaedria to find the money for his *citharistria*, has agreed to sell her to another customer, who is prepared to pay cash for her next day. Appeals to Dorio's compassion fail, but he eventually agrees to let Phaedria have the girl, if he can produce the money before the other customer. The task of finding the necessary funds is thrust upon the reluctant Geta, who at last agrees to try to get the money out of Demipho—on condition that he is allowed to have Phormio's services to help him carry out the scheme he has in mind.

Demipho now reappears with Chremes, who has just returned from Lemnos, where his wife has some estates. We quickly learn, however, that Chremes' visit has had another motive; by a bigamous marriage in Lemnos, which he has managed to keep secret from everyone but his brother, he has had a daughter. As she is now of marriageable age, Chremes had gone to bring her back to Athens, where he and Demipho had agreed to marry her to Antipho. But Chremes informs his brother that his journey had been unsuccessful because mother and daughter had already left Lemnos to come to search for him in Athens, and the fact that Antipho has already got himself married threatens to be a grave obstacle to their scheme. Geta now enters and tells the *senes* that he has just had a private interview with Phormio and persuaded him to accept Phanium as his wife (after she has been divorced from Antipho) for the sum of thirty minae (this is, of course, the exact sum that Phaedria requires for his *citharistria*). Demipho goes off with Geta to the forum to hand over the money to Phormio.

As Chremes stands alone on the stage, Phanium's nurse, Sophrona, comes out of Demipho's house, sees Chremes, and recognizes him as Phanium's father. Chremes goes in to meet his daughter, having first adjured Sophrona not to reveal the secret of Phanium's parentage to anyone. Shortly afterwards, while Demipho is conversing with Nausistrata, Chremes' wife, Chremes rushes excitedly out of the house and, failing at first to see his wife, almost gives away his secret. After Nausistrata has been persuaded to go back home, Chremes tells Demipho that he has found his daughter and that she is none other than the girl Antipho has already married. They both go into Demipho's house.

After Antipho and Phormio have entered separately, Geta bursts out of Demipho's house, where he has overheard by eavesdropping the astounding news that Chremes is Phanium's father. He has been sent by the *senes* to fetch Antipho and to tell him that they no longer object to his marriage to Phanium. Geta and Antipho go in together, leaving Phormio alone. In a soliloquy he announces that Geta's news will enable him to avoid having to pay back the thirty minae he has received from the *senes*. When the latter accost him and ask for the return of the money, Phormio refuses, saying that he is quite willing to carry out his promise to marry Phanium. When the *senes* rush to seize him to take him to law for the recovery of the thirty minae, he shouts for Nausistrata to come out of her house, and acquaints her with her husband's double life. He also tells Nausistrata that the money which he has got out of the old men has gone to pay for a *citharistria* with whom Phaedria is in love. Chremes' protest at his son's behaviour is cut short by Nausistrata with the remark that it ill becomes a man with *two* wives to criticize his son for having *one* mistress. Salt is rubbed in Chremes' wound when Nausistrata announces that she will leave it to her son, Phaedria, to decide whether she shall pardon her husband or not, and accedes to the request of Phormio that he be invited to dinner.

Although the main outline of the plot is straightforward, a number of passages where Terence is known or thought to have departed from his Greek original raise interesting problems. The more notable of these may be conveniently discussed in the order in which they occur in the play.

The *Phormio*, like all Terence's plays, begins with a non-dramatic prologue, which relates to the production of the Latin version of the play; therefore it cannot have existed in the Greek original. But did the Greek original have its own prologue? It has generally been held that it was normal for plays of Greek New Comedy to have an expository prologue, and that in plays involving an *anagnorisis* such a prologue was essential.[1] The

---

[1] Cf. Jachmann in Pauly-Wissowa RE VA 608-9.

question is not without interest, for the attitude of an audience forewarned of the outcome of the play is different from that of an audience kept in suspense as to how the play will develop. Duckworth (op. cit., pp. 211–18) analyses the plays of Plautus with reference to this question, and concludes that the general statement that an expository prologue was a necessity in a Greek play with an *anagnorisis* is highly questionable. In any case, the general argument would seem to prove nothing for the *Phormio*, for the *Phormio* is not, in the normal sense of the term, a play of *anagnorisis*, but of deception and intrigue. Furthermore, a knowledge of Chremes' Lemnian liaison has no relevance before the scenes immediately succeeding its first mention in 567 f. Thus whatever may be the case in Terence's other plays, for the *Phormio*, at least, it does not seem proved that Terence has excised an expository prologue from its Greek original.

Two points in Scenes i and ii of Act I deserve note: (*a*) Donatus' note on line 49 makes it fairly certain that the obscure reference there to initiation has been substituted by Terence for what was a specific reference in the Greek original to the Samothracian mysteries. If this is so, we are probably right in regarding the present passage as one example of Terence's tendency to eliminate specifically Greek minor details. (*b*) Donatus in his note on 91–2 asserts that Terence has substituted an *adulescens lacrimans* where the Greek had a barber cutting the girl's hair as a sign of mourning—*ne externis moribus spectatorem Romanum offenderet*. Jachmann holds that Donatus is wrong. According to him, the reason for the alteration is Terence's desire to increase the pathos of the passage.[1] But while it is true that the effect of the change is to heighten the pathos, this does not prove that this was the reason for making the change. In any case it is worth noting that,

[1] Leo, *Geschichte d. römischen Literatur*, pp. 247 f.; Jachmann's criticism (RE VA 616, 43 f.) does not seem to me to be well founded.

where Terence alters, the result is not always (as some have argued) less forceful than the Greek original.

The mention at 311 of *deos Penatis* seems to be a further instance of Terence's tendency, just noted, to eliminate minor Greek details. For the slight complication in staging caused by the substitution of the Roman allusion, see the note on line 311.

Scene ii of Act II, in which Phormio appears for the first time, raises interesting questions. Phormio enters with Geta, who has been telling the parasite of the complications that have arisen as a result of Demipho's return from abroad. The opening lines of the scene (315-23) show us the rapidity with which Phormio can prepare to act. Next, after assuring Geta that he fears no foe (324-9), Phormio goes on to explain the reasons for his fearlessness. It is this section that raises difficulties. The passage may be considered in two parts, (1) 330-6, (2) 337-45. In lines 330-4a Phormio explains by the tale of the hawk and the kite that, although, like them, he is dangerous, also, like them, he is not worth catching. Why this is so he goes on to explain (334b-6). The only punishment he could suffer would be to be made a judgement debtor (*addictus, obaeratus*) in the house of his adversary; but in that case his adversary would have to feed him. What better punishment, he asks, could a parasite want? Now if, as the evidence seems conclusively to suggest, enslavement for debt was illegal in post-Solonian Athens,[1] 334b-6 could not have stood in the Greek original. But it is just these lines that afford the only explicit link between the two aspects of Phormio's character—those of sycophant and parasite: Phormio is fearless as a *sycophanta* because the only punishment that his adversary could inflict on him is one that, as *parasitus*, he would welcome.[2] Line

---

[1] Lipsius (*Das Attische Recht und Rechtsverahren*, p. 948, note 21) says of *Phormio* 334, 'Offenbar römisches Recht vorliegt'.

[2] As often, Donatus seizes on the vital point: ducent damnatum domum—mire iuris usus est uerbis ad extenuandam poenam et rem ad commodum transferendam; nam quod obaeratis inimicum, id parasitus maxime optat: duci ab aliquo

337 forms a bridge between the two parts; Geta expresses
Antipho's indebtedness to Phormio. There is a slight awkwardness in that *illo* must refer to Antipho (cf. Donatus on 337, 3),
but the line does not necessarily imply either the exclusion or
the inclusion of the immediately preceding lines.

   The second section (338–45) elaborates on the happy lot of the
parasite, but no longer follows the idea (of 334b–6) that the
parasite will be happy even as a judgement debtor. In fact, these
lines give a picture of the *parasitus* as *parasitus* (even the language
and the pun of 342 are in keeping), and have no direct bearing
on the plot. In the first line of this section (338) *gratiam . . .
refert* picks up *referri gratia* of the previous line, but there is
an awkwardness in the sequence of thought, for Antipho is not
the *rex* of Phormio. Lines 339–42a, according to the explicit
testimony of Donatus, are not from the Greek original but
from a Latin author (? Ennius; cf. note ad loc.). 342b leads to a
frigid pun on *cena dubia*, a joke that is much more Plautine than
Terentian in character. If lines 334b–6 (which provide the connecting link between the aspects of *sycophanta* and *parasitus* in
Phormio) and lines 338–45 (the eulogy of the parasite's way of
life) are Roman additions, it is clear—since it is only in these
lines that prominence is given to the parasitic side of Phormio's
character—that in the Greek original that aspect of his character
was completely overshadowed by his function as a sycophant.
Whether the Terentian addition is an improvement is doubtful.
Perhaps the lines are justified as underlining Phormio's com-
posure on the threshold of battle, but already in 322 (or 334a)
the audience is adequately convinced that Phormio cannot fail.

   Donatus' note on 482 reads *non optat saluum patruum uenire
secundum Apollodorum, et ostendit non congruere salutem eius cum
commodo suo.* Whereas Philolaches (Plautus *Most.* 233 f.) wishes

---

domum. The alliteration (*d*ucent *d*amnatum *d*omum) would not in itself prove any
more than that the form of words was not taken from the Greek.

for his father's death so that he can bestow his inheritance on his mistress, Ctesipho in Terence's *Adelphoe* cannot bring himself to wish more than that for three days his father should be too tired to get out of bed. In the present passage also we see Terence toning down the Greek original in order not to violate the sense of *pietas* that the *adulescens* should feel towards his elders.

Lines 567–8 mention Chremes' Lemnian daughter for the first time, and this is taken by some as evidence that the Greek original must have had an expository prologue, in which the spectators were earlier acquainted with her existence. Reasons for doubting this argument have already been given. To the modern critic it is dramatically much more effective that news of the Lemnian intrigue should be deferred to the point where knowledge of it can be used to extricate *both adulescentes* from their troubles. If the Greek original had an expository prologue, Terence has made an improvement by eliminating it.

In his note on line 647 Donatus says *in Graeca fabula senex hoc dicit: 'quid interest me non suscepisse filiam, si modo dos dabitur alienae?'* Why, we may ask, has Terence transferred the words from Demipho to Geta? Two answers, not mutually exclusive, might be suggested: (1) Terence may have felt that in Demipho's mouth the remark was too harsh, and offended against the canon of decorum; (2) Terence may have thought that the remark was dramatically more effective in the mouth of the slave. That Terence could tone down or eliminate expressions in the Greek original that seemed to him too extravagant or unworthy of the character that uttered them is shown, e.g. by *Phormio* 482, *Adelphoe* 275, and the same motive may have led him to regard the present passage as more suited to the coarser slave temperament. But though Pataikos, in Menander's *Perikeiromene* (350 f.), thinks that the exposure of his child was a somewhat shameful operation, calling for an explanation, Chremes, in the *Hautontimorumenos* of Terence, does not seem to regard the exposure of a female child as reprehensible, and, in the *Phormio*, it is hard to see how the opprobrium, if such it were, could be entirely removed by transferring the phrase from Demipho to Geta. Moreover, parsimony is one of the strongest traits in Demipho's character, and his refusal to rear girl children (contrast the more tender-hearted Chremes) is exactly in keeping with that trait. It seems unlikely, therefore, that the main reason for assigning the passage to Geta was a desire to whitewash Demipho's character. There is, however, a gain in dramatic effectiveness in transferring the words to Geta. In Apollodorus we have merely an ill-tempered comment made by Demipho to his slave Geta: in Terence Geta claims to have used the words to support his indignant rejection of Phormio's demand. He thereby makes the old men more ready to believe in his loyalty to them—a belief that is essential to the successful execution of the intrigue that is being practised on them.

The instances where Terence has deviated from the Greek original seem to be few in number, and the alterations are almost all small ones.[1] The evidence thus suggests that in his adaptation of Apollodorus' comedy Terence did not make major alterations to the plot. But it is not for his plot construction that Terence was renowned in antiquity, but for his depicting of character. The most important question we must seek to answer about the *Phormio* is whether the characters are mere puppets introduced to satisfy the demands of the plot, or whether they have personal qualities that make us take an interest in them as human beings.

It must first be remembered that Terence's characters are not to be judged by modern standards: as has already been said, the *fabula palliata* uses stock characters. But whereas it is often true of Plautus' characters that they are exaggerated to the point of caricature, that they hold up the dramatic action to indulge in

---

[1] The most substantial alterations seem to have been made in II. ii.

buffoonery, or that they exist merely to fulfil the demands of the plot—to mislead or be misled—Terence's characters, besides being the agents through whom the plot develops, also conform to the reasonable standard of behaviour of the types to which they belong. Within the structure of the society of the *palliata* they remain plausible human beings. Terence's characters are not distorted to emphasize the farcical aspects of the plot: rather, the plot has to be developed in such a way as not to do violence to the humanity of the characters.

The *Phormio*, like all Terence's plays except the *Hecyra*, has a double plot; but it not only has two sets of young lovers, it also has a contrasting pair of *senes*, the brothers Demipho and Chremes. In this respect it resembles the *Adelphoe*. But whereas Micio and Demea in the *Adelphoe* hold diametrically opposed views on how to educate their respective sons, Demipho and Chremes are united in their aim of marrying Chremes' Lemnian daughter to Demipho's son without having to reveal the truth of her parentage. Yet, though agreed on what they wish to achieve, because they are men of a very different temperament, they have different ideas about the methods to be employed. The chief trait of Demipho is his 'nearness' (cf. Donatus on line 69) and his consequent determination not to let himself be done out of money (cf. 713–15). It is one of the finer points of the play that Demipho, who so prides himself on his financial acumen, is the one who actually hands over the thirty minae which Phormio's trick has extracted from the *senes*, and that in the last scene it is his determination not to be defeated by Phormio that produces the ultimate triumph of the parasite's cause and the total discomfiture of Chremes.

The character of Chremes is conventionally drawn. He first appears at line 567, and his subsequent actions are adequately accounted for by his desire to get his Lemnian daughter (when he has found her!) married to Antipho and by his fear that his wife,

Nausistrata, will discover the truth about the girl's parentage. The hen-pecked husband and the domineering wife are traditional elements of the *fabula palliata*: what individuality Chremes possesses comes from the contrast between his character and his brother's (e.g. Chremes' eagerness, even at great personal risk, to rear and provide for his illegitimate daughter contrasts with Demipho's mercenary attitude at 645–7; so too in 724 Chremes shows interest in preserving his reputation: Demipho is for doing the bare minimum prescribed by law).

Chremes behaves towards Nausistrata as though she were the traditional *uxor dotata* of the *fabula palliata*. Certainly in the last scene of the play, where her function is merely to be the means of Chremes' final discomfiture, her behaviour conforms to this pattern. Similarly from V. iii our chief impression is of an able and domineering woman: we are left in no doubt who is the ruling partner in *her* home. Two sentences, however (803, 814–15), show her in a more sympathetic light. It may be only the conventional morality of one woman siding with another against the male sex, but in spite of her strictures in the preceding scene upon her husband she is prepared to support the more humane course of action he proposes against that which Demipho had advocated (814 *sic pol commodius esse in omnis arbitror quam ut coeperas*).

Sophrona, the *nutrix*, has an important part to play in the development of the plot, but her character is purely conventional. She is utterly loyal to her mistress, Phanium, to whom she shows a selfless devotion; within the limits possible to a serving woman she shows great resourcefulness in safeguarding the interests of her charge.

Like the *Adelphoe* the *Phormio* has two *adulescentes* around whose love affairs the plot revolves. But whereas in the *Adelphoe* there is a marked contrast between the spinelessness of Ctesipho and the resolution of Aeschinus, it is less certain in the *Phormio*

that Terence wishes us to see so complete a contrast between
Antipho and Phaedria. The character of Antipho presents no
difficulty. His love for Phanium is completely overshadowed in
the play by his dread of meeting his father. It is not unusual in
Terence for sons to feel a sense of shame before their fathers for
their misconduct, but Antipho is timorous to a degree unparalleled in Terence. Completely without courage where his
own love affair is concerned, Antipho expresses his readiness to
help Phaedria in his, but his help for the most part consists in
urging the slave Geta to devise some way of helping Phaedria.
His offer (at 556) to share equally in any punishments the plotters
may incur, in view of his conduct so far in the play, carries no
conviction. Later (712) he does give some slight assistance by
taking a message to Phaedria informing him that the necessary
thirty minae have been found, but Phaedria's good fortune does
not allow him to forget his own sorrows. In short, Antipho cuts
a sorry figure and the practical help he gives his cousin is small
compared with Phaedria's exertions on his behalf.

   That Phaedria is spirited and courageous in his defence of
Antipho's cause is abundantly clear. But where his own love
affair is concerned, Phaedria is almost as ready as his cousin to
give way to despair. In 164–72 he refuses to admit that his predicament is less grave than Antipho's, while his language during
the scene with the *leno* and immediately afterwards (485–566) is
typical of the pitiful behaviour of the *adulescens* of the *palliata*
in this situation.[1] This suggests that it is possible to exaggerate
the difference between the two youths. It can be admitted that
Antipho shows himself both more terrified than Phaedria when
his own love affair seems to be in jeopardy and less effective in
lending aid when his cousin's is in danger; yet they have one
essential point of similarity. Love has caused them both to lose
a sense of proportion; their readiness to surrender to despair when

---

[1] Cf. Duckworth, op. cit., p. 239, footnotes 5 and 6.

things threaten to go wrong makes them slightly ridiculous. Though we wish, as we watch the play, for the ultimate success of their cause, their helplessness in the face of trouble prevents us from taking them too seriously and reminds us that it is a comedy we are witnessing.

Only a brief word is necessary about Dorio, the *leno*. The *leno* appears in Terence only in the *Phormio* and the *Adelphoe*, and in neither play has he a prominent part. The element of coarse abuse that centres on him in Plautus is almost completely lacking in Terence. Both Terentian *lenones* are conscious of the unsavouriness of their trade, and their behaviour, once granted the necessity of the existence of their profession, is, ironically enough, more reasonable than that of the freeborn *adulescentes* who deal with them. Whereas Plautus exaggerates his *lenones* to the point of farcical grotesqueness, in Terence the humour lies rather in the fact that the young men treat them as though they were the grotesques of the Plautine stage, while in fact they behave reasonably and try to do no more than uphold their minimum legal rights. In the upshot Dorio is paid his money in full. The scene in which he appears, apart from being necessary to set the second stage of the plot in motion, shows us rather the unreasonableness of the love-distracted Phaedria than any inhumanity in the *leno*.

The function of the slave Davos is discussed in the introduction to Scene i of Act I in the commentary, nor need anything be said about the three *aduocati* who appear in II. (iii and) iv. This leaves only Geta and Phormio to be discussed. In the plays of Terence the role of the slave is much less prominent than in such plays as Plautus' *Epidicus*, *Miles Gloriosus* (Palaestrio), *Mostellaria* (Tranio), *Pseudolus*, where the whole web of the intrigue radiates from the *seruus* as *architectus doli*. This is partly because Terence does not use the slave, as Plautus does, as an agent of farce and boisterous fun, and partly because Terence is less interested in the intrigue and deception that the *seruus callidus* practises than in how the freeborn members of the family or families involved in the play react to changing circumstances. The *Hautontimorumenos* is a good example of Terence's method. The plans for the deception of Chremes, which is essential to the plot, are the work of the slave Syrus, but it is not the intrigue, but its result— Chremes' self-deception—that provides the main interest of the play, and the role of Syrus is not allowed to obtrude itself. In the *Phormio* the nature of the plot limits Geta's role to that of lieutenant to the parasite. But the importance of Geta to the play must not be underestimated. From the time when he first enters (line 51), till he departs with Demipho for the forum to pay over the thirty minae to Phormio (line 727), he is continuously on the stage but for two short scenes (153–78 and 568–90). His continued presence during all this time is largely accounted for by the fact that his part is to run with the hare and hunt with the hounds. But although he plays an important part in the development of the plot,[1] it is still fair to say that his character is purely conventional and lacking in individuality; his main function is to bring events to a point where Phormio's intervention becomes necessary.

The consideration of Phormio's character has been left to the last. The parasite appears in Terence only here and in the *Eunuchus*, but in the latter play Gnatho is a typical *edax parasitus* (though lacking the boisterous fun of the Plautine type), who is prepared to flatter and wheedle to win a meal for himself. With this kind of parasite Phormio has absolutely nothing in common: such interest in food as he has is mentioned only incidentally apart from lines 330 to 345. It is true that in Plautus' *Curculio* the

---

[1] E.g. I. ii exposition; I, iv Geta as the *seruus currens* brings the news that leads to Antipho's flight; II. i he offers to fetch Phormio for an interview with Demipho; III. iii he devises the plot for getting the thirty minae that Phaedria needs; IV. iii he baits the trap that is to persuade the *senes* to part with the thirty minae; V. vi he brings the news of the secret of Phanium's parentage: this is the weapon that enables Phormio to achieve total victory over the *senes*.

parasite Curculio works the necessary deceptions like a *seruus callidus*, but from his language and behaviour in other scenes it is clear that Curculio is basically the *edax parasitus*. Not so Phormio: there is nothing of the buffoon about him (except, possibly, his pun on *cena dubia* in 342) and though he may be a rogue, he does not lack a certain air of dignity. Lofberg[1] is certainly right in regarding him as primarily an orthodox Athenian sycophant (so Donatus calls him in his notes on 319, 348, 352). From the moment he appears he is completely in command of the situation. We are never for a moment in doubt that Phormio will come out on top. The air of sure success that attends him is important for the understanding of the nature of the play to which he gives his name. By relieving us of all anxiety about the outcome of the intrigue the poet shows us that he wishes us to concentrate on the 'bravura' with which the intrigue is conducted, rather than on the characters who are involved in it.

If Phormio is meant to be no more than the invincible agent of intrigue, we should not expect there to be any attempt to fill in his character. Apart from one scene (II. ii, 315–47) this is indeed true; Phormio appears only when the action has reached a stage of complexity that requires the intervention of the *architectus doli*. And even though lines 315–45 do not further the action,[2] their function is not so much to give any real depth to Phormio's character as to let us know from his own lips that no task is too difficult for him and that he has absolutely no fear of failure.

The *Adelphoe* shows that Terence could invest traditional characters with a greater significance than they usually enjoyed in the *palliata*, but it would be a mistake to think that what is true of one play must be true of another. To search in the *Phormio* for depths of character is to miss the lightness of touch, the rapidity and

---

[1] *Classical Weekly*, XXII (1928–9), pp. 183–4.
[2] There is some evidence that parts at least of the scene did not appear in the Greek original (see notes on 334 and 339–41).

liveliness of action, which are the play's chief merit. Less than six months earlier Terence had achieved his greatest success with the *Eunuchus*, which, in its farce and boisterousness, is the most Plautine of all his plays. We need not wonder if with his next play Terence tried to maintain the reputation he had won by displaying his skill in the handling of a pure comedy of intrigue.

LIFE AND WORKS OF TERENCE

Our knowledge of the life and career of Terence is derived principally from Suetonius' life of the poet, preserved in the fourth-century commentary of Donatus, and from the production notices (*didascaliae*) and prologues to the plays. Unfortunately, since writers of biography in classical antiquity had a tendency to fabricate episodes, the personal details recorded by Suetonius must be accepted with reserve. Terence was born at Carthage, early in the second century B.C. Suetonius says of Terence in the year 160 or 159 B.C., *nondum quintum atque uicesimum* (*uulgo*: some manuscripts have *tricesimum*) *egressus annum.* If he was only twenty-five at that time, his first play must have been produced when he was only nineteen; this seems improbable. If, (reading *tricesimum*), he was born *c.* 195 B.C., the *Andria* was produced when he was twenty-nine. At an early age he was brought as a slave to Rome; there he was educated and later manumitted by his master, the Roman senator Terentius Lucanus. It was presumably at that date that, taking the *nomen* of his manumitter, he became known as P. Terentius Afer. His literary talent won him friendship and patronage from the Scipionic Circle, a group of aristocrats interested in Greek culture, and numbering among its members Scipio Africanus Minor (born 185 B.C.) and C. Laelius (born 186 B.C.). He wrote six plays (all of which we possess), which were performed between the years 166 and 160 B.C. After the production of the last of these plays he went to Greece, and died on his way home (possibly by

shipwreck) in 159 B.C. The following list of dates for the production of his plays commands general, though not universal,
assent.

166 B.C.	*Andria*	performed at the	Ludi Megalenses.
165 B.C.	*Hecyra*		Ludi Megalenses (with-drawn as a failure).
163 B.C.	*Hautontimorumenos*		Ludi Megalenses.
161 B.C.	*Eunuchus*		Ludi Megalenses.
	Phormio		Ludi Romani.
160 B.C.	*Hecyra*	booed out of the theatr.	Ludi funebres for L. Aemilius Paullus (second failure).
	Adelphoe	which brother has the downfall?	Ludi funebres for L. Aemilius Paullus.
	Hecyra		Ludi Romani (third, successful presenta-tion).

Terence's success and aristocratic patronage made him the
object of envious criticism, especially from a rival playwright
named Luscius Lanuvinus (cf. note on *poeta uetus* in line 1). The
reception given to his plays by the Roman public varied; the
Eunuchus was greeted with enthusiasm,[1] but the *Hecyra* succeeded
only on its third presentation, having twice failed to secure a
hearing.

The productive period of the *palliata* virtually ended with
Terence's death,[2] but the *didascaliae* attest performances of his
plays in the generation after his death, and in the time of Cicero
comedies of Plautus, Terence, and Turpilius were still being
performed. Already by the end of the second century B.C. the

[1] Suetonius 3. *Eunuchus quidem †bis die† acta est, meruitque pretium quantum nulla antea cuiusquam comoedia, id est octo milia nummorum.*

[2] Sextus Turpilius, who died as an old man in 103 B.C., is the only notable writer of the *palliata* after Terence's death.

writings of Terence had become a subject of scholarly study, and, although their works are lost, we know of a series of grammarians and commentators during succeeding centuries who interested themselves in his works. In the schools, too, possibly at an early date in the Christian era, Terence became a standard author for study, and throughout the rest of classical antiquity his plays were assured at least of a reading public.

SOURCES OF THE TEXT

The extant manuscripts of Terence belong to two families. The first family consists of a single manuscript, the Codex Bembinus, designated A in the *apparatus criticus* of the Oxford Text; it is a manuscript of the fourth or fifth century A.D., written without word division in Rustic Capitals. It derives its name from one of its owners in the fifteenth century, the father of Cardinal Bembo. It lacks most of the *Andria* (1–888) and small parts of the *Hecyra* and *Adelphoe*. All the other manuscripts, written in minuscules, belong to the second family, designated Σ; the earliest of them were written in the ninth century. In manuscripts of the Σ family there occurs the *subscriptio* 'Calliopius recensui' or 'feliciter Calliopio bono scholastico'. We cannot be sure when Calliopius lived or that he actually made the recension from which all manuscripts of the Σ family derive, but it is convenient to use the adjective 'Calliopian' as referring to all manuscripts of the Σ family. The presence in Σ as well as in A of the *argumenta* of Sulpicius Apollinaris (fl. A.D. 150) shows that the Calliopian recension is later than the middle of the second century A.D.: in fact, although scholars dispute whether the Calliopian recension should be placed earlier or later than the date of A (fourth or fifth century) and Donatus (mid-fourth century), it is generally agreed that the recension was made between about A.D. 300 and the fifth century.

The Σ family is sub-divided into two branches, γ and δ.

Members of the γ class are numerous and only a small selection of them is represented in the *apparatus criticus* of the Oxford Text: the δ class consists of half a dozen manuscripts, two of them only small fragments. The most important formal difference between the γ and δ branches of the Σ family is the different order in which the plays occur: in addition it should be noted that three manuscripts of the γ branch (CPF) are illustrated.[1] In general the text of δ is superior to that of γ. How and when the Σ family came to divide into these two branches is still a subject of dispute among scholars, though it now seems established that the γ branch is not later than the fifth century.

The claim of A to be regarded as the best manuscript of Terence rests, not on the fact that it is over four centuries older than any other Terentian manuscript, but on the fact that it represents a comparatively pure tradition, whereas the Σ family has suffered many alterations (often rendering the Latin unmetrical), whose main purpose is to make the text easier and more readily intelligible. Though A follows a good tradition, it is not by any means a perfect example of that tradition. A scholar of the fifth or sixth century, who signs his name 'Iouiales' (Jovialis), corrected a number of scribal errors in the manuscript itself, and also introduced a number of corrections from a Σ family manuscript, thus demonstrating that the Σ family of manuscripts was already in existence in the sixth century.

The evidence of the manuscripts of Terence can often be supplemented or corrected from information recorded by ancient commentators and grammarians. The most important ancient commentary of Terence is that of Aelius Donatus (fl. A.D. 350). His commentary, which is referred to frequently in the notes, not only discusses questions of subject matter and points of

---

[1] Volume VIII of *Codices Graeci et Latini* (ed. de Vries, Leiden, 1903) contains a photographic facsimile of the whole of F and illustrative pages from C and P. Some photographs of the illustrated manuscripts may also be found in G. Duckworth, *The Nature of Roman Comedy* (Princeton, 1952).

interpretation: it gives (unfortunately, rather rarely) precious references to the Greek originals of Terence's plays, and, not infrequently, offers evidence on the Latin text; so, for example, in the *Phormio* at lines 330 and 1028 Donatus offers readings which, although they are found in no Terentian manuscript, are almost certainly correct.

METRE

The rhythms of Terence's verse are almost entirely iambic or trochaic. Less than thirty out of more than 6,000 lines have other rhythms. The most common metres, in order of frequency, are:

1. IAMBIC SENARIUS (Greek iambic trimeter acatalectic[1]) consists of six iambic feet ($\cup\,\acute{-}$);[2] in all feet except the sixth which *must* be an iambus [or, by *syllaba anceps*,[1] a pyrrhic ($\cup\,\overset{\vee}{}$)], other feet may be substituted as follows: tribrach ($\cup\,\acute{\cup}\,\cup$), spondee ($-\,\acute{-}$), anapaest ($\cup\,\cup\,\acute{-}$), dactyl ($-\,\acute{\cup}\,\cup$), proceleusmatic ($\cup\,\cup\,\acute{\cup}\,\cup$) [comparatively rare and most commonly in the first foot—80 out of 119 exx. (Laidlaw, p. 38)]. The regular caesura is penthemimeral (immediately before the ictus of the third foot) or hephthemimeral (immediately before the ictus of the fourth foot). About half of all the lines in Terence are in this metre; it is used in the prologues and opening lines of all six plays. It

[1] For technical terms, see glossary (p. 32).

[2] Each foot in an iambic or trochaic line has a metrical ictus. The syllable on which the ictus falls may conventionally be marked by the sign / , and many editors since the time of Richard Bentley (ed. Terence, 1726) have so marked the metrical ictus in *alternate* feet in their text. Whether the syllable bearing the ictus was emphasized in pronunciation is uncertain (see now W. Beare, 'The meaning of *ictus* as applied to Latin verse, *Hermathena*, No. LXXXI (1953), pp. 29 ff.), and the present text follows the Oxford Text of Kauer and Lindsay in omitting ictus marks from the text. Ictus marks are, however, sometimes used in the notes, especially to explain the operation of the law of Brevis Brevians. The ictus is always on the first syllable in trochaic feet; in the iambic feet it falls on the long syllable of the iambus or, as marked above, on the corresponding syllable of a foot substituted for an iambus.

may be observed that an iambus- (or pyrrhic-) word at the end of a senarius may not be preceded by an iambus unless the penultimate word is a monosyllable.

2. TROCHAIC SEPTENARIUS (Greek trochaic tetrameter catalectic) consists of 7½ trochaic feet ($-\smile$); in all feet except the seventh, which *must* be a trochee (or its exact metrical equivalent, a tribrach), other feet may be substituted as follows: tribrach ($\smile\smile\smile$), spondee ($--$), anapaest ($\smile\smile-$), dactyl ($-\smile\smile$). Terence, unlike Plautus, does not seem to admit the proceleusmatic in his trochaic lines (Laidlaw, p. 42). The line normally divides with diaeresis at the end of the fourth foot. Hiatus occurs at the diaeresis in Plautus about once in twenty lines: there is no sure example in Terence (Laidlaw, pp. 109–10). Diaeresis sometimes occurs at the end of the fifth foot; in about one line in thirteen it is missing altogether. Trochaic Septenarii are 'the vehicle for excited talk, as the Senarii for quiet talk' (Lindsay). All six plays end in this metre, of which there are about 1,350 lines in Terence.

3. IAMBIC OCTONARIUS (iambic tetrameter acatalectic) accounts for about 870 lines in Terence. The line may have diaeresis at the end of the fourth foot (which, in this case, *must* be a pure iambus (or pyrrhic, with *syllaba anceps*)), but more commonly does not (Laidlaw, p. 107, n. 3). Hiatus, *syllaba anceps*, and change of speaker at the diaeresis are rare (Laidlaw, pp. 115–16).

4. IAMBIC SEPTENARIUS (iambic tetrameter catalectic). Terence has 384 lines in this metre. 'For Terence, as for Plautus, the fourth foot is normally an iambus' (Laidlaw, p. 104), i.e. the iambic character of the line is proclaimed in the middle, not in the seventh foot, where a spondee (over 150 exx.) is about as common as an iambus. 'Some twenty [sc. lines] show *syllaba anceps* or hiatus, or both, at the diaeresis' (ibid.). In all these cases the fourth foot is an iambus.

5. TROCHAIC OCTONARII occur in ninety lines, mostly with diaeresis.

PROSODY

Prosody is the system of rules that govern the scansion of the actual words that go to make up the metrical lines. It is assumed that the main rules are already known by which, in the classical hexameter or elegiac couplet of Virgil or Ovid, it is determined whether a syllable is long or short. Briefly speaking, a syllable is long either when it contains a long vowel (or diphthong) or when the vowel is immediately succeeded by two consonants or more, not necessarily in the same word. In Plautus and Terence these rules are modified as follows:

1. Final 's' following a short vowel does not necessarily make position with a following consonant. It is impossible to determine how widely Plautus and Terence used this licence. In many cases the line scans only if the 's' is dropped; more often the line scans with the 's' either dropped or retained. Except at a pause or diaeresis there are relatively few examples where the line scans only if the 's' is retained, e.g. (in the fifth foot) *Phormio* 32, 89.

2. A mute followed by 'l' or 'r' never makes position, e.g. *pătrem*, never *pātrem*.

3. Synizesis: two vowels not separated by a consonant *may* coalesce into one syllable, e.g. *huius*, *cuius* (*quoius*), *meos*, *deos*, *fuisse*, *rei*, *ait*.

4. Hiatus (cf. Laidlaw, c. VII, pp. 82 f.) may occur:

(*a*) in word groups like *quĭ ămant*. 'Monosyllables ending in a long vowel (or *-m*) were left in "Prosodic Hiatus" (i.e. with shortening of the final) before iambic words which began with a vowel (or *h-*)' (Lindsay, *E.L.V.* 229), e.g. *Phormio* 883, 954, *dĭ ăment*.

(*b*) after an emphatic monosyllable; an emphatic monosyllable 'always, and an unemphatic often, is left in Prosodic Hiatus before an initial short vowel (or "*h*" + short vowel) . . . ; even before a long syllable Prosodic Hiatus is possible' (*E.L.V.* 245–6), e.g. *Phormio* 191, *quăm hic.*

(*c*) after emphatic iambic words (sts. unemphatic also), which may be left in Prosodic Hiatus, e.g. *Phormio* 318, *tute hoc intristi*; *tibĭ omnest.*

(*d*) at Diaeresis in the middle of longer lines (cf. note on Trochaic Septenarius); e.g. *Adelphoe* 947, *Hegiō | est*; there is no certain example in the *Phormio*—529 and 1028 (both in Troch. Sept.) are doubtful.

(*e*) at Change of Speaker, e.g. *Phormio* 146, *fortassĕ?—immo* . . . ; 882, *fecerō.—heus Phormio.*

(*f*) at a Sense Pause, e.g. 633, *inquăm: eho* . . . ; perhaps 656, *debeō: etiamnunc* . . .

(*g*) with Interjections, e.g. 212, *ĕm ĭstuc serua* (*ĭst-* by B–B); 360, *ŏ ăudaciam* (*ău-* by B–B); 754, *ău obsecro.*

(*a*), (*b*), (*c*), and (*g*) are instances of Prosodic Hiatus, the others of true Hiatus. Hiatus is usual in (*a*), (*b*), and (*g*), permissible in the other cases.

5. *Breuis breuians* (*breues breuiantes*): a long syllable (i) immediately preceded by a short syllable, and (ii) immediately preceded or succeeded by a metrical ictus (or word-accent[1]) may itself be shortened. With very few exceptions the *breuis breuians* (i.e. the 'short' that precedes the 'long-to-be-shortened') is either a monosyllable (or elided disyllable) or begins an iambic

---

[1] It is disputed whether B–B is merely a metrical law owing its operation to metrical ictus, or a phonetic law occasioned by word accent. The shortening in classical Latin of a number of common iambic words (e.g. *modŏ, cauĕ*) and the fact that some forms, which on the metrical theory might be allowed (e.g. *monĕre, amăre, uenĭre*), are in practice avoided support the view that B–B is a phonetic law. However, for the practical purposes of scanning Plautus or Terence it is not necessary to takes sides in this dispute. In the verse of both authors a metrical ictus always does precede or succeed the syllable-to-be-shortened. Cf. Laidlaw, pp. 23–5, and the literature cited on p. 24.

word (hence the German term *Iambenkürzung*). Less often B-B (this abbreviation for *breuis breuians* is used throughout the commentary) shortens the second syllable of a longer word.[2] The operation of B-B may be illustrated with examples from the *Phormio*. The B-B is

(i) a monosyllable: 648, *ut ăd pauca*; 707, *per ĭnpluuium*.

(ii) an elided disyllable: 154, *ub(i) ĭn mentem*; 439, *tib(i) ĭnpingam*.

(iii) the first syllable of an iambic word: 601, *patĕr*; 553, *uidĕ*; 342, *priŏr*.

(iv) the first syllable of a longer word: 434, *senĕctutem*; 666, *supĕllectile*; 901, *uerĕbamini* (see note ad loc.).

6. (*a*) A small group of words ending in short -*e* requires special note: *nempe* always scans *nemp'*, *ille* sts. (esp. at beginning of a Senarius) *ill'*, *unde* sts. *und'*; (*b*) *eccum* regularly, *immo* sts., shorten the first syllable; (*c*) enclitic *quidem* may shorten a preceding monosyllable, e.g. *sĭquidem* or *sī quidem*.

Examples of the commonest metres are scanned below:

IAMBIC SENARII (*Phormio* 80–6)

noster | mali | nil quic|quam pri|m(o); hic Phae|dria

continu|o quan|dam nac|tus est | puel|lulam

citharis|tri(am), hanc | arde|re coe|pit per|dite.

ea ser|uie|bat le|non(i) in|puris|simo,

neque quod | dare|tur quic|qu(am); id cu|rarant | patres.

resta|bat ali|ud nil | nis(i) ocu|los pas|cere,

secta|r(i), in lu|dum du|cer(e) et | reddu|cere.

---

[1] In such cases the syllable to be shortened is more often long only by position (e.g. *uolŭptati*) than by nature (e.g. *uerĕbamini*).

In line 82 the caesura is hephthemimeral (after *ardere*): in the other lines it is in the third foot (penthemimeral).

IAMBIC OCTONARIUS (*Phormio* 176)

ut neque | mihi[1] | sit a|mitten|di nec | retinen|di co|pia

IAMBIC SEPTENARIUS (*Phormio* 177)

sed quid hoc[2] | est? uide|on ego | Getam | curren|t(em) huc

ad|ueni|re?

TROCHAIC SEPTENARII (*Phormio* 196–200)

satis pr(o) im|perio, | quisquis | es—Ge|t(a)—ipsest | quem

uolu|(i) obui|am.

cedo quid | portas, | obse|cr(o?) atqu(e) id, | si po|tes, uer|

b(o) expe|di.

faci(am)—e|loquere | —mod(o) apud[3] | portum | —meum

n(e?)[4]—in | tellex|t(i) occi|d(i) hem

quid agam? | —quid ais? | —huius pa|trem ui|disse | m(e) et

patru|om tu|om.

nam quod e|g(o) huic nunc | subit(o) ex|itio | remedi(um) |

inueni|am mi | ser?

---

[1] *mihi* usually scans *mĭhĭ*. [2] *hoc* by B-B. [3]—*ĭd* by B-B is also possible

[4] *meumne–ŭmn* by B-B, or *meumne* by synizesis.

GLOSSARY

acatalectic implies that the last foot of the line is complete, e.g. in the
Iambic Senarius the last foot is an iambus (or, by *syllaba anceps*, a
pyrrhic); contrast catalectic.

caesura; a word break in the middle of a foot, e.g. 83, *ĕă sēr|uĭē|băt } lē-*.

catalectic implies that the last foot of the line is incomplete, as in the
Trochaic Septenarius, where the first syllable only of the eighth foot
remains.

diaeresis: a word break at the end of a foot, e.g. 198, *făcĭ(am)ē|lŏquĕrĕ;
mŏd(o) ăpŭd | pōrtŭm. }|*

hephthemimeral caesura [Gk. ἐφθημιμερὴς τομή, lit. caesura after seven
half feet (3½ feet)] e.g. 82, *cĭthărīs|trĭ(am) hānc | ārdē|rĕ } cōe-*.

hiatus occurs when a final vowel or syllable ending in *-m* is not elided
before an initial vowel or 'h'.

impure foot: a foot in which a long syllable is substituted for a short
syllable, e.g. a spondee (— —) instead of a trochee (— ◡) in a trochaic
line, or instead of an iambus (◡ —) in an iambic line.

mora: a term used to designate the duration of one short syllable (◡);
a long syllable (—) is equivalent to two *morae* (◡ ◡).

penthemimeral caesura [Gk. πενθημιμερὴς τομή, lit. caesura after five half
feet (2½ feet)], e.g. 83, *ĕă sēr|uĭē|băt } lē|nōn(i).*

prosodic hiatus occurs when 'a final long vowel or syllable ending in *-m*
is neither elided nor wholly unaffected before an initial vowel or
"h", but is scanned as a short syllable' (Lindsay, *Captiui*, pp. 46–7).

pure foot: a foot in which there is no substitution, unless one that is the
exact equivalent in duration to the basic foot of the line, e.g. in
an iambic line an iambus (◡ —) or a tribrach (◡ ◡ ◡) is a pure foot.

resolution: the subsititution of two short syllables for one long.

resolved foot: a foot containing a resolution (q.v.), e.g. — ◡ ◡ for — —.

syllaba anceps: a syllable (most often at end of line) that may by the rules
of versification be either short or long.

word-accent: the rule governing the word-accent in Latin is simple: in
all polysyllables the accent is (1) on the penult (second last syllable)
if that syllable is long, or (2) on the pro-penult if the penult is short,
e.g. *pópŭlus Rōmânus.* Disyllables are accented on the first syllable.

CONSPECTVS METRORVM

1–152	iamb. senar.		479–80	troch. octonar.
153	troch. octonar.		481–2, 484	troch. septenar.
154–5	troch. septenar.		483, 486	iamb. octonar.
156–7	troch. octonar.		487–9	troch. septenar.
158–9	troch. septenar.		490	iamb. senar.
160–2	iamb. octonar.		491	iamb. septenar.
163	iamb. dim. acatal.		492–5	troch. septenar.
164–76	iamb. octonar.		496	iamb. octonar.
177–8	iamb. septenar.		497–501	troch. septenar.
179	troch. octonar.		502–3	iamb. octonar.
180	troch. septenar.		504–14	troch. septenar.
181–2, 184	iamb. octonar.		515–16	iamb. octonar.
183	troch. dim. catal.		517–66	troch. septenar.
185	troch. septenar.		567–712	iamb. senar.
186	iamb. octonar.		713–27	iamb. octonar.
187–8	troch. octonar.		728	troch. octonar.
189–90	troch. septenar.		729	troch. dim. catal.
191	troch. dim. catal.		730–1	troch. octonar.
192–3	iamb. octonar.		732	troch. septenar.
194	troch. trim. catal.		733–4	iamb. octonar.
195	iamb. dim acatal.		735–8	troch. octonar.
196–215	troch. septenar.		739–41	troch. septenar.
216–30	iamb. senar.		742–7	iamb. octonar.
231–2	troch. septenar.		748–64	iamb. septenar.
233–51	iamb. octonar.		765	iamb. senar.
252–3	troch. septenar.		766–94	iamb. septenar.
254–314	iamb. senar.		795–819	iamb. octonar.
315–47	troch. septenar.		820–8	iamb. septenar.
348–464	iamb. senar.		829–40	iamb. octonar.
465–8	troch. octonar.		841–83	troch. septenar.
469–70	troch. septenar.		884–1010	iamb. senar.
471–8	iamb. octonar.		1011–55	troch. septenar.

[iamb. = iambic, troch. = trochaic; catal. = catalectic, acatal. = acatalectic; dim. = dimeter, trim. = trimeter, senar. = senarius, septenar. = septenarius, octonar. = octonarius.]

Phormio

DIDASCALIA

INCIPIT TERENTI PHORMIO: ACTA LVDIS ROMANIS

L. POSTVMIO ALBINO L. CORNELIO MERVLA AEDI-

LIBVS CVRVLIBVS: EGERE L. AMBIVIVS TVRPIO L.

HATILIVS PRAENESTINVS: MODOS FECIT FLACCVS

CLAVDI TIBIIS INPARIBVS TOTA: GRAECA APOLLO-

DORV EPIDICAZOMENOS: FACTA IIII C. FANNIO

M. VALERIO COS.

C. SVLPICI APOLLINARIS
PERIOCHA

Chremetis frater aberat peregre Demipho
relicto Athenis Antiphone filio.
Chremes clam habebat Lemni uxorem et filiam,
Athenis aliam coniugem et amantem unice
fidicinam gnatum. mater e Lemno aduenit
Athenas; moritur; uirgo sola (aberat Chremes)
funus procurat. ibi eam uisam Antipho
cum amaret, opera parasiti uxorem accipit.
pater et Chremes reuersi fremere. dein minas
triginta dant parasito, ut illam coniugem
haberet ipse: argento hoc emitur fidicina.
uxorem retinet Antipho a patruo adgnitam.

PERSONAE

[PROLOGVS]	HEGIO
DAVOS SERVOS	CRATINVS ⎱ ADVOCATI *(lawyers)*
GETA SERVOS	CRITO
ANTIPHO ADVLESCENS	DORIO LENO
PHAEDRIA ADVLESCENS	CHREMES SENEX
DEMIPHO SENEX	SOPHRONA NVTRIX — *nurse*
PHORMIO PARASITVS	NAVSISTRATA MATRONA
	[CANTOR] *God woman*

(handwritten annotations)
young nerd in love (by ANTIPHO / PHAEDRIA)
↳ *playing the tricky slave role*
– *needs to be able to bring a law suit*
✳ *common name* (by DAVOS)

PROLOGVS

POSTQVAM poeta uetus poetam non potest
retrahere a studio et transdere hominem in otium,
maledictis deterrere ne scribat parat;
qui ita dictitat, quas ante hic fecit fabulas
5 tenui esse oratione et scriptura leui,   5
quia nusquam insanum scripsit adulescentulum
ceruam uidere fugere et sectari canes
et eam plorare, orare ut subueniat sibi.
quod si intellegeret, quom stetit olim noua,
10 actoris opera mage stetisse quam sua,   10
minus multo audacter quam nunc laedit laederet.
11a [et mage placerent quas fecisset fabulas].
nunc siquis est qui hoc dicat aut sic cogitet,
'uetus si poeta non lacessisset prior,
nullum inuenire prologum posset nouos   15
15 quem diceret, nisi haberet cui male diceret',
is sibi responsum hoc habeat, in medio omnibus
palmam esse positam qui artem tractent musicam.
ille ad famem hunc a studio studuit reicere:
hic respondere uoluit, non lacessere.   20
20 benedictis si certasset, audisset bene:
quod ab illo adlatumst, sibi esse rellatum putet.
de illo iam finem faciam dicundi mihi,
peccandi quom ipse de se finem non facit.
nunc quid uelim animum attendite: adporto nouam   25
25 Epidicazomenon quam uocant comoediam
Graeci, Latini Phormionem nominant,
quia primas partis qui aget, is erit Phormio
parasitus, per quem res geretur maxume,
uoluntas uostra si ad poetam accesserit.   30
30 date operam, adeste aequo animo per silentium,
ne simili utamur fortuna atque usi sumus

quom per tumultum noster grex motus locost:
quem actoris uirtus nobis restituit locum
35 bonitasque uostra adiutans atque aequanimitas.

ACTVS I

DAVOS

35 Amicus summus meus et popularis Geta
  heri ad me uenit. erat ei de ratiuncula
  iampridem apud me relicuom pauxillulum
  nummorum: id ut conficerem. confeci: adfero.
  nam erilem filium eius duxisse audio   5
40 uxorem: ei credo munus hoc conraditur.
  quam inique comparatumst, i qui minus habent
  ut semper aliquid addant ditioribus!
  quod ille unciatim uix de demenso suo
  suom defrudans genium conpersit miser,   10
45 id illa uniuorsum abripiet, haud existumans
  quanto labore partum. porro autem Geta
  ferietur alio munere ubi era pepererit;
  porro autem alio ubi erit puero natalis dies;
  ubi initiabunt. omne hoc mater auferet: 15
50 puer causa erit mittundi. sed uideon Getam?

GETA DAVOS

  GE. Siquis me quaeret rufus . . DA. praestost, desine.
    GE. oh,
  at ego obuiam conabar tibi, Daue. DA. accipe, em:
  lectumst; conueniet numerus quantum debui.
  GE. amo te et non neglexisse habeo gratiam.
55 DA. praesertim ut nunc sunt mores: adeo res redit: 5
  siquis quid reddit, magna habendast gratia.
  sed quid tu es tristis? GE. egone? nescis quo in metu et
  quanto in periclo simus! DA. quid istuc est? GE. scies,
  modo ut tacere possis. DA. abi sis, insciens:
60 quoius tu fidem in pecunia perspexeris,   10
  uerere uerba ei credere, ubi quid mihi lucrist

te fallere? GE. ergo ausculta. DA. hanc operam tibi
   dico.
GE. senis nostri, Daue, fratrem maiorem Chremem
nostin? DA. quidni? GE. quid? eius gnatum Phaedriam?
15 DA. tam quam te. GE. euenit senibus ambobus simul   65
iter illi in Lemnum ut esset, nostro in Ciliciam
ad hospitem antiquom. is senem per epistulas
pellexit, modo non montis auri pollicens.
DA. quoi tanta erat res et supererat? GE. desinas:
20 sic est ingenium. DA. oh regem me esse oportuit.   70
GE. abeuntes ambo hic tum senes me filiis
relinquont quasi magistrum. DA. o Geta, prouinciam
cepisti duram. GE. mi usu uenit, hoc scio:
memini relinqui me deo irato meo.
25 coepi aduorsari primo: quid uerbis opust?   75
seni fidelis dum sum, scapulas perdidi.
DA. uenere in mentem mi istaec: 'namque inscitiast
aduorsum stimulum calces.' GE. coepi is omnia
facere, obsequi quae uellent. DA. scisti uti foro.
30 GE. noster mali nil quicquam primo; hic Phaedria   80
continuo quandam nactus est puellulam
citharistriam, hanc ardere coepit perdite.
ea seruiebat lenoni inpurissimo,
neque quod daretur quicquam; id curarant patres.
35 restabat aliud nil nisi oculos pascere,   85
sectari, in ludum ducere et redducere.
nos otiosi operam dabamus Phaedriae.
in quo haec discebat ludo, exaduorsum ilico
tonstrina erat quaedam: hic solebamus fere
40 plerumque eam opperiri, dum inde iret domum.   90
interea dum sedemus illi, interuenit
adulescens quidam lacrumans. nos mirarier;
rogamus quid sit. 'numquam aeque' inquit 'ac modo
paupertas mihi onus uisumst et miserum et graue.
45 modo quandam uidi uirginem hic uiciniae   95

78 O.T. aduorsus

    miseram suam matrem lamentari mortuam.
    ea sita erat exaduorsum neque illi beniuolus
    neque notus neque uicinus extra unam aniculam
    quisquam aderat qui adiutaret funus: miseritumst.
100 uirgo ipsa facie egregia.' quid uerbis opust?   50
    commorat omnis nos. ibi continuo Antipho
    'uoltisne eamus uisere?' alius 'censeo:
    eamus: duc nos sodes.' imus, uenimus,
    uidemus. uirgo pulchra, et quo mage diceres,
105 nil aderat adiumenti ad pulchritudinem: 55
    capillus passus, nudus pes, ipsa horrida,
    lacrumae, uestitus turpis: ut, ni uis boni
    in ipsa inesset forma, haec formam exstinguerent.
    ille qui illam amabat fidicinam tantummodo
110 'satis' inquit 'scitast'; noster uero .. DA. iam scio: 60
    amare coepit. GE. scin quam? quo euadat uide.
    postridie ad anum recta pergit: obsecrat
    ut sibi eius faciat copiam. illa enim se negat
    neque eum aequom facere ait: illam ciuem esse Atticam,
115 bonam bonis prognatam: si uxorem uelit,   65
    lege id licere facere; sin aliter, negat.
    noster quid ageret nescire: et illam ducere
    cupiebat et metuebat absentem patrem.
    DA. non, si redisset, ei pater ueniam daret?
120 GE. ille indotatam uirginem atque ignobilem   70
    daret illi? numquam faceret. DA. quid fit denique?
    GE. quid fiat? est parasitus quidam Phormio,
    homo confidens: qui illum di omnes perduint!
    DA. quid is fecit? GE. hoc consilium quod dicam dedit:
125 'lex est ut orbae, qui sint genere proxumi,   75
    is nubant, et illos ducere eadem haec lex iubet.
    ego te cognatum dicam et tibi scribam dicam;
    paternum amicum me adsimulabo uirginis:
    ad iudices ueniemus: qui fuerit pater,
130 quae mater, qui cognata tibi sit, omnia haec   80
    confingam quod erit mihi bonum atque commodum;

quom tu horum nil refelles, uincam scilicet.
pater aderit: mihi paratae lites: quid mea?
illa quidem nostra erit.' DA. iocularem audaciam!
85 GE. persuasumst homini: factumst: uentumst: uincimur: 135
duxit. DA. quid narras? GE. hoc quod audis. DA. o
    Geta,
quid te futurumst? GE. nescio hercle; unum hoc scio,
quod fors feret feremus aequo animo. DA. placet:
em istuc uirist officium. GE. in me omnis spes mihist.
90 DA. laudo. GE. ad precatorem adeam credo qui mihi   140
sic oret: 'nunc amitte quaeso hunc; ceterum
posthac si quicquam, nil precor.' tantummodo
non addit: 'ubi ego hinc abiero, uel occidito.'
DA. quid paedagogus ille qui citharistriam,
95 quid rei gerit? GE. sic, tenuiter. DA. non multum habet   145
quod det fortasse? GE. immo nil nisi spem meram.
DA. pater eius rediit an non? GE. nondum. DA. quid?
    senem
quoad exspectatis uostrum? GE. non certum scio,
sed epistulam ab eo adlatam esse audiui modo
100 et ad portitores esse delatam: hanc petam.   150
DA. numquid, Geta, aliud me uis? GE. ut bene sit tibi.
puer, heus. nemon hoc prodit? cape, da hoc Dorcio.

iii   ANTIPHO PHAEDRIA

AN. Adeon rem redisse ut qui mi consultum optume uelit
    esse,
Phaedria, patrem ut extimescam ubi in mentem eius
    aduenti uenit!
quod ni fuissem incogitans, ita eum exspectarem ut par   155
    fuit.
PH. quid istuc? AN. rogitas, qui tam audacis facinoris
    mihi conscius sis?
5 quod utinam ne Phormioni id suadere in mentem incidis-
    set

    neu me cupidum eo inpulisset, quod mihi principiumst
      mali!
    non potitus essem: fuisset tum illos mi aegre aliquot dies,
160 at non cotidiana cura haec angeret animum.   PH. audio.
    AN. dum exspecto quam mox ueniat qui adimat hanc mi
      consuetudinem.
    PH. aliis quia defit quod amant aegrest; tibi quia superest   10
      dolet:
          amore abundas, Antipho.
    nam tua quidem hercle certo uita haec expetenda optanda-
      que est.
165 ita me di bene ament ut mihi liceat tam diu quod amo frui,
    iam depecisci morte cupio: tu conicito cetera,
    quid ego ex hac inopia nunc capiam et quid tu ex ista   15
      copia,
    ut ne addam quod sine sumptu ingenuam, liberalem
      nactus es,
    quod habes, ita ut uoluisti, uxorem sine mala fama palam:
170 beatus, ni unum desit, animus qui modeste istaec ferat.
    quod si tibi res sit cum eo lenone quo mihist, tum sentias.
    ita plerique ingenio sumus omnes: nostri nosmet paenitet.   20
    AN. at tu mihi contra nunc uidere fortunatus, Phaedria,
    quoi de integro est potestas etiam consulendi quid uelis:
175 retinere amare mittere; ego in eum incidi infelix locum
    ut neque mihi sit amittendi nec retinendi copia.
    sed quid hoc est? uideon ego Getam currentem huc   25
      aduenire?
    is est ipsus. ei, timeo miser quam hic mihi nunc nuntiet
      rem.

        GETA ANTIPHO PHAEDRIA   iv

    GE. Nullus es, Geta, nisi iam aliquod tibi consilium celere
      reperis:
180 ita nunc inparatum subito tanta te inpendent mala;
    quae neque uti deuitem scio neque quo modo me inde
      extraham,

quae si non astu prouidentur me aut erum pessum 181*a*
  dabunt;
5 nam non potest celari nostra diutius iam audacia.
       AN. quid illic commotus uenit?
  GE. tum temporis mihi punctum ad hanc rem est: erus
    adest. AN. quid illuc malist?
  GE. quod quom audierit, quod eius remedium inueniam 185
    iracundiae?
loquarne? incendam; taceam? instigem; purgem me?
  laterem lauem.
10 heu me miserum! quom mihi paueo, tum Antipho me
    excruciat animi:
eius me miseret, ei nunc timeo, is nunc me retinet; nam
    absque eo esset,
recte ego mihi uidissem et senis essem ultus iracundiam:
aliquid conuasassem atque hinc me conicerem protinam 190
    in pedes.
       AN. quam hic fugam aut furtum parat?
15 GE. sed ubi Antiphonem reperiam, aut qua quaerere in-
    sistam uia?
  PH. te nominat. AN. nescioquod magnum hoc nuntio
    exspecto malum. PH. ah.
sanus es? GE. domum ire pergam: ibi plurimumst.
  PH. reuocemus hominem. AN. sta ilico. GE. hem, 195
satis pro imperio, quisquis es. AN. Geta. GE. ipsest quem
  uolui obuiam.
20 AN. cedo quid portas, obsecro? atque id, si potes, uerbo
    expedi.
  GE. faciam. AN. eloquere. GE. modo apud portum..
  AN. meumne? GE. intellexti. AN. occidi. PH. hem..
  AN. quid agam? PH. quid ais? GE. huius patrem uidisse
    me et patruom tuom.
  AN. nam quod ego huic nunc subito exitio remedium 200
    inueniam miser?
quod si eo meae fortunae redeunt, Phanium, abs te ut dis-
  trahar,

nullast mihi uita expetenda. GE. ergo istaec quom ita   25
   sunt, Antipho,
tanto mage te aduigilare aequomst: fortis fortuna adiuuat.
AN. non sum apud me. GE. atqui opus est nunc quom
   maxume ut sis, Antipho;
205 nam si senserit te timidum pater esse, arbitrabitur
commeruisse culpam. PH. hoc uerumst. AN. non possum inmutarier.
GE. quid faceres si aliud quid grauius tibi nunc faciundum   30
   foret?
AN. quom hoc non possum, illud minus possem. GE.
   hoc nil est, Phaedria: ilicet.
quid hic conterimus operam frustra? quin abeo? PH. et
   quidem ego? AN. obsecro,
210 quid si adsimulo? satinest? GE. garris. AN. voltum contemplamini: em,
satine sic est? GE. non. AN. quid si sic? GE. propemodum. AN. quid sic? GE. sat est:
em istuc serua; et uerbum uerbo, par pari ut respondeas,   35
ne te iratus suis saeuidicis dictis protelet. AN. scio.
GE. ui coactum te esse inuitum. PH. lege, iudicio. GE.
   tenes?
215 sed hic quis est senex quem uideo in ultima platea? ipsus
   est.
AN. non possum adesse. GE. ah quid agis? quo abis,
   Antipho?
mane inquam. AN. egomet me noui et peccatum meum: 40
uobis commendo Phanium et uitam meam. —
PH. Geta, quid nunc fiet? GE. tu iam litis audies;
220 ego plectar pendens nisi quid me fefellerit.
sed quod modo hic nos Antiphonem monuimus,
id nosmet ipsos facere oportet, Phaedria.   45
PH. aufer mi 'oportet': quin tu quid faciam impera.
GE. meministin, olim ut fuerit uostra oratio
225 in re incipiunda ad defendendam noxiam,
iustam illam causam, facilem, uincibilem, optumam?

50 PH. memini. GE. em nunc ipsast opus ea aut, siquid potest,
    meliore et callidore. PH. fiet sedulo.
GE. nunc prior adito tu, ego in insidiis hic ero
    succenturiatus siquid deficias. PH. age. 230

ACTVS II

i
DEMIPHO PHAEDRIA GETA

DE. Itane tandem uxorem duxit Antipho iniussu meo?
nec meum imperium—ac mitto imperium—non simulta-
    tem meam
reuereri saltem! non pudere! o facinus audax, o Geta
    monitor! GE. uix tandem. DE. quid mihi dicent aut
    quam causam reperient?
5 demiror. GE. atqui reperiam: aliud cura. DE. an hoc 235
    dicet mihi:
'inuitus feci. lex coegit'? audio, fateor. GE. places.
DE. uerum scientem, tacitum causam tradere aduorsariis,
etiamne id lex coegit? PH. illud durum. GE. ego ex-
    pediam: sine!
DE. incertumst quid agam, quia praeter spem atque incre-
    dibile hoc mi optigit:
10 ita sum inritatus animum ut nequeam ad cogitandum 240
    instituere.
quam ob rem omnis, quom secundae res sunt maxume,
    tum maxume
meditari secum oportet quo pacto aduorsam aerumnam
    ferant,
pericla damna exsilia: peregre rediens semper cogitet
aut fili peccatum aut uxoris mortem aut morbum filiae,
15 communia esse haec, fieri posse, ut ne quid animo sit 245
    nouom;
quidquid praeter spem eueniat, omne id deputare esse in
    lucro.

GE. o Phaedria, incredibile quantum erum ante eo sapi-
    entia.

meditata mihi sunt omnia mea incommoda, erus si re-
    dierit:

molendum esse in pistrino, uapulandum; habendae com-
    pedes,

250 opus ruri faciundum, horum nil quicquam accidet animo   20
    nouom.

quidquid praeter spem eueniet, omne id deputabo esse in
    lucro.

sed quid cessas hominem adire et blande in principio
    adloqui?

DE. Phaedriam mei fratris uideo filium mi ire obuiam.

PH. mi patrue, salue.   DE. salue; sed ubist Antipho?

255 PH. saluom uenire . . .   DE. credo; hoc responde mihi.   25

PH. ualet, hic est; sed satin omnia ex sententia?

DE. uellem quidem.   PH. quid istuc est?   DE. rogitas,
    Phaedria?

bonas me absente hic confecistis nuptias.

PH. eho, an id suscenses nunc illi?   GE. artificem probum!

260 DE. egon illi non suscenseam? ipsum gestio   30

dari mi in conspectum, nunc sua culpa ut sciat

lenem patrem illum factum me esse acerrimum.

PH. atqui nihil fecit, patrue, quod suscenseas.

DE. ecce autem similia omnia! omnes congruont:

265 unum quom noris omnis noris.   PH. haud itast.   35

DE. hic in noxast, ille ad defendundam causam adest;

quom illest, hic praestost: tradunt operas mutuas.

GE. probe horum facta inprudens depinxit senex.

DE. nam ni haec ita essent, cum illo haud stares, Phaedria.

270 PH. si est, patrue, culpam ut Antipho in se admiserit,   40

ex qua re minus rei foret aut famae temperans,

non causam dico quin quod meritus sit ferat.

sed siquis forte malitia fretus sua

insidias nostrae fecit adulescentiae

275 ac uicit, nostra culpa east an iudicum,   45

qui saepe propter inuidiam adimunt diuiti
aut propter misericordiam addunt pauperi?
GE. ni nossem causam, crederem uera hunc loqui.
DE. an quisquam iudex est qui possit noscere
50 tua iusta, ubi tute uerbum non respondeas,   280
ita ut ille fecit? PH. functus adulescentulist
officium liberalis: postquam ad iudices
uentumst, non potuit cogitata proloqui;
ita eum tum timidum ibi obstupefecit pudor.
55 GE. laudo hunc, sed cesso adire quam primum senem?   285
ere, salue: saluom te aduenisse gaudeo. DE. oh,
bone custos, salue, columen uero familiae,
quoi commendaui filium hinc abiens meum.
GE. iamdudum te omnis nos accusare audio
60 inmerito et me omnium horunc inmeritissumo.   290
nam quid me in hac re facere uoluisti tibi?
seruom hominem causam orare leges non sinunt
neque testimoni dictiost. DE. mitto omnia.
do istuc 'inprudens timuit adulescens'; sino
65 'tu seruo's'; uerum si cognatast maxume,   295
non fuit necessum habere; sed id quod lex iubet,
dotem daretis, quaereret alium uirum.
qua ratione inopem potius ducebat domum?
GE. non ratio, uerum argentum deerat. DE. sumeret
70 alicunde. GE. alicunde? nil est dictu facilius.   300
DE. postremo si nullo alio pacto, fenore.
GE. hui, dixti pulchre! siquidem quisquam crederet
te uiuo. DE. non, non sic futurumst: non potest.
egon illam cum illo ut patiar nuptam unum diem?
75 nil suaue meritumst. hominem conmonstrarier   305
mihi istum uolo aut ubi habitet demonstrarier.
GE. nempe Phormionem? DE. istum patronum mulieris.
GE. iam faxo hic aderit. DE. Antipho ubi nunc est? GE.
foris.
DE. abi, Phaedria, eum require atque huc adduc. PH. eo:

309 O.T. adduce

310 recta uia quidem—illuc. GE. nempe ad Pamphilam.   80
DE. ego deos Penatis hinc salutatum domum
deuortar; inde ibo ad forum atque aliquot mihi
amicos aduocabo ad hanc rem qui adsient,
ut ne inparatus sim si ueniat Phormio.

PHORMIO   GETA   ii

315 PH. Itane patris ais conspectum ueritum hinc abiisse? GE.
admodum.
   PH. Phanium relictam solam? GE. sic. PH. et iratum
senem?
   GE. oppido. PH. ad te summa solum, Phormio rerum
redit:
tute hoc intristi: tibi omnest exedendum: accingere.
   GE. obsecro te. PH. si rogabit . . . GE. in te spes est.   5
     PH. eccere,
320 quid si reddet? GE. tu inpulisti. PH. sic opinor. GE.
subueni.
   PH. cedo senem: iam instructa sunt mi in corde consilia
omnia.
   GE. quid ages? PH. quid uis, nisi uti maneat Phanium
atque ex crimine hoc
Antiphonem eripiam atque in me omnem iram deriuem
senis?
   GE. o uir fortis atque amicus. uerum hoc saepe, Phormio,   10
325 uereor, ne istaec fortitudo in neruom erumpat denique.
     PH. ah,
non itast: factumst periclum, iam pedum uisast uia.
quot me censes homines iam deuerberasse usque ad necem,
hospites, tum ciuis? quo mage noui, tanto saepius.
cedo dum, enumquam iniuriarum audisti mihi scriptam   15
dicam?
330 GE. qui istuc? PH. quia non rete accipitri tennitur neque
miluo,
qui male faciunt nobis: illis qui nihil faciunt tennitur,

315 O.T. ais aduentum

quia enim in illis fructus est, in illis opera luditur.
aliis aliunde est periclum unde aliquid abradi potest:
20 mihi sciunt nil esse. dices 'ducent damnatum domum':
alere nolunt hominem edacem et sapiunt mea sententia, 335
pro maleficio si beneficium summum nolunt reddere.
GE. non potest satis pro merito ab illo tibi referri gratia.
PH. immo enim nemo satis pro merito gratiam regi refert.
25 ten asymbolum uenire unctum atque lautum e balineis,
otiosum ab animo, quom ille et cura et sumptu absumitur! 340
dum tibi fit quod placeat, ille ringitur: tu rideas,
prior bibas, prior decumbas; cena dubia apponitur.
GE. quid istuc uerbist? PH. ubi tu dubites quid sumas
potissimum.
30 haec quom rationem ineas quam sint suauia et quam cara
sint,
ea qui praebet, non tu hunc habeas plane praesentem deum? 345
GE. senex adest: uide quid agas: prima coitiost acerrima.
si eam sustinueris, postilla iam ut lubet ludas licet.

iii DEMIPHO HEGIO CRATINVS CRITO
PHORMIO GETA

DE. Enumquam quoiquam contumeliosius
audistis factam iniuriam quam haec est mihi?
adeste quaeso. GE. iratus est. PH. quin tu hoc age: 350
iam ego hunc agitabo. pro deum inmortalium,
5 negat Phanium esse hanc sibi cognatam Demipho?
hanc Demipho negat esse cognatam? GE. negat.
PH. neque eius patrem se scire qui fuerit? GE. negat.
DE. ipsum esse opinor de quo agebam: sequimini. 355
PH. nec Stilponem ipsum scire qui fuerit? GE. negat.
10 PH. quia egens relictast misera, ignoratur parens,
neglegitur ipsa: uide auaritia quid facit.
GE. si erum insimulabis malitiae, male audies.
DE. o audaciam! etiam me ultro accusatum aduenit. 360
PH. nam iam adulescenti nil est quod suscenseam,
15 si illum minus norat; quippe homo iam grandior,

    pauper, quoi opera uita erat, ruri fere
    se continebat; ibi agrum de nostro patre
365 colendum habebat. saepe interea mihi senex
    narrabat se hunc neglegere cognatum suom:
    at quem uirum! quem ego uiderim in uita optumum.   20
    GE. uideas te atque illum ut narras! PH. in' malam
        crucem!
    nam ni ita eum existumassem, numquam tam grauis
370 ob hanc inimicitias caperem in uostram familiam,
    quam is aspernatur nunc tam inliberaliter.
    GE. pergin ero absenti male loqui, inpurissime?   25
    PH. dignum autem hoc illost. GE. ain tandem carcer?
    DE. Geta.
    GE. bonorum extortor, legum contortor! DE. Geta.
375 PH. responde. GE. quis homost? ehem. DE. tace. GE.
        absenti tibi
    te indignas seque dignas contumelias
    numquam cessauit dicere hodie. DE. desine.   30
    adulescens, primum abs te hoc bona uenia peto,
    si tibi placere potis est, mi ut respondeas:
380 quem amicum tuom ais fuisse istum, explana mihi,
    et qui cognatum me sibi esse diceret.
    PH. proinde expiscare quasi non nosses. DE. nossem?   35
        PH. ita.
    DE. ego me nego: tu qui ais redige in memoriam.
    PH. eho tu, sobrinum tuom non noras? DE. enicas.
385 dic nomen. PH. nomen? maxume. DE. quid nunc taces?
    PH. perii hercle, nomen perdidi. DE. quid ais? PH.
        (Geta,
    si meministi id quod olim dictumst, subice.) hem   40
    non dico: quasi non nosses, temptatum aduenis.
    DE. ego autem tempto? GE. (Stilpo.) PH. atque adeo
        quid mea?
390 Stilpost. DE. quem dixti? PH. Stilponem inquam
        noueras.
    DE. neque ego illum noram neque mihi cognatus fuit

45 quisquam istoc nomine.   PH. itane? non te horum pudet?
at si talentum rem reliquisset decem,
DE. di tibi malefaciant!   PH. primus esses memoriter
progeniem uostram usque ab auo atque atauo proferens.   395
DE. ita ut dicis. ego tum quom aduenissem, qui mihi
50 cognata ea esset dicerem: itidem tu face.
cedo qui est cognata?   GE. eu noster, recte. heus tu, caue.
PH. dilucide expediui quibus me oportuit
iudicibus: tum id si falsum fuerat, filius   400
quor non refellit?   DE. filium narras mihi?
55 quoius de stultitia dici ut dignumst non potest.
PH. at tu qui sapiens es magistratus adi,
iudicium de eadem causa iterum ut reddant tibi,
quandoquidem solus regnas et soli licet   405
hic de eadem causa bis iudicium adipiscier.
60 DE. etsi mihi facta iniuriast, uerum tamen
potius quam litis secter aut quam te audiam,
itidem ut cognata si sit, id quod lex iubet
dotis dare, abduc hanc, minas quinque accipe.   410
PH. hahahae, homo suauis.   DE. quid est? num iniquom
  postulo?
65 an ne hoc quidem ego adipiscar quod ius publicumst?
PH. itan tandem, quaeso, item ut meretricem ubi abusus
  sis,
mercedem dare lex iubet ei atque amittere?
an, ut ne quid turpe ciuis in se admitteret   415
propter egestatem, proxumo iussast dari,
70 ut cum uno aetatem degeret? quod tu uetas.
DE. ita, proxumo quidem; at nos unde? aut quam ob rem?
  PH. ohe,
'actum' aiunt 'ne agas.'   DE. non agam? immo haud
  desinam,
donec perfecero hoc.   PH. ineptis.   DE. sine modo.   420
PH. postremo tecum nil rei nobis, Demipho, est:
75 tuos est damnatus gnatus, non tu; nam tua

410 O.T. abduce

praeterierat iam ducendi aetas. DE. omnia haec
illum putato quae ego nunc dico dicere;
425 aut quidem cum uxore hac ipsum prohibebo domo.
    GE. (iratus est.) PH. tu te idem melius feceris.
    DE. itan es paratus facere me aduorsum omnia,   80
    infelix? PH. (metuit hic nos, tam etsi sedulo
    dissimulat.) GE. (bene habent tibi principia.) PH. quin
       quod est
430 ferundum fers? tuis dignum factis feceris,
    ut amici inter nos simus. DE. egon tuam expetam
    amicitiam? aut te uisum aut auditum uelim?   85
    PH. si concordabis cum illa, habebis quae tuam
    senectutem oblectet: respice aetatem tuam.
435 DE. te oblectet, tibi habe. PH. minue uero iram. DE.
      hoc age:
    satis iam uerborumst: nisi tu properas mulierem
    abducere, ego illam eiciam. dixi, Phormio.   90
    PH. si tu illam attigeris secus quam dignumst liberam,
    dicam tibi inpingam grandem. dixi, Demipho.
440 siquid opus fuerit, heus, domo me. GE. intellego.

    DEMIPHO GETA HEGIO CRATINVS CRITO   iv

    DE. Quanta me cura et sollicitudine adficit
    gnatus, qui me et se hisce inpediuit nuptiis!
    neque mi in conspectum prodit, ut saltem sciam
    quid de hac re dicat quidue sit sententiae.
445 abi, uise redieritne iam an nondum domum.   5
    GE. eo. — DE. uidetis quo in loco res haec siet:
    quid ago? dic, Hegio. HE. ego? Cratinum censeo,
    si tibi uidetur. DE. dic, Cratine. CRA. mene uis?
    DE. te. CRA. ego quae in rem tuam sint ea uelim facias.
      mihi
450 sic hoc uidetur: quod te absente hic filius   10
    egit, restitui in integrum aequomst et bonum,
    et id impetrabis. dixi. DE. dic nunc, Hegio.
    HE. ego sedulo hunc dixisse credo; uerum itast,

quot homines tot sententiae: suos quoique mos.
15 mihi non uidetur quod sit factum legibus　　　　　　455
rescindi posse; et turpe inceptust. DE. dic, Crito.
CRI. ego amplius deliberandum censeo:
res magnast. HE. numquid nos uis? DE. fecistis probe:
incertior sum multo quam dudum. — GE. negant
20 redisse. DE. frater est exspectandus mihi:　　　　　　460
is quod mihi dederit de hac re consilium, id sequar.
percontatum ibo ad portum, quoad se recipiat. —
GE. at ego Antiphonem quaeram, ut quae acta hic sint
　　sciat.
sed eccum ipsum uideo in tempore huc se recipere.

ACTVS III

i　　　　　　　ANTIPHO GETA

AN. Enimuero, Antipho, multimodis cum istoc animo es 465
　　uituperandus:
itane te hinc abisse et uitam tuam tutandam aliis dedisse!
alios tuam rem credidisti mage quam tete animum aduor-
　　suros?
nam utut erant alia, illi certe quae nunc tibi domist
　　consuleres,
5 nequid propter tuam fidem decepta poteretur mali.
quoius nunc miserae spes opesque sunt in te uno omnes 470
　　sitae.
GE. et quidem, ere, nos iamdudum hic te absentem
　　incusamus qui abieris.
AN. te ipsum quaerebam. GE. sed ea causa nihilo mage
　　defecimus.
AN. loquere obsecro, quonam in loco sunt res et fortunae
　　meae?
10 numquid patri subolet? GE. nil etiam. AN. ecquid spei
　　porrost? GE. nescio. AN. ah.

475 GE. nisi Phaedria haud cessauit pro te eniti. AN. nil fecit
noui.
GE. tum Phormio itidem in hac re ut in aliis strenuom
hominem praebuit.
AN. quid is fecit? GE. confutauit uerbis admodum
iratum senem.
AN. eu Phormio. GE. ego (quod potui) porro. AN. mi
Geta, omnis uos amo.
GE. sic habent principia sese ut dico: adhuc tranquilla res   15
est,
480 mansurusque patruom pater est, dum huc adueniat. AN.
quid eum? GE. ut aibat,
de eius consilio sese uelle facere quod ad hanc rem attinet.
AN. quantum metus est mihi uidere huc saluom nunc
patruom, Geta!
nam per eius unam, ut audio, aut uiuam aut moriar sententiam.
GE. Phaedria tibi adest. AN. ubinam? GE. eccum ab sua   20
palaestra exit foras.

PHAEDRIA   DORIO   ANTIPHO   GETA   ii

485 PH. Dorio,
audi obsecro . . DO. non audio. PH. parumper . . DO.
quin omitte me.
PH. audi quod dicam. DO. at enim taedet iam audire
eadem miliens.
PH. at nunc dicam quod lubenter audias. DO. loquere,
audio.
PH. non queo te exorare ut maneas triduom hoc? quo
nunc abis?
490 DO. mirabar si tu mihi quicquam adferres noui. AN. ei,   5
metuo lenonem nequid suo suat capiti. GE. idem ego
uereor.
PH. non mihi credis? DO. hariolare. PH. sin fidem do?
DO. fabulae!

491 O.T. nequid . . GE. suo suat *etc.*   492 O.T. nondum mihi

PH. feneratum istuc beneficium pulchre tibi dices. DO. logi!

PH. crede mihi, gaudebis facto: uerum hercle hoc est. DO. somnium!

10 PH. experire: non est longum. DO. cantilenam eandem 495 canis.

PH. tu mihi cognatus, tu parens, tu amicus, tu . . . DO. garri modo.

PH. adeon ingenio esse duro te atque inexorabili, ut neque misericordia neque precibus molliri queas!

DO. adeon te esse incogitantem atque inpudentem, Phaedria,

15 me ut phaleratis ducas dictis et meam ductes gratiis! 500

AN. miseritumst. PH. ei, ueris uincor! GE. quam uter-quest similis sui!

PH. neque Antipho alia quom occupatus esset sollicitudine, tum hoc esse mihi obiectum malum! AN. quid istuc est autem, Phaedria?

PH. o fortunatissime Antipho. AN. egone? PH. quoi quod amas domist,

20 neque cum huius modi umquam usus uenit ut conflictares 505 malo.

AN. mihin domist? immo, id quod aiunt, auribus teneo lupum:

nam neque quo pacto a me amittam neque uti retineam scio.

DO. ipsum istuc mi in hoc est. AN. heia, ne parum leno sies.

numquid hic confecit? PH. hicine? quod homo in-humanissimus:

· 25 Pamphilam meam uendidit. AN. quid? uendidit? GE. 510 ain? uendidit?

PH. uendidit. DO. quam indignum facinus, ancillam aere emptam suo!

PH. nequeo exorare ut me maneat et cum illo ut mutet fidem

triduom hoc, dum id quod est promissum ab amicis
argentum aufero.

si non tum dedero, unam praeterea horam ne oppertus
sies.

515 DO. optunde. AN. haud longumst id quod orat: Dorio   30
exoret sine.

idem hic tibi, quod boni promeritus fueris, conduplicauerit.

DO. uerba istaec sunt. AN. Pamphilamne hac urbe priuari
sines?

tum praeterea horunc amorem distrahi poterin pati?

DO. neque ego neque tu. GE. di tibi omnes id quod es
dignus duint!

520 DO. ego te compluris aduorsum ingenium meum mensis   35
tuli

pollicitantem et nil ferentem, flentem; nunc contra omnia
haec

repperi qui det neque lacrumet: da locum melioribus.

AN. certe hercle, ego si satis commemini, tibi quidem est
olim dies,

quam ad dares huic, praestituta. PH. factum. DO. num
ego istuc nego?

525 AN. iam ea praeteriit? DO. non, uerum haec ei antecessit.   40
AN. non pudet

uanitatis? DO. minime, dum ob rem. GE. sterculinum!
PH. Dorio,

itane tandem facere oportet? DO. sic sum: si placeo,
utere.

AN. sicin hunc decipis?. DO. immo enimuero, Antipho,
hic me decipit:

nam hic me huius modi scibat esse, ego hunc esse aliter
credidi;

530 iste me fefellit, ego isti nihilo sum aliter ac fui.   45
sed utut haec sunt, tamen hoc faciam: cras mane argentum
mihi

516 O.T. idem hoc   525 O.T. haec ei — antecessit.

miles dare se dixit: si tu prior attuleris, Phaedria,
mea lege utar, ut potior sit qui prior ad dandumst. uale.

iii   PHAEDRIA ANTIPHO GETA

PH. Quid faciam? unde ego nunc tam subito huic argen-
    tum inueniam miser,
quoi minus nihilost? quod, hic si pote fuisset exorarier   535
triduom hoc, promissum fuerat. AN. itane hunc patie-
    mur, Geta,
fieri miserum, qui me dudum ut dixti adiuerit comiter?
5 quin, quom opust, beneficium rursum ei experiemur
    reddere?
GE. scio equidem hoc esse aequom. AN. age ergo, solus
    seruare hunc potes.
GE. quid faciam? AN. inuenias argentum. GE. cupio;   540
    sed id unde edoce.
AN. pater adest hic. GE. scio; sed quid tum? AN. ah,
    dictum sapienti sat est.
GE. itane? AN. ita. GE. sane hercle pulchre suades: etiam
    tu hinc abis?
10 non triumpho, ex nuptiis tuis si nil nanciscor mali,
ni etiamnunc me huius causa quaerere in malo iubeas
    crucem?
AN. uerum hic dicit. PH. quid? ego uobis, Geta, alienus   545
    sum? GE. haud puto;
sed parumne est quod omnibus nunc nobis suscenset
    senex,
ni instigemus etiam ut nullus locus relinquatur preci?
15 PH. alius ab oculis meis illam in ignotum abducet locum?
    hem
tum igitur, dum licet dumque adsum, loquimini mecum,
    Antipho,
contemplamini me. AN. quam ob rem? aut quidnam   550
    facturu's? cedo.
PH. quoquo hinc asportabitur terrarum, certumst per-
    sequi

    aut perire. GE. di bene uortant quod agas! pedetemptim
      tamen.

    AN. uide siquid opis potes adferre huic. GE. 'siquid'? 20
      quid? AN. quaere obsecro,

nequid plus minusue faxit quod nos post pigeat, Geta.

555 GE. quaero.—saluos est, ut opinor; uerum enim metuo
      malum.

    AN. noli metuere: una tecum bona mala tolerabimus.

    GE. quantum opus est tibi argenti, loquere. PH. solae
      triginta minae.

    GE. triginta? hui, percarast, Phaedria. PH. istaec uero 25
      uilis est.

    GE. age age, inuentas reddam. PH. o lepidum! GE. aufer
      te hinc. PH. iam opust. GE. iam feres:

560 sed opus est mihi Phormionem ad hanc rem adiutorem
      dari.

    AN. praestost: audacissime oneris quiduis inpone et feret;

solus est homo amico amicus. GE. eamus ergo ad eum
      ocius.

    AN. numquid est quod opera mea uobis opus sit? GE. 30
      nil; uerum abi domum

et illam miseram, quam ego nunc intus scio esse exanima-
      tam metu,

565 consolare. cessas? AN. nil est aeque quod faciam lubens.—

    PH. qua uia istuc facies? GE. dicam in itinere: modo te
      hinc amoue.

ACTVS IV

DEMIPHO CHREMES   i

    DE. Quid? qua profectus causa hinc es Lemnum, Chreme,
    adduxtin tecum filiam? CH. non. DE. quid ita non?

    CH. postquam uidet me eius mater esse hic diutius,

570 simul autem non manebat aetas uirginis

5 meam neglegentiam, ipsam cum omni familia
  ad me profectam esse aibant.   DE. quid illi tam diu
  quaeso igitur commorabare, ubi id audiueras?
  CH. pol me detinuit morbus.   DE. unde? aut qui?   CH.
  rogas?
  senectus ipsast morbus. sed uenisse eas   575
10 saluas audiui ex nauta qui illas uexerat.
  DE. quid gnato optigerit me absente audistin, Chreme?
  CH. quod quidem me factum consili incertum facit.
  nam hanc condicionem siquoi tulero extrario,
  quo pacto aut unde mihi sit dicundum ordinest.   580
15 te mihi fidelem esse aeque atque egomet sum mihi
  scibam. ille si me alienus adfinem uolet,
  tacebit dum intercedet familiaritas;
  sin spreuerit me, plus quam opus est scito sciet.
  uereorque ne uxor aliqua hoc resciscat mea: 585
20 quod si fit, ut me excutiam atque egrediar domo,
  id restat; nam ego meorum solus sum meus.
  DE. scio ita esse, et istaec mihi res sollicitudinist,
  neque defetiscar usque adeo experirier,
  donec tibi id quod pollicitus sum effecero.   590

ii   GETA DEMIPHO CHREMES

  GE. Ego hominem callidiorem uidi neminem
  quam Phormionem. uenio ad hominem ut dicerem
  argentum opus esse, et id quo pacto fieret.
  uixdum dimidium dixeram, intellexerat:
5 gaudebat, me laudabat, quaerebat senem.   595
  dis gratias agebat tempus sibi dari
  ubi Phaedriae esse ostenderet nihilo minus
  amicum sese quam Antiphoni. hominem ad forum
  iussi opperiri: eo me esse adducturum senem.
10 sed eccum ipsum. quis est ulterior? attat Phaedriae   600
  pater uenit. sed quid pertimui autem belua?
  an quia quos fallam pro uno duo sunt mihi dati?
  commodius esse opinor duplici spe utier.

petam hinc unde a primo institi: is si dat, sat est;
605 si ab eo nil fiet, tum hunc adoriar hospitem.

ANTIPHO GETA CHREMES DEMIPHO iii

AN. Exspecto quam mox recipiat sese Geta.
sed patruom uideo cum patre astantem. ei mihi,
quam timeo aduentus huius quo inpellat patrem!
GE. adibo hosce: o noster Chreme . . CH. salue, Geta.
610 GE. uenire saluom uolup est. CH. credo. GE. quid   5
    agitur?
multa aduenienti, ut fit, noua hic? CH. compluria.
GE. ita. de Antiphone audistin quae facta? CH. omnia.
GE. tun dixeras huic? facinus indignum, Chreme,
sic circumiri! CH. id cum hoc agebam commodum.
615 GE. nam hercle ego quoque id quidem agitans mecum   10
    sedulo
inueni, opinor, remedium huic rei. CH. quid, Geta?
DE. quod remedium? GE. ut abii abs te, fit forte obuiam
mihi Phormio. CH. qui Phormio? DE. is qui istanc . .
    CH. scio.
GE. uisumst mihi ut eius temptarem sententiam.
620 prendo hominem solum: 'quor non' inquam 'Phormio,   15
uides inter nos sic haec potius cum bona
ut componamus gratia quam cum mala?
erus liberalis est et fugitans litium;
nam ceteri quidem hercle amici omnes modo
625 uno ore auctores fuere ut praecipitem hanc daret.'   20
AN. quid hic coeptat aut quo euadet hodie? GE. 'an
    legibus
daturum poenas dices, si illam eiecerit?
iam id exploratumst: heia, sudabis satis,
si cum illo inceptas homine: ea eloquentiast.
630 uerum pone esse uictum eum; at tandem tamen   25
non capitis eius res agitur sed pecuniae.'
postquam hominem his uerbis sentio mollirier,
'soli sumus nunc hic' inquam: 'eho, quid uis dari

tibi in manum, ut erus his desistat litibus,
30 haec hinc facessat, tu molestus ne sies?'   635
     AN. satin illi di sunt propitii?   GE. 'nam sat scio,
   si tu aliquam partem aequi bonique dixeris,
   ut est ille bonus uir, tria non commutabitis
   uerba hodie inter uos.'   DE. quis te istaec iussit loqui?
35 CH. immo non potuit melius peruenirier   640
   eo quo nos uolumus.   AN. occidi!   DE. perge eloqui.
     GE. a primo homo insanibat.   CH. cedo quid postulat?
     GE. quid? nimium; quantum libuit.   CH. dic.   GE. si quis
          daret
   talentum magnum.   DE. immo malum hercle: ut nil
          pudet!
40 GE. quod dixi adeo ei: 'quaeso, quid si filiam   645
   suam unicam locaret? parui retulit
   non suscepisse: inuentast quae dotem petat.'
   ut ad pauca redeam ac mittam illius ineptias,
   haec denique eius fuit postrema oratio:
45 'ego' inquit 'a principio amici filiam,   650
   ita ut aequom fuerat, uolui uxorem ducere;
   nam mihi ueniebat in mentem eius incommodum,
   in seruitutem pauperem ad ditem dari.
   sed mi opus erat, ut aperte tibi nunc fabuler,
50 aliquantulum quae adferret qui dissoluerem   655
   quae debeo: et etiamnunc, si uolt Demipho
   dare quantum ab hac accipio quae sponsast mihi,
   nullam mihi malim quam istanc uxorem dari.'
     AN. utrum stultitia facere ego hunc an malitia
55 dicam, scientem an inprudentem, incertus sum.   660
     DE. quid si animam debet?   GE. 'ager oppositus pignori
          ob
   decem minas' inquit.   DE. age age, iam ducat: dabo.
     GE. 'aediculae item sunt ob decem alias.'   DE. oiei,
   nimiumst.   CH. ne clama: repetito hasce a me decem.
60 GE. 'uxori emunda ancillulast; tum pluscula   665
   supellectile opus est; opus est sumptu ad nuptias:

his rebus pone sane' inquit 'decem minas.'
DE. sescentas perinde scribito iam mihi dicas:
nil do. inpuratus me ille ut etiam inrideat?
670 CH. quaeso, ego dabo, quiesce: tu modo filium   65
fac ut illam ducat nos quam uolumus.   AN. ei mihi,
Geta, occidisti me tuis fallaciis.
CH. mea causa eicitur: me hoc est aequom amittere.
GE. 'quantum potest me certiorem' inquit 'face,
675 si illam dant, hanc ut mittam, ne incertus siem;   70
nam illi mihi dotem iam constituerunt dare.'
CH. iam accipiat: illis repudium renuntiet;
hanc ducat.   DE. quae quidem illi res uortat male!
CH. opportune adeo argentum nunc mecum attuli,
680 fructum quem Lemni uxoris reddunt praedia: 75
inde sumam; uxori tibi opus esse dixero.

ANTIPHO   GETA   iv

AN. Geta.   GE. hem.   AN. quid egisti?   GE. emunxi
argento senes.
AN. satin est id?   GE. nescio hercle: tantum iussus sum.
AN. eho, uerbero, aliud mihi respondes ac rogo?
685 GE. quid ergo narras?   AN. quid ego narrem? opera tua
ad restim miquidem res redit planissume.   5
ut tequidem omnes di deaeque, superi inferi,
malis exemplis perdant! em siquid uelis,
huic mandes quod quidem recte curatum uelis.
690 quid minus utibile fuit quam hoc ulcus tangere
aut nominare uxorem? iniectast spes patri   10
posse illam extrudi. cedo nunc porro: Phormio
dotem si accipiet, uxor ducendast domum:
quid fiet? GE. non enim ducet. AN. noui. ceterum
695 quom argentum repetent, nostra causa scilicet
in neruom potius ibit. GE. nil est, Antipho,   15
quin male narrando possit deprauarier:
tu id quod bonist excerpis, dicis quod malist.
audi nunc contra: iam si argentum acceperit,

ducendast uxor, ut ais, concedo tibi: 700
20 spatium quidem tandem apparandi nuptias,
uocandi, sacruficandi dabitur paullulum.
interea amici quod polliciti sunt dabunt:
inde iste reddet. AN. quam ob rem? aut quid dicet?
    GE. rogas?
'quot res postilla monstra euenerunt mihi!   705
25 intro iit in aedis ater alienus canis;
anguis per inpluuium decidit de tegulis;
gallina cecinit; interdixit hariolus:
haruspex uetuit; ante brumam autem noui
negoti incipere!' quae causast iustissima.   710
30 haec fient. AN. ut modo fiant! GE. fient: me uide.
pater exit: abi, dic esse argentum Phaedriae.

v   DEMIPHO   CHREMES   GETA

DE. Quietus esto, inquam: ego curabo nequid uerborum
    duit.
hoc temere numquam amittam ego a me quin mihi testis
    adhibeam.
quoi dem et quam ob rem dem commemorabo. GE. ut   715
    cautust, ubi nil opust!
CH. atque ita opus factost: et matura, dum lubido eadem
    haec manet;
5 nam si altera illaec magis instabit, forsitan nos reiciat.
GE. rem ipsam putasti. DE. duc me ad eum ergo. GE.
    non moror. CH. ubi hoc egeris,
transito ad uxorem meam, ut conueniat hanc prius quam
    hinc abit.
dicat eam dare nos Phormioni nuptum, ne suscenseat;   720
et magis esse illum idoneum qui ipsi sit familiarior;
· 10 nos nostro officio non digressos esse: quantum is uoluerit,
datum esse dotis. DE. quid tua, malum, id refert? CH.
    magni, Demipho.

     715 O.T. quom dem et   717 O.T. fors sit an

    non sat est tuom te officium fecisse, si non id fama ad-
      probat:
725 uolo ipsius quoque uoluntate haec fieri, ne se eiectam
      praedicet.
    DE. idem ego istuc facere possum.   CH. mulier mulieri
      mage conuenit.
    DE. rogabo.   CH. ubi illas nunc ego reperire possim   15
      cogito.

ACTVS V

SOPHRONA CHREMES   i

    SO. Quid agam? quem mi amicum inueniam misera? aut
      quoi consilia haec referam?
                 aut unde auxilium petam?
730 nam uereor era ne ob meum suasum indigne iniuria ad-
      ficiatur:
    ita patrem adulescentis facta haec tolerare audio uiolenter.
    CH. nam quae haec anus est exanimata a fratre quae   5
      egressast meo?
    SO. quod ut facerem egestas me inpulit, quom scirem
      infirmas nuptias
    hasce esse, ut id consulerem, interea uita ut in tuto foret.
735 CH. certe edepol, nisi me animus fallit aut parum pro-
      spiciunt oculi,
    meae nutricem gnatae uideo.   SO. neque ille inuestigatur,
    CH. quid ago?
    SO. qui est pater eius.   CH. adeo, maneo dum haec quae   10
      loquitur mage cognosco?
    SO. quodsi eum nunc reperire possim, nil est quod uerear.
    CH. east ipsa:
    conloquar.   SO. quis hic loquitur?   CH. Sophrona.   SO.
    et meum nomen nominat?
740 CH. respice ad me.   SO. di obsecro uos, estne hic Stilpo?
    CH. non.   SO. negas?

CH. concede hinc a foribus paullum istorsum sodes,
    Sophrona.

15 ne me istoc posthac nomine appellassis. SO. quid? non
    obsecro es

quem semper te esse dictitasti? CH. st. SO. quid has
    metuis fores?

CH. conclusam hic habeo uxorem saeuam. uerum istoc
    de nomine

eo perperam olim dixi ne uos forte inprudentes foris   745
effuttiretis atque id porro aliqua uxor mea rescisceret.

20 SO. em istoc pol nos te hic inuenire miserae numquam
    potuimus.

CH. eho dic mihi, quid rei tibist cum familia hac unde
    exis?

ubi illae sunt? SO. miseram me! CH. hem quid est?
    uiuontne? SO. uiuit gnata.

matrem ipsam ex aegritudine hac miseram mors con-   750
secutast.

CH. male factum. SO. ego autem, quae essem anus
    deserta egens ignota,

25 ut potui nuptum uirginem locaui huic adulescenti,
harum qui est dominus aedium. CH. Antiphonin? SO.
    em istic ipsi.

CH. quid? duasne uxores habet? SO. au obsecro, unam
    illequidem hanc solam.

CH. quid illam alteram quae dicitur cognata? SO. haec   755
ergost. CH. quid ais?

SO. composito factumst, quo modo hanc amans habere
    posset

30 sine dote. CH. di uostram fidem, quam saepe forte temere
eueniunt quae non audeas optare! offendi adueniens
quicum uolebam et ut uolebam conlocatam amari:
quod nos ambo opere maxumo dabamus operam ut fieret,   760
sine nostra cura, maxuma sua cura haec sola fecit.

35 SO. nunc quid opus facto sit uide: pater adulescentis uenit

761 O.T. sua cura solus fecit

eumque animo iniquo hoc oppido ferre aiunt.   CH. nil
    periclist.
sed per deos atque homines meam esse hanc caue resciscat
    quisquam.
765 SO. nemo e me scibit.   CH. sequere me: intus cetera.

DEMIPHO   GETA   ii

DE. Nostrapte culpa facimus ut malis expediat esse,
    dum nimium dici nos bonos studemus et benignos.
    ita fugias ne praeter casam, quod aiunt. nonne id sat erat,
    accipere ab illo iniuriam? etiam argentumst ultro obiec-
      tum,
770 ut sit qui uiuat dum aliud aliquid flagiti conficiat.   5
    GE. planissime.   DE. is nunc praemiumst qui recta praua
      faciunt.
    GE. uerissime.   DE. ut stultissime quidem illi rem ges-
      serimus.
    GE. modo ut hoc consilio possiet discedi, ut istam ducat.
    DE. etiamne id dubiumst?   GE. haud scio hercle, ut
      homost, an mutet animum.
775 DE. hem mutet autem?   GE. nescio; uerum, si forte, dico.   10
    DE. ita faciam, ut frater censuit, ut uxorem eius huc
      adducam,
    cum ista ut loquatur. tu, Geta, abi prae, nuntia hanc uen-
      turam.—
    GE. argentum inuentumst Phaedriae; de iurgio siletur;
    prouisumst ne in praesentia haec hinc abeat: quid nunc
      porro?
780 quid fiet? in eodem luto haesitas; uorsuram solues,   15
    Geta: praesens quod fuerat malum in diem abiit: plagae
      crescunt,
    nisi prospicis. nunc hinc domum ibo ac Phanium edocebo
    nequid uereatur Phormionem aut eius orationem.

iii   DEMIPHO NAVSISTRATA

DE. Agedum, ut soles, Nausistrata, fac illa ut placetur
   nobis,
ut sua uoluntate id quod est faciundum faciat. NA. 785
   faciam.
DE. pariter nunc opera me adiuues ac re dudum opitulata
   es.
NA. factum uolo. ac pol minus queo uiri culpa quam me
   dignumst.
5 DE. quid autem? NA. quia pol mei patris bene parta in-
   diligenter
tutatur; nam ex is praediis talenta argenti bina
statim capiebat: uir uiro quid praestat! DE. bina quaeso? 790
NA. ac rebus uilioribus multo tamen duo talenta. DE.
   hui.
NA. quid haec uidentur? DE. scilicet. NA uirum me
   natum uellem:
10 ego ostenderem. DE. certo scio. NA. quo pacto . . .
   DE. parce sodes,
ut possis cum illa, ne te adulescens mulier defetiget.
NA. faciam ut iubes. sed meum uirum abs te exire uideo. 795

              NAVSISTRATA CHREMES DEMIPHO
                              CH. Ehem Demipho,
iam illi datumst argentum? DE. curaui ilico. CH. nollem datum.
ei, uideo uxorem: paene plus quam sat erat. DE. quor
   nolles, Chreme?
15 CH. iam recte. DE. quid tu? ecquid locutu's cum istac
   quam ob rem hanc ducimus?
CH. transegi. DE. quid ait tandem? CH. abduci non
   potest. DE. qui non potest?
CH. quia uterque utrique est cordi. DE. quid istuc nostra? 800
   CH. magni. praeterhac

cognatam comperi esse nobis.   DE. quid? deliras.   CH. sic
    erit.

non temere dico: redii mecum in memoriam.   DE. satin
    sanus es?

NA. au obsecro, uide ne in cognatam pecces.   DE. non   20
    est.   CH. ne nega:

patris nomen aliud dictumst: hoc tu errasti.   DE. non
    norat patrem?

805   CH. norat.   DE. quor aliud dixit?   CH. numquamne
    hodie concedes mihi

neque intelleges?   DE. si tu nil narras?   CH. perdis.   NA.
    miror quid hoc siet.

DE. equidem hercle nescio.   CH. uin scire? at ita me
    seruet Iuppiter,

ut propior illi quam ego sum ac tu homo nemost.   DE. di   25
    uostram fidem,

eamus ad ipsam: una omnis nos aut scire aut nescire hoc
    uolo.   CH. ah.

810   DE. quid est?   CH. itan paruam mihi fidem esse apud te!
    DE. uin me credere?

uin satis quaesitum mi istuc esse? age, fiat. quid illa filia
amici nostri? quid futurumst?   CH. recte.   DE. hanc igitur
    mittimus?

CH. quidni?   DE. illa maneat?   CH. sic.   DE. ire igitur   30
    tibi licet, Nausistrata.

NA. sic pol commodius esse in omnis arbitror quam ut
    coeperas,

815   manere hanc; nam perliberalis uisast, quom uidi, mihi.—
    DE. quid istuc negotist?   CH. iamne operuit ostium?   DE.
    iam.   CH. o Iuppiter,

di nos respiciunt: gnatam inueni nuptam cum tuo filio.
    DE. hem

quo pacto potuit?   CH. non satis tutus est ad narrandum   35
    hic locus.

DE. at tu intro abi.   CH. heus ne filii quidem hoc nostri
    resciscant uolo.

iv   ANTIPHO

Laetus sum, utut meae res sese habent, fratri optigisse   820
    quod uolt.
quam scitumst eius modi in animo parare cupiditates
quas, quom res aduorsae sient, paulo mederi possis!
hic simul argentum repperit, cura sese expediuit;
5 ego nullo possum remedio me euoluere ex his turbis
quin, si hoc celetur, in metu, sin patefit, in probro sim.   825
neque me domum nunc reciperem ni mi esset spes ostenta
huiusce habendae. sed ubinam Getam inuenire possim, ut
rogem quod tempus conueniundi patris me capere iubeat?

v   PHORMIO ANTIPHO

PH. Argentum accepi, tradidi lenoni, abduxi mulierem,
curaui propria ut Phaedria poteretur; nam emissast manu.   830
nunc una mihi res etiam restat quae est conficiunda, otium
ab senibus ad potandum ut habeam; nam aliquot hos
    sumam dies.
5 AN. sed Phormiost. quid ais? PH. quid? AN. quidnam
    nunc facturust Phaedria?
quo pacto satietatem amoris ait se uelle absumere?
PH. uicissim partis tuas acturus est. AN. quas? PH. ut   835
    fugitet patrem.
te suas rogauit rursum ut ageres, causam ut pro se diceres;
nam potaturus est apud me. ego me ire senibus Sunium
10 dicam ad mercatum, ancillulam emptum dudum quam
    dixit Geta:
ne quom hic non uideant me conficere credant argentum
    suom.
sed ostium concrepuit abs te. AN. uide quis egreditur.   840
PH. Getast.

vi   GETA ANTIPHO PHORMIO

GE. O Fortuna, o Fors Fortuna, quantis commoditatibus,
quam subito meo ero Antiphoni ope uostra hunc onerastis
    diem!

AN. quidnam hic sibi uolt? GE. nosque amicos eius
     exonerastis metu!

sed ego nunc mihi cesso qui non umerum hunc onero
     pallio

845 atque hominem propero inuenire, ut haec quae conti-   5
     gerint sciat.

AN. num tu intellegis quid hic narret? PH. num tu? AN.
     nil. PH. tantundem ego.

GE. ad lenonem hinc ire pergam: ibi nunc sunt. AN.
     heus Geta! GE. em tibi:

num mirum aut nouomst reuocari cursum quom in-
     stiteris? AN. Geta.

GE. pergit hercle. numquam tu odio tuo me uinces. AN.
     non manes?

850 GE. uapula. AN. id quidem tibi iam fiet nisi resistis,   10
     uerbero.

GE. familiariorem oportet esse hunc: minitatur malum.

sed isne est quem quaero an non? ipsust. congredere actu-
     tum. AN. quid est?

GE. o omnium quantumst qui uiuont homo hominum
     ornatissime!

nam sine controuorsia ab dis solus diligere, Antipho.

855 AN. ita uelim; sed qui istuc credam ita esse mihi dici   15
     uelim.

GE. satine est si te delibutum gaudio reddo? AN. enicas.

PH. quin tu hinc pollicitationes aufer et quod fers cedo.
     GE. oh,

tu quoque aderas, Phormio? PH. aderam. sed tu cessas.
     GE. accipe, em:

ut modo argentum tibi dedimus apud forum, recta
     domum

860 sumus profecti; interea mittit erus me ad uxorem tuam.   20

AN. quam ob rem? GE. omitto proloqui; nam nil ad
     hanc rem est, Antipho.

ubi in gynaeceum ire occipio, puer ad me adcurrit Mida,

pone reprendit pallio, resupinat: respicio, rogo

quam ob rem retineat me: ait esse uetitum intro ad eram
accedere.

25 'Sophrona modo fratrem huc' inquit 'senis introduxit   865
Chremem'

eumque nunc esse intus cum illis. hoc ubi ego audiui, ad
fores

suspenso gradu placide ire perrexi, accessi, astiti,

animam compressi, aurem admoui: ita animum coepi
attendere,

hoc modo sermonem captans. PH. eu Geta. GE. hic
pulcherrimum

30 facinus audiui: itaque paene hercle exclamaui gaudio.   870

AN. quod? GE. quodnam arbitrare? AN. nescio. GE.
atqui mirificissimum:

patruos tuos est pater inuentus Phanio uxori tuae. AN.
hem

quid ais? GE. cum eius consueuit olim matre in Lemno
clanculum.

PH. somnium! utine haec ignoraret suom patrem? GE.
aliquid credito,

35 Phormio, esse causae. sed censen me potuisse omnia   875
intellegere extra ostium intus quae inter sese ipsi egerint?

AN. atque ego quoque inaudiui hercle illam fabulam.
GE. immo etiam dabo

quo mage credas: patruos interea inde huc egreditur foras:
haud multo post cum patre idem recipit se intro denuo:

40 ait uterque tibi potestatem eius adhibendae dari.   880
denique ego sum missus te ut requirerem atque addu-
cerem.

AN. quin ergo rape me: quid cessas? GE. fecero. AN.
heus Phormio,

uale. PH. uale, Antipho. bene, ita me di ament, factum:
gaudeo.

PHORMIO

Tantam fortunam de inprouiso esse his datam!
885 summa eludendi occasiost mihi nunc senes
et Phaedriae curam adimere argentariam,
ne quoiquam suorum aequalium supplex siet.
    nam idem hoc argentum, ita ut datumst, ingratiis   5
ei datum erit: hoc qui cogam re ipsa repperi.
890 nunc gestus mihi uoltusque est capiundus nouos.
sed hinc concedam in angiportum hoc proxumum,
inde hisce ostendam me, ubi erunt egressi foras.
quo me adsimularam ire ad mercatum, non eo.   10

DEMIPHO CHREMES PHORMIO

DE. Dis magnas merito gratias habeo atque ago,
895 quando euenere haec nobis, frater, prospere.
quantum potest nunc conueniundust Phormio,
prius quam dilapidat nostras triginta minas
ut auferamus. PH. Demiphonem si domist   5
uisam, ut quod . . . DE. at nos ad te ibamus, Phormio.
900 PH. de eadem hac fortasse causa? DE. ita hercle. PH.
    credidi:
quid ad me ibatis? DE. ridiculum. PH. uerebamini
ne non id facerem quod recepissem semel?
heus quanta quanta haec mea paupertas est, tamen   10
adhuc curaui unum hoc quidem, ut mi esset fides.
905 CH. estne ita uti dixi liberalis? DE. oppido.
PH. idque ad uos uenio nuntiatum, Demipho,
paratum me esse: ubi uoltis, uxorem date.
nam omnis posthabui mihi res, ita uti par fuit,   15
postquam id tanto opere uos uelle animum aduorteram.
910 DE. at hic dehortatus est me ne illam tibi darem:
'nam qui erit rumor populi' inquit, 'si id feceris?
olim quom honeste potuit, tum non est data:
eam nunc extrudi turpest.' ferme eadem omnia   20
quae tute dudum coram me incusaueras.

PH. satis superbe inluditis me. DE. qui? PH. rogas?   915
quia ne alteram quidem illam potero ducere;
nam quo redibo ore ad eam quam contempserim?
25 CH. ('tum autem Antiphonem uideo ab sese amittere
inuitum eam' inque.) DE. tum autem uideo filium
inuitum sane mulierem ab se amittere.   920
sed transi sodes ad forum atque illud mihi
argentum rursum iube rescribi, Phormio.
30 PH. quodne ego discripsi porro illis quibus debui?
DE. quid igitur fiet? PH. si uis mi uxorem dare
quam despondisti, ducam; sin est ut uelis   925
manere illam apud te, dos hic maneat, Demipho.
nam non est aequom me propter uos decipi,
35 quom ego uostri honoris causa repudium alterae
remiserim, quae dotis tantundem dabat.
DE. in' hinc malam rem cum istac magnificentia,   930
fugitiue? etiamnunc credis te ignorarier
aut tua facta adeo? PH. irritor! DE. tune hanc duceres,
40 si tibi daretur? PH. fac periclum. DE. ut filius
cum illa habitet apud te, hoc uostrum consilium fuit.
PH. quaeso quid narras? DE. quin tu mi argentum cedo. 935
PH. immo uero uxorem tu cedo. DE. in ius ambula.
PH. enim uero si porro esse odiosi pergitis . . .
45 DE. quid facies? PH. egone? uos me indotatis modo
patrocinari fortasse arbitramini:
etiam dotatis soleo. CH. quid id nostra? PH. nihil.   940
hic quandam noram, quoius uir uxorem CH. hem. DE.
    quid est?
PH. Lemni habuit aliam: CH. nullus sum. PH. ex qua
    filiam
50 suscepit, et eam clam educat. CH. sepultus sum.
PH. haec adeo ego illi iam denarrabo. CH. obsecro,
ne facias. PH. oh, tune is eras? DE. ut ludos facit!   945
CH. missum te facimus. PH. fabulae! CH. quid uis tibi?
argentum quod habes condonamus te. PH. audio.
55 quid uos, malum, ergo me sic ludificamini

  inepti uostra puerili sententia?
950 nolo uolo; uolo nolo rursum; cape cedo;
  quod dictum indictumst; quod modo ratum erat inritumst.
  CH. quo pacto aut unde hic haec resciuit? DE. nescio;
  nisi me dixisse nemini certo scio.   60
   CH. monstri, ita me di ament, simile. PH. inieci scrupulum. DE. hem,
955 hicine ut a nobis hoc tantum argenti auferat
  tam aperte inridens? emori hercle satius est.
  animo uirili praesentique ut sis para.
  uides peccatum tuom esse elatum foras   65
  neque iam id celare posse te uxorem tuam:
960 nunc quod ipsa ex aliis auditura sit, Chreme,
  id nosmet indicare placabilius est.
  tum hunc inpuratum poterimus nostro modo
  ulcisci. PH. attat, nisi mi prospicio, haereo.   70
  hi gladiatorio animo ad me adfectant uiam.
965 CH. at uereor ut placari possit. DE. bono animo es:
  ego redigam uos in gratiam, hoc fretus, Chreme,
  quom e medio excessit unde haec susceptast tibi.
  PH. itan agitis mecum? satis astute adgredimini. 75
  non hercle ex re istius me instigasti, Demipho.
970 ain tu? ubi quae lubitum fuerit peregre feceris
  neque huius sis ueritus feminae primariae
  quin nouo modo ei faceres contumeliam,
  uenias nunc precibus lautum peccatum tuom? 80
  hisce ego illam dictis ita tibi incensam dabo
975 ut ne restinguas lacrumis si exstillaueris.
  DE. malum quod isti di deaeque omnes duint.
  tantane adfectum quemquam esse hominem audacia!
  non hoc publicitus scelus hinc asportarier 85
  in solas terras! CH. in id redactus sum loci
980 ut quid agam cum illo nesciam prorsum. DE. ego scio:
  in ius eamus. PH. in ius? huc, siquid lubet.
   CH. adsequere, retine dum ego huc seruos euoco.
   DE. enim nequeo solus: accurre. PH. una iniuriast 90

tecum. DE. lege agito ergo. PH. alterast tecum, Chreme.
CH. rape hunc. PH. sic agitis? enimuero uocest opus: 985
Nausistrata, exi. CH. os opprime inpurum: uide
quantum ualet. PH. Nausistrata! inquam. DE. non taces?
95 PH. taceam? DE. nisi sequitur, pugnos in uentrem ingere.
   PH. uel oculum exclude: est ubi uos ulciscar probe.

ix   NAUSISTRATA CHREMES DEMIPHO PHORMIO

   NA. Qui nominat me? hem quid istuc turbaest, obsecro, 990
   mi uir? PH. ehem quid nunc obstipuisti? NA. quis hic
     homost?
   non mihi respondes? PH. hicine ut tibi respondeat,
   qui hercle ubi sit nescit? CH. caue isti quicquam creduas.
 5 PH. abi, tange: si non totus friget, me enica.
   CH. nil est. NA. quid ergo? quid istic narrat? PH. iam 995
     scies:
   ausculta. CH. pergin credere? NA. quid ego obsecro
   huic credam, qui nil dixit? PH. delirat miser
   timore. NA. non pol temerest quod tu tam times.
10 CH. egon timeo? PH. recte sane: quando nil times,
   et hoc nil est quod ego dico, tu narra. DE. scelus,   1000
   tibi narret? PH. ohe tu, factumst abs te sedulo
   pro fratre. NA. mi uir, non mihi narras? CH. at . . .
     NA. quid 'at'?
   CH. non opus est dicto. PH. tibi quidem; at scito huic
     opust.
15 in Lemno NA. hem quid ais? CH. non taces? PH. clam
     te CH. ei mihi!
   PH. uxorem duxit. NA. mi homo, di melius duint!   1005
   PH. sic factumst. NA. perii misera! PH. et inde filiam
   suscepit iam unam, dum tu dormis. CH. quid agimus?
   NA. pro di inmortales, facinus miserandum et malum!
20 PH. hoc actumst. NA. an quicquam hodiest factum in-
     dignius?
   qui mi, ubi ad uxores uentumst, tum fiunt senes.   1010
   Demipho, te appello: nam cum hoc ipso distaedet loqui:

haecin erant itiones crebrae et mansiones diutinae
Lemni? haecin erat ea quae nostros minuit fructus uilitas?
DE. ego, Nausistrata, esse in hac re culpam meritum non   25
    nego;
1015 sed ea qui sit ignoscenda. PH. uerba fiunt mortuo.
DE. nam neque neglegentia tua neque odio id fecit tuo.
uinolentus fere abhinc annos quindecim mulierculam
eam compressit unde haec natast; neque postilla umquam
    attigit.
ea mortem obiit, e medio abiit qui fuit in re hac scrupulus.   30
1020 quam ob rem te oro, ut alia facta tua sunt, aequo animo
    hoc feras.
NA. quid ego aequo animo? cupio misera in hac re iam
    defungier;
sed quid sperem? aetate porro minus peccaturum putem?
iam tum erat senex, senectus si uerecundos facit.
an mea forma atque aetas magis nunc expetendast,   35
    Demipho?
1025 quid mi hic adfers quam ob rem exspectem aut sperem
    porro non fore?
PH. exsequias Chremeti quibus est commodum ire, em
    tempus est.
sic dabo: age nunc, Phormionem qui uolet lacessito:
faxo tali sum mactatum atque hic est infortunio.
PH. redeat sane in gratiam iam: supplici satis est mihi.   40
1030 habet haec ei quod, dum uiuat, usque ad aurem ogganniat.
NA. at meo merito credo. quid ego nunc commemorem,
    Demipho,
singulatim qualis ego in hunc fuerim? DE. noui aeque
    omnia
tecum. NA. merito hoc meo uidetur factum? DE.
    minime gentium.
uerum iam, quando accusando fieri infectum non potest,   45
1035 ignosce: orat confitetur purgat: quid uis amplius?
PH. enimuero prius quam haec dat ueniam, mihi prospi-
    ciam et Phaedriae.

heus Nausistrata, prius quam huic respondes temere, audi.
    NA. quid est?
PH. ego minas triginta per fallaciam ab illoc abstuli:
50 eas dedi tuo gnato: is pro sua amica lenoni dedit.
    CH. hem quid ais?   NA. adeone hoc indignum tibi uide- 1040
    tur, filius
homo adulescens si habet unam amicam, tu uxores duas?
nil pudere! quo ore illum obiurgabis? responde mihi.
    DE. faciet ut uoles.   NA. immo ut meam iam scias senten-
    tiam,
55 neque ego ignosco neque promitto quicquam neque re-
    spondeo
prius quam gnatum uidero: eius iudicio permitto omnia. 1045
quod is iubebit faciam.   PH. mulier sapiens es, Nausistrata.
NA. satin tibi est?   CH. immo uero pulchre discedo et
    probe
et praeter spem.   NA. tu tuom nomen dic mihi quid est.
    PH. mihin? Phormio:
60 uostrae familiae hercle amicus et tuo summus Phaedriae.
    NA. Phormio, at ego ecastor posthac tibi quod potero, 1050
    quae uoles
faciamque et dicam.   PH. benigne dicis.   NA. pol meri-
    tumst tuom.
PH. uin primum hodie facere quod ego gaudeam, Nausi-
    strata,
et quod tuo uiro oculi doleant?   NA. cupio.   PH. me ad
    cenam uoca.
65 NA. pol uero uoco.   DE. eamus intro hinc.   NA. fiat. sed
    ubist Phaedria
iudex noster?   PH. iam hic faxo aderit.   CANTOR. uos 1055
    ualete et plaudite.

       1047 O.T. *PH.* immo uero *etc.*

BIBLIOGRAPHY AND LIST OF ABBREVIA-
TIONS USED IN THE COMMENTARY

References to the other plays of Terence are given, without the author's name prefixed, by the following abbreviations:
Ad. = *Adelphoe. An.* = *Andria. Eun.* = *Eunuchus. Haut.* (or *Ht.*) = *Hautontimorumenos. Hec.* = *Hecyra.*

The plays of Plautus[1] are similarly abbreviated (usually) to the first syllable of the title (e.g. *Amph.* = *Amphitruo*), and Plautus' name is omitted where the reference is unambiguous.

The names Ashmore, Bond and Walpole, Marouzeau, Sargeaunt, Sloman refer to their respective editions of the play or of Terence's works; details are given below.

For the meaning of A and Σ, abbreviations referring to Terentian manuscripts, see Introduction, Section IV.

The customary abbreviations (mostly initial letters only) are used for the titles of classical periodicals.

Allardice	J. T. Allardice, *Syntax of Terence* (St Andrews University Publications), 1929.
Ashmore	S. G. Ashmore, *The Comedies of Terence*, 2nd edition, 1908.
B-B	'Breuis breuians' (Laidlaw (*vid. infra*) commonly abbreviates B.-B.).
Beare	W. Beare, *The Roman Stage*, 2nd edition, 1955.
Bennett	C. E. Bennett, *Syntax of Early Latin* (2 vols.), 1910.
Bond and Walpole	*The Phormio of Terence*, 3rd edition, 1889, etc.
Duckworth	G. E. Duckworth, *The Nature of Roman Comedy*, 1952.
Dz-H	*Phormio*, ed. Dziatzko-Hauler (Teubner), 1913.
E.L.V.	W. M. Lindsay, *Early Latin Verse*, 1922.
L & S	Lewis and Short, *A Latin Dictionary*.
Laidlaw	W. A. Laidlaw, *The Prosody of Terence* (St Andrews University Publications), 1938.

[1] *Amphitruo, Asinaria, Aulularia, Bacchides, Captiui, Casina, Cistellaria, Curculio, Epidicus, Menaechmi, Mercator, Miles Gloriosus, Mostellaria, Persa, Poenulus, Pseudolus, Rudens, Stichus, Trinummus, Truculentus.*

Lindsay, Syntax W. M. Lindsay, *Syntax of Plautus*, 1907.
Marouzeau   J. Marouzeau, *Térence* (Budé edition, 3 vols.), 1947–9.
Neue   F. Neue-C. Wagener, *Formenlehre d. lat. Sprache*, 3rd
                 edition, 1902.
O.C.D.   *The Oxford Classical Dictionary*, 1949.
O.T.   *P. Terenti Afri Comoediae*: R. Kauer and W. M.
                 Lindsay (Oxford Classical Text), 1926.
Otto   A. Otto, *Die Sprichwörter u. sprichwortlichen Redens-
                 arten der Römer*, 1890.
Sargeaunt   J. Sargeaunt, *P. Terenti Phormio*, 1914.
Sloman   A. Sloman, *P. Terenti Phormio*, 2nd edition, 1890, etc.
Tyrrell   R. Y. Tyrrell, *P. Terenti Afri Comoediae* (Oxford
                 Classical Text), 1902.
Umgsspr.   J. B. Hofmann, *Lateinische Umgangssprache*, 3rd
                 edition, 1951.

Commentary

DIDASCALIA

Though the word is not found in classical Latin, *didascalia* is conventionally used of the 'production notices' that are found in our manuscripts of Terence and, paraphrased, in Donatus' commentary. The notices clearly purport to record the first production of the individual plays, but in their present form they have suffered from much accretion —derived, presumably, from the records of subsequent productions. Their origin is unknown.

INCIPIT. 'Here begins'.

TERENTI. The gen. sing. of nouns in *-ius* and *-ium* was written with a single *-i* until the end of the Republic: the form in *-ii* begins to be common in the Augustan Age and regular from the Flavian era.

PHORMIO. This is the only play of Terence that does not retain the title of the Greek original. The changed title is a happy innovation; the name of Phormio became a synonym for a bare-faced rascal.

LVDIS ROMANIS. In the time of Terence four series of public games, *ludi scaenici*, were available for dramatic productions. These included the *Ludi Romani* held by the curule aediles in honour of Jupiter in September. Dramatic performances might also be given at the funeral games of individuals (*ludi funebres*). The last play that Terence wrote, the *Adelphoe*, and the second (unsuccessful) production of the *Hecyra* were given at the funeral games of Aemilius Paullus in 160 B.C.

AEDILIBVS CVRVLIBVS. Organization of the public games (*cura ludorum*) was one of the tasks of the aediles.

EGERE. *Agere* here has the technical sense 'to produce', 'to put on' a play. L. Ambivius Turpio was the original producer of Terence's plays, and we should have expected the notice to read *egit L. Ambiuius Turpio*. L. Hatilius Praenestinus must have been responsible for some subsequent production of the play. Ambivius Turpio was still remembered as a famous actor in the times of Cicero and Tacitus. The producer (*dominus gregis*) was a freedman, in contrast to the rest of the actors (and the composer of the music) who were slaves.

MODOS FECIT. 'Composed the music'. All metres except iambic senarii were accompanied by music played on *tibiae. Tibia* (Gk. αὐλός) is usually (mis-)translated as 'flute': it was, in fact, a reed instrument for which 'oboe' or, simply, 'pipe' would be a better translation. The music was played on a pair of *tibiae* operated by one player. The general impression to be gained from ancient writers is that the two pipes could be played simultaneously, though this implies a degree of polyphony that many modern authorities can scarcely credit. More than one pair of pipes might be used in a single play; this is so in the *Ht.* whose didascalia reads *acta primo (-um* A) *tibiis inparibus deinde duabus dextris.* In the other plays only one pair of pipes is used throughout. *Tota* (sc. *fabula*), 'throughout', refers to this continuous use of one type of pipes only.

FLACCVS CLAVDI. 'Flaccus, slave of Claudius'. The gen. *Claudi* depends on a noun *(seruos)* understood.

GRAECA APOLLODORV EPIDICAZOMENOS. 'The Greek play "The Claimant at Law" of Apollodorus'. *Apollodoru* represents the Greek gen. Ἀπολλοδώρου. Apollodorus of Carystus, author also of the original of the *Hecyra*, was a writer of New Comedy active in the first half of the third century B.C. A reference in line 114 (q.v.) may perhaps enable us to fix a closer limit for the dates within which the *Epidicazomenos* was written.

FACTA QVARTA. 'Composed fourth'. This interest in the order of composition of the plays implies the collection and preservation of the author's works in a single corpus. The transmission of a small body of numbered plays is in marked contrast to the history of the text of Plautus, under whose name Varro, in the first century B.C., found current 130 plays, of which only 21 were universally admitted to be genuine.

C. FANNIO M. VALERIO COS. 'In the consulship of Gaius Fannius and Marcus Valerius'. This dates the original production to 161 B.C., the year in which the successful *Eunuchus* also was produced. *Cos.* (or *coss.*), rather than *cons.* (*conss.*) is the usual abbreviation of *consule* (*consulibus*).

C. SVLPICI APOLLINARIS PERIOCHA

Prefixed to each of the plays of Terence is a summary (*periocha*) of the plot in twelve iambic senarii, composed in the second century A.D. by Gaius Sulpicius Apollinaris of Carthage.

4–. *fidicinam* is governed by *amantem*, which agrees with *gnatum.*

5–. *aduenit . . . moritur . . . procurat . . . accipit* are historic presents.

cum amaret. After an historic present indicative either primary or historic sequence is permissible.

9. *fremere*, historic infinitive.

PERSONAE

A list of dramatis personae is inserted in accordance with the custom of printed editions. Such a list (entitled τὰ τοῦ δϱάματος πϱόσωπα) is the rule in manuscripts of Greek plays, but is found in no manuscript of Terence (or Plautus). It can however be reconstructed from the scene-headings, where the names of the speakers with their roles are given.

PROLOGVS

Terence rejected the expository prologue, which was a feature of Greek and Roman drama from at least the time of Euripides. Preferring to unfold the plot within the play itself, Terence used the prologue instead as the equivalent of an author's preface, in which he could reply to the criticisms made against him by his older rivals and appeal to the audience for a fair hearing. The expository prologue had sometimes been dispensed with by earlier authors,[1] but to Terence, apparently, belongs the credit of being the first to eliminate it from all his works.

The prologue was delivered by one of the actors, wearing woollen fillets and carrying an olive branch to show that he came as an intercessor on behalf of the author. The part was usually given to a young actor, who refers to the author in the third person (*poeta, hic noster, hominem,* etc.). Exceptionally the part might be taken by the *dominus gregis* himself; in this case, the *dominus gregis* speaks in his own person.

1. **postquam** is causal, as in *Ad.* 1. The causal sense, 'since', is sometimes found in classical Latin also, e.g. Livy III. 60, 4; XXI. 13, 4.

poeta uetus. Luscius Lanuvinus is meant. He was an older contemporary and rival of Terence, and had attempted to get the aediles to withdraw the production of the *Eunuchus* on the ground of plagiarism.

poeta . . . poetam. The repetition of the same word in the same clause is a rhetorical device; cf. Virg. *Aen.* I. 684, *notos pueri puer indue uultus.* The prologues of Terence are full of rhetorical devices, particularly

---

[1] Cf. Plautus, *Trin.* 16–17:

> sed de argumento ne exspectetis fabulae:
> senes qui huc uenient, i rem uobis aperient.

This should be compared with Terence, *Ad.* 22–3.

word-play, to an extent that contrasts markedly with their infrequency in the plays themselves.

2. **studio,** used of application to the dramatic art also at line 18; cf. *Ht.* 23, *studium musicum.* **transdere** is restored from Donatus; all MSS. read *tradere.* **hominem,** sc. *Terentium.*

3. **parat,** 'endeavours'.

4. **qui,** connecting relative, trans. 'he'. **ita,** 'as follows', merely anticipates the acc. and inf. **dictitat,** frequentative, 'goes on saying'. **quas . . . fabulas.** The antecedent *eas fabulas* has to be understood from the rel. cl. **ante hic** is Bentley's emendation of the MS. *antehac*; *hic* (sc. *Terentius*) indicates that the subject of *fecit* (Terence) is different from the subject of *dictitat* (Luscius).

5. **tenui esse oratione et scriptura leui,** 'the language is poor and the writing trivial': *oratione* and *scriptura* are abl. of description. Some editors take *oratio* to refer to the subject-matter, but it should be given its normal meaning, 'language': *scriptura,* 'writing', can refer either to the manner of the writing or to its content (cf. Nepos *praef. genus scripturae leue*); in the present passage a reference to subject-matter gives a better antithesis to *oratione.* This is supported by the comment of Eugraphius (sixth century A.D.) ORATIONE ET SCRIPTVRA LEVI *hoc est*: *soliditatem in uerbis nullam, nullam in rebus.*

6f. This may describe a situation in which a young man, out of his senses through love, imagines that his beloved is a hind, and hunts her with his dogs, as in the episode of Cephalus and Procris—though here it is not certain that the dogs belong to the *adulescentulus.* Terence considered such themes unsuitable for comedy and carefully avoided them.

7f. *ceruam fugere, sectari canes, eam plorare, orare* are all acc. and inf., constructions depending on *scripsit.*

9. **quod si,** 'but if'; *quod* is adverbial acc. of the connecting rel., 'if with respect to this (the foregoing statement)'. **quom,** the usual spelling during the Republic, *cum* from the Augustan Age; *quum* is a late hybrid. With *quom* (temporal) in Terence 'the Indic. is the normal Mood. All cases of the Subj. seem to be capable of special explanation. The classical Latin rules for the use of the Imperf. and Pluperf. Subj. do not hold' (Allardice, p. 144). **stetit.** The final long syllable (*-īt*) is most simply explained as an archaism, a retention of an original long vowel; cf. *Ad.* 25, *augeāt, An.* 682, *concrepuīt. Stare,* 'hold its ground', 'succeed'; for its opposite, cf. *loco moueri, Ph.* 32. **noua.** Though Luscius was *uetus poeta,* his play was *noua,* i.e. had never been done before.

10. **actoris,** i.e. *dominus gregis,* 'actor-manager'; cf. note on *egere* in the didascalia.

11*a.* This line, apparently based on *An.* 3 and missing in A, does not fit the context and should be omitted.

12. **hoc** and **sic,** 'as follows', anticipate the quotation in the next three lines. **dicat . . . cogitet.** With 'Characterising or Generic Relatives' (Allardice, p. 151), especially in 'indefinite, negative, or generic expressions' the mood in Plautus and Terence, as in classical Latin, is normally subjunctive, e.g. 15, 565.

13–15. For a similar form of sentence (*si . . .* main cl. *. . . nisi*), cf. *Aul.* 380–1, *festo die si quid prodegeris, profesto egere liceat, nisi peperceris.*

13. **uetus** is emphatic by its initial position and by its separation from its noun *poeta.*

14. **prologum,** prō-, though Gk. πρόλογος has a short first syllable. **nouos** (nom. masc. sing.), sc. *poeta.* The 2nd decl. nom. and acc. sing. in *-uos* and *-uom* are the correct forms during the Republican period. From Quintilian (I. 7, 26) we learn that the forms in *-uus* and *-uum* came in during the first century A.D. See also 29n. (*uostra*).

15. **diceret . . . male diceret.** For mood, cf. 12n.

16. **hoc** anticipates the following acc. and inf. **habeat,** jussive subj.

17. **palmam,** here used metaphorically as 'the prize', 'victory', of pre-eminence among the ranks of dramatists. **artem . . . musicam,** 'the art of poetry'; here, more specifically, of dramatic art—in which the music still played an important part. *Ars . . . musica,* also at *Hec.* 23, 46; *studium musicum, Ht.* 23. **tractent.** Since the classical rule that subordinate clauses in Oratio Obliqua have subjunctive is not firmly established in Plautus and Terence, it is difficult to decide whether *tractent* (A) or *tractant* (Σ) is the correct reading here.

18. **reicere,** rēi-, by synizesis, as *reiciat* (717).

18*f.* *ille . . . ab illo . . . de illo* refer to Luscius, *hunc . . . hic* to Terence.

20. **audisset bene,** *Bene* (*male*) *audire* reproduce the Greek καλῶς or εὖ (κακῶς) ἀκούειν, 'to be well or ill spoken of', with ἀκούειν idiomatically used as the passive of λέγειν.

21. **adlatumst . . . rellatum.** Note the rhyme, 'tit for tat'; Donatus *prouerbiale est: quod dedit, recepit.* **adlatumst** for *-um est;* so *locost* (32) for *loco est.* **sibi esse.** Scan *sĭb(i) ĕs | sĕ (ĕs-* by B–B).

22. **de ill-,** *dĕ ĭll-* (*de* shortened by prosodic hiatus, *ill-* by B–B) is preferable to total elision of *de, d(e) ĭll-.* **dicundi.** The forms *-undus,* etc., for the gerundive and gerund of 3rd and 4th conj. verbs are archaic

(hence often retained in legal formulae); but after -*u*- the form is always -*endus*, etc. (e.g. *restituendus*).

23. **quom** 'although'; both indicative and subjunctive are found in Terence with *quom* meaning 'although'. **de se** contrasts chiefly with *mihi*, 'for my part', not with *de illo*: 'Now *I for my part* (*mihi*) will stop talking about him, though *he for his part* (*de se*) does not stop doing wrong.'

24. **nouam,** not simply, as Donatus says, 'Latin', but 'for the first time in Latin'. The stress laid on the epithet *noua* is designed at the same time to win the attention of the audience and to refute any charge of plagiarism.

25. **Epidicazomenon.** 'The (male) claimant at law'. **Latini . . . nominant** seems to imply that the Latins are already in the habit of calling the play by the name *Phormio*, yet line 24 insists that this is the play's first performance. How then have the *Latini* got into the habit of calling it the *Phormio*? Bentley sought to restore logic by reading, against all manuscript authority, *Graece, Latine hic* (sc. *poeta noster*) . . . *nominat*. This is the only play of Terence with a title different from that of its Greek original.

27. **qui aget, is.** The position of the rel. cl. and its antecedent are inverted, as often in Terence. **primas partis** belongs to the rel. cl. *qui aget* and gains emphasis by appearing before the rel. pronoun; cf. the position of *uoluntas uostra* before *si* in 29. Don. *primas partes . . . hoc est summas, non priores partes.* **qui aget** prosodic hiatus, *quĭ ă | get.*

28. **maxume.** -*u*- is found for later -*i*- in *lubet, lacrumare*, and in superlatives after 't' or 's' [so *proxumi* (125)], but not after 'r' and 'n'; so always *minime* (e.g. 1033).

29. **uoluntas uostra.** This clause is attached loosely to the foregoing sentence and provides a transition to the final appeal for a sympathetic hearing. **uostra.** Cf. 14n. *uo*- changes to *ue*- before 'r', 's', 't', *c.* 150 B.C. (Quint. I. 7, 25).

30. The appeal for attention, a fair hearing, and silence is a frequent one, e.g. *Eun.* 44, *date operam, cum silentio animum attendite, adeste aequo animo.* Similar appeals are found in several of Plautus' plays.

31*f.* The reference is to the unsuccessful first production of the *Hecyra* (165 B.C.) when the alternative attraction of boxers and tight-rope dancers (cf. Mayor on Juvenal XIV. 272) removed Terence's audience (*Hec.* 33–4). The second production of the *Hecyra* (160 B.C.) likewise failed because of the prospect of a gladiatorial show (*Hec.* 39–40).

33. Note the emphasis on the importance of the actor-manager.

restituit, perfect, 'has restored (since then)', viz. in the successful productions of the *Hautontimorumenos* (163 B.C.) and the *Eunuchus* (161 B.C.).

34. **bonitas . . . atque aequanimitas,** hendiadys 'your kind attention'; *aequanimitas* first occurs in Terence; cf. *Ad.* 24.

ACT I. SCENE 1

The Act divisions which are printed in most editions of the plays of Plautus and Terence are the work of Renaissance editors endeavouring to apply to the *fabula palliata* the 5-Act division enjoined by Horace (*Ars Poetica* 189) and mentioned in some passages of Donatus. The Scene divisions are ancient and an integral feature of our earliest manuscripts of Plautus and Terence (fourth–fifth centuries A.D.). Their function was not to mark a break in the action of the play, but to indicate the exit or entrance of one or more characters.

In the *fabula palliata* the scene, which remains unchanged throughout the play, usually represents a street in Athens, while the back wall of the stage has three doors, which represent, according to the demands of the plot, the front entrances of one, two, or three houses. When the play takes place elsewhere than in Athens, the audience is informed of the fact (e.g. Plaut. *Men.* 7–9, and 72 *haec urbs Epidamnus est dum haec agitur fabula*). Five of the six plays of Terence, including the *Phormio*, take place in the city of Athens; the scene of the sixth, the *Hautontimorumenos*, is laid on a country road, outside Athens. In addition to the three door entrances and, possibly (cf. 891 n.), an *angiportum* running back between the houses at right angles to the main street, there is a side entrance at each end of the stage. When the plot involves departures to or arrivals from the town and harbour, the town is thought of as lying to the spectators' right hand, the harbour to the left. In those plays that require in addition an exit to the country this was probably, like the exit to the harbour, to the spectators' left.

The *Phormio* requires three[1] houses on the stage, those of Demipho, Chremes, and Dorio, and has references to harbour and town. The house of Dorio is certainly on the spectators' right hand nearest the forum, while Demipho's is probably on the left hand with Chremes' in the centre.[2]

[1] Probably: Dorio's house must be visible from the stage (484), but is not necessarily on it.

[2] Cf. Mary Johnston, *Exits and Entrances in Roman Comedy*, pp. 32–3, 52–3.

Since Terence uses the prologue as an author's preface, the exposition of the plot must be made within the play itself. In the *Andria, Hecyra* and *Phormio* the opening scenes include a πρόσωπον προτατικόν (prosōpon protatikon—a character introduced to facilitate the exposition of the plot), whose only dramatic function is to have the facts of the situation explained to him. Davos is such a character; his function fulfilled, he disappears at 151–2.

Davos, a slave, enters along the street (probably from the forum), carrying a bag of money; he has come to repay a debt to Geta, slave of Demipho. He surmises that Geta's need of the money may have something to do with the recent marriage, about which he has heard, of Antipho, Demipho's son.

35. **summus,** with or without *amicus*, 'my very good friend'. **popularis** probably means 'fellow-townsman', as it certainly does in the only other passages in which it occurs in Terence (*Eun.* 1031, *Ad.* 155).

36. **de ratiuncula,** after *relicuom* 'outstanding on (lit. "from") the account'. The diminutives *ratiuncula* and *pauxillulum* are appropriate in the speech of slaves.

37. **relicuom** scans as four syllables.

38. **id ut conficerem.** Editors usu. say 'understand *orauit*', but to explain the syntax by the ellipse of a main verb is, historically speaking, to put the cart before the horse. The Subj. in independent sentences precedes its use in dependent clauses (cf. 102n.); *conficerem* here is probably a past jussive, 'I was to find the money'. With an independent subjunctive *ut* usually need not be translated; in origin it is an indefinite adverb (mostly enclitic) meaning 'in some way', 'in any way'. *Conficerem* must mean, as *confeci* does, 'get it together', not 'settle the account' (Sloman); cf. Cic. *pro Flacc.* 20, *duae rationes conficiendae pecuniae*. **adfero** almost 'Here it is!' Davos holds the purse up for the audience to see.

39. **erilem filium eius** = *filium eri eius*.

40. **ei,** feminine. **credo,** parenthetic 'I suppose'. **munus hoc** Davos touches the purse. **conraditur** a homely metaphor, Eng. 'scrape together'.

41. **quam inique comparatumst.** 'What an unfair arrangement it is!' Construe *i qui habent* inside the *ut* clause; *i* is nom. masc. pl. of *is*.

43. **quod . . . id,** inverted rel. cl. **demenso.** Donatus tells us that slaves received four *modii* of grain a month as their *dimensum*; according to Polybius VI. 39. 13 this was also the grain ration of the Roman legionary. **quod ille un-,** ïlle by B-B.

44. genium. *Genius* is the attendant spirit of a man during his life-time; as *genio indulgere* is 'to give oneself a good time', so *genium defrudare* is 'to deny oneself pleasures'; cf. Pl. *Aul. 724, egomet me defraudaui animumque meum geniumque.*

45. uniuorsum contrasts with *unciatim.* **illa,** 'she' emphatic.

46. partum. sc. *sit.* For similar omissions in subordinate clauses, cf. 540, 612. **porro autem,** cf. 48; *porro* (as Greek πόρρω), 'going straight on', is used of both place and time, 'immediately after', 'next thing you'll know', 'then again'.

47. ferietur, 'will be stung for another present', 'will be touched'; cf. Pl. *Poen,* 1286, *aere militari tetigero lenunculum.* **munere,** abl. instr.

48. alio, sc. *munere ferietur; ălĭ(o) ŭb(i) ĕr-,* proceleusmatic. **natalis dies,** cf. Becker's *Gallus* I³, 127–8 and *O.C.D.,* s.v. Birthday. The earliest evidence for the giving of birthday presents is Pl. *Epid.* 639f.

49. ubi initiabunt, sc. *puerum, alio munere ferietur Geta.* The Roman audience did not need to know which Greek initiation ceremony was meant, though Donatus informs us that the reference is to the Samo-thracian mysteries.

50. causa, 'pretext', as opposed to the real reason. **mittundi,** sc. *aliud munus, alia munera; mittere,* as often, virtually = *donare.* **sed uideon Getam?** '(But) Is this Geta I see?' References to players' entrances and exits are usually contained in the text itself. **uideon.** After a word ending in a long vowel *-ne* always becomes *-n* (or elides), except when it is enclitic upon a monosyllable bearing the ictus, e.g. 448 *mene uis.*

ACT I. SCENE 2

Enter Geta from Demipho's house; Davos comes up and hands over the money to him; noticing that Geta is looking worried, he asks him what is the matter. Geta explains that during the absence abroad of Demipho and Chremes, his old master and his master's brother, he has been entrusted with the care of their respective sons, Antipho and Phaedria. His initial attempts to exercise a strict control over them earned him nothing but beatings, so he decided to let the young men have their own way. Phaedria thereupon began an affair with a music-girl belonging to their neighbour, the *leno* Dorio, but lacked the money to buy her and Antipho fell in love with a penniless orphan, Phanium. As she was said to be an Athenian citizen, an illicit liaison was out of the question. Fearing to marry her without his father's consent Antipho allowed the parasite Phormio to trump up a charge that he was the girl's nearest relative and thus obliged, by Athenian law, to marry her. Antipho made no effective defence to Phormio's allegation and has been compelled by the court's decision to marry Phanium. The imminent prospect of Demipho's return now fills Geta with terror—as it does Antipho, whom he has aided and abetted.

51. As Geta turns back to give instructions to someone within the house, he does not see Davos come up behind him. **rufus.** In Greek New Comedy all actors wore masks and the red hair formed part of the slave's mask: in Roman *palliatae* masks were certainly worn from the time of Roscius (first century B.C.). It is disputed whether previously they wore masks or merely wigs and make-up (Beare 184-). **oh.** An ejaculation mostly expressing surprise (as here, 945), sometimes a wish, e.g. 70. It is to be distinguished from *o* + voc. or acc. exclamation.

52. **obuiam conabar.** 'I was wanting to meet you'. Take *conabar* absolutely ('I was making an effort in your direction'); Terence has no example of *conari* with an infinitive. **accipe, em:** Davos hands over the bag. **em,** 'there, take it!' is probably for *eme*, imperative of *emere*, in its original sense of 'take'; it is most often used with imperatives and *tibi* (847). It has nothing to do with *en* 'lo!' 'behold!' which does not occur in Terence. *Em* must be distinguished from two other particles that Terence uses freely, (1) *hem*, an ejaculation, usu. expressing surprise, 'Eh?' 'What?' 'What's that?' (2) *ehem*, more exclamatory than *hem*, 'Ah!' 'What!'

53. **lectumst.** 'It is good money', 'in mint condition', lit. 'picked'. **conueniet,** 'you'll find it's the right amount', lit. 'it will correspond to'; sc. *tanto argento*.

54. **amo te,** formula equivalent to 'Thank you', cf. 478. Similarly in making a request *si me amas*, 'Please'. *Amabo*, used parenthetically, expresses a polite request, 'pray', and is used almost exclusively by women or by men when addressing women. **neglexisse,** sc. *te* (easily understood from preceding *amo te*). The acc. and inf. after *habeo gratiam* seems not to be classical, and not to occur earlier than Terence.

55f. The division of speakers is uncertain; another possible solution is (54) GE. *amo te . . . mores.* DA. *adeo res . . . tristis?* Davos' remarks would then be spoken ironically, 'A fine state things have reached etc.' **adeo res redit,** cf. *Ht.* 113, *postremo adeo res rediit.*

58. **quid istuc est.** 'What's that you say?' 'What d'you mean?' is to be distinguished from *quid est?* ('What is it?' 'What's up?'), which is a common reaction to sighs, exclamations etc., cf. 749, 810, 852, 941,

1037. **istuc** (for *istud-ce*) rather than *istud* or *istoc* is the commonest form of the nom. and acc. neuter sing. in Plautus, and probably the only form in Terence.

59. **modo ut,** 'if only' (lit. 'provided only that'); cf. 773. **abi sis, insciens,** 'Go on (with you), you fool!' *Abi* is a remonstrance not necessarily implying a command to move, e.g. *Eun.* 221, *abi, nil dicis.* **sis** (= *si uis*), usu. subjoined to imperative and emphasizing it: its force varies, according to context, from civil request to peremptory command.

60. **quoius . . . ei,** inverted rel. cl. 'When you've found a man can be trusted in money matters, d'you hesitate to trust him with a secret?' **perspexeris,** Perf. Subj. but the reason for the subjunctive is obscure, since here, as in 536-7, and in 917 the antecedent is definite and the verb refers to a fact.

61f. **quid . . . lucrist?** is equivalent to *nil . . . lucrist*; construe as *verere* ⟨*ibi*⟩ *uerba ei credere, ubi nil mihi lucrist*: ⟨*ibi*⟩ *. . . ubi*, 'in a matter wherein'. The best parallels for a question inside a rel. cl. are Greek, e.g. Demosth. *de Cor.* 126, 209, παλαιὰ ἔργ᾽ ἔλεγες, ὧν τίνος προσεδεῖθ᾽ ὁ παρὼν ἀγὼν οὑτοσί; Many editors punctuate with a question mark after *credere*, making *ubi . . . fallere?* a separate question. In that case *ubi* is still connecting rel. (= 'in this matter') and *quid* interrogative.

62. **dico,** *dīcare* is a solemn word, and the phrase carries a mock solemnity; cf. Pl. *Bacch.* 995, *aurium operam tibi dico.*

63. **Chremem,** the usual acc. of *Chremes* in Terence (but *-etem* in *An.* 472, 553); *Ph.* 1026 has dative *-eti*.

64. **nostin** for *-n*, cf. 5on. **quidni** 'Why not?' 'Of course!' *ni* = *non* and may be separated from *quid* by *ego* or *ille*. *Quidni*, answering a question, is to be distinguished from *cur non* asking one and equivalent to 'you ought to have', e.g. *An.* 518, *quor non dixti?* **quid?,** 'Well, d'you know . . . ?' *Quid* does no more than prepare the listener for the question that follows. **eius . . . Phaedriam?,** sc. *nostine*.

66. **in Lemnum.** Except here Terence always omits the preposition of 'motion towards' with names of towns and islands (cf. 567, 837) and always inserts it with names of countries. Here *in Lemnum* doubtless because of parallelism with *in Ciliciam.* **euenit,** impersonal; construe *euenit ut ambobus senibus iter esset, illi in Lemnum, nostro in Ciliciam.* 'Both the old men happened to have to make a journey at the same time, he to Lemnos, our master . . .'

67. **antiquom,** 'of long standing'. **epistulas,** not just one letter.

68. **modo non,** 'all but', Gk. μόνον οὐ. **montis auri pollicens,**

a proverbial expression; cf. Sall. *Cat.* 23.3, *maria montisque polliceri coepit.* For golden mountains, cf. Pl. *Aul.* 701; Aristoph. *Ach.* 82, ἐπὶ χρυσῶν ὀρῶν; cf. Eng. 'El Dorado'.

69. **quoi** is relative, not interrogative; there is an ellipse of a preceding *eumne pellexit . . .* ? We may translate, 'And him with wealth and enough to spare?' As Donatus remarks, Demipho's *auaritia* is important to the plot; cf. 120 f. **desinas,** jussive subjunctive, 'Oh, shut up!'

70. **sic est ingenium,** sc. *eius,* 'That's his nature.' **sic** = predicative *tale.* **oh, regem me,** scan *mĕ ĕss(e),* with emphasis on *me,* 'It's *I* should have been the *rex*!' Sargeaunt maintains that *regem,* not *me,* must be the emphatic word, 'It's a king I should have been.' **oh,** 5in. **regem** (metaphorically) = *patronus,* cf. 338.

71. **hic,** with *relinquont: hinc* (some MSS.) would have to be taken with *abeuntes.*

72. **quasi,** 'to act as'. **magistrum,** for Gk. παιδαγωγός. **prouincia,** 'sphere of duty, influence', also used at *Ht.* 516. Plautus, who is more ready than Terence to admit Roman allusions, uses *prouincia* (always metaphorically 'sphere of duty') several times.

73–8. The division of speakers in these lines is uncertain; the notes refer only to the text as printed.

73. **mi usu uenit, hoc scio,** 'It has been my experience, that I know.'

74. **memini** is taken by some editors to mean 'I am sure that', but no parallel is given for the meaning. *Memini* has its normal sense, 'I remember my luck was out the day I was left'. **relinqui.** Present tense may be used after *memini* where English would use a past tense; cf. L & S, s.v. **deo irato meo,** abl. of attendant circumstances, cf. Pl. *Poen.* 452, *ego deis meis iratissumis sex immolaui agnos.* English gets the emphasis by inversion 'the gods were against me when I . . .' **deo . . . meo,** virtually *genio meo;* cf. 44n.

75. **quid uerbis opust?,** formula 'need I say more?' **opust** = *opus* + *'st* (prodelision of *est*). This combination is so common that editors print *opust.* The combination of -*s* + *'s* (prodelision of *es*) is less common, and is printed (e.g. 295, 550) *seruo's, facturu's.*

76. **scapulas perdidi,** 'I ruined my shoulder-blades.' Cf. Pl. *Asin.* 545 and *Ep.* 91, *corium perdidi.*

77. 'I thought of those (well-known) words "It's folly to kick against the pricks".' With the text as printed *istaec* refers to the following words *namque . . . calces* and *namque* is an asseverative particle, 'indeed', like *etenim.* Elsewhere in Terence *namque* is explanatory, 'for', rather than

asseverative, and an explanatory force can be given to it here if the inverted commas are removed from *namque . . . calces* and *istaec* referred to the preceding words, 'I thought of what you've just said. For it's folly etc.'

78. **aduorsum stimulum calces,** Don. *deest 'iactare'*, 'to kick against the pricks'. The proverb is Greek; cf. Aesch. *Ag.* 1624, πρὸς κέντρα μὴ λάκτιζε. Latin grammarians frequently quote the present passage, but no other. **aduorsum.** Metre never requires *-us* in T. and the form in *-um* is better attested in the MSS. **is,** dat. pl. for *iis.* With *facere* the dative is one of advantage; for *is omnia obsequi,* cf. Pl. *Asin.* 76, *id ego percupio obsequi gnato meo.* **uellent,** 'anything they wanted'; *uelim, nolim, malim* are often used indistinguishably from the indic. even in subordinate clauses, e.g. Pl. *Amph.* 39, *debetis uelle quae uelimus.*

79. **scisti uti foro.** Note the tense, 'You were a wise man', 'You knew how to play your cards', 'work the market' (Ashmore). The reference, according to Donatus, is to market vendors, who do not offer goods at a fixed price, but adapt their charges according to the temper of the market.

80. **noster,** sc. *erilis filius,* 'our young gentleman', cf. 110, 117 etc., sc. *fecit;* for omission of verb in lively narration, cf. (*esse* omitted) 84, 100, 104, 106; (verb of saying) 101, 102; (*arcesse*) 440. **nil quicquam.** The pronoun *quisquam* is colloquially used to emphasize *nil* (250), *nemo* (*Hec.* 67). **primo,** but not for long! Cf. 110 f. Don., *bene additum primo, quia non perpetuo.* **hic,** 'Phaedria here', pointing to Chremes' house; Allardice, p. 41, 'The deictic use of this pronoun is conspicuous, and often refers to a person whose house is close by the speaker.'

81. **continuo,** i.e. no sooner had his father left town. **puellulam,** once again the diminutive in a slave's speech.

82. **citharistriam,** cf. 144; *citharistria* and *psaltria,* Greek loan words, occur first in Terence. Plautus uses instead the Latin word *fidicina* (used by T. in *Ph.* 109 as synonym for *citharistria*). **ardere** is restored from the grammarian Charisius, although all MSS. of Terence read *amare* (cf. *Ht.* 97, *eius filiam ille amare coepit perdite*). By a *constructio ad sensum* the intrans. *ardere* (= *amare*) governs a direct object as in Virg. *Ecl.* II. 1, *Formosum pastor Corydon ardebat Alexim.* Similarly in *Ht.* 525, *hanc si deperit* the intrans. *deperire* = *deamare.* **perdite,** 'to distraction'; cf. *Ht.* 97 (quoted above); Catullus 45.3, *ni te perdite amo.*

83. **inpurissimo,** a common epithet of the *leno,* whose trade made him a social outcast.

84. **neque . . . quicquam,** sc. *erat apud nos.* **patres,** 'both

fathers'. **quod daretur,** potential, 'that might be given' (to offer to the *leno*); Eng., 'And there wasn't a penny to give'.

85. **restabat.** Impersonal *restat* is more often followed by *ut* with the Subj., e.g. 587, 831. For the Inf. (mostly poetical), cf. Livy XLIV. 4. 8, *nec aliud restabat quam . . . corrigere.* **oculos pascere.** Note the metaphorical use of *pascere*; cf. Sen. *Ep.* LVIII. 25, *oculos . . . ut dici solet pascit.*

86. **sectari,** frequentative of *sequi.* **ludum.** The *leno* regarded the education of his girls as a good investment.

87. **otiosi,** 'being at a loose end'.

88. **in quo . . . ludo,** inverted rel. cl., the inverted antecedent being understood from *exaduorsum ilico.* **ilico,** 'straight opposite'; *ilico,* in classical Latin an adverb of time ('straightway'), is used in the ante-classical period also as an adverb of place, especially when, as here, combined with another adverb of place.

89. **tonstrina.** In both Greek and Roman times the barber's shop was a well-known clearing-house for gossip; cf. 'Greek and Roman Barbers' by F. W. Nicolson in *H.S.C.P.* II (1891), 41–56 (esp. p. 42). **solebamus fere plerumque,** cumulative pleonasm.

90. **iret,** prospective Subj. as frequently after verbs of awaiting, expecting.

91. **illi,** 'there', locative from *ille.* The classical adverb *illic* is *illi +ce.* **interuenit,** historic present; the scansion (-*uĕnit*) shows that it cannot be past definite.

92. **adulescens . . . lacrumans.** Donatus notes an interesting point. In the Greek original Apollodorus caused this news to be given by the barber who had just cut the girl's hair as a sign of mourning. As this was not the custom among the Romans (cf. 106, *capillus passus*), Terence altered the incident, as Donatus says, *scilicet . . . ne externis moribus spectatorem Romanum offenderet*; for a discussion of Donatus' statement, see Introduction, section II. **lacrumans,** orthography 28n. **mirarier.** The archaic present Inf. passive is mostly used *metri gratia* at the end of a line or at an iambic diacresis. *Mirarier* is historic Inf. This is generally found in simple sentences in narrative or descriptive passages, and signifies action that is continuous (as here) or repeated, rather than single and momentary.

93. **quid sit,** oblique form of *quid est?* Cf. 58n.

94. **uisumst,** for concord, cf. Allardice, pp. 4–6; here, as the predicate, the neuter *onus*, precedes the verb, there is no difficulty in the attraction. **et . . . et,** 'both . . . and'.

95. **hic uiciniae,** *uiciniae* may be partitive genitive dependent on the adverb *hic,* but *Bacch.* 205, *proxumae uiciniae,* suggests rather that *uiciniae* is locative in apposition to the adverb *hic.* Note alliteration *uidi . . . uirginem . . . uiciniae* and also in 96.

96. **miseram** agrees with *uirginem,* but its position shows that it is used predicatively; translate by an adverb, 'piteously weeping'.

97. **ea,** i.e. *mater mortua.* **illi,** i.e. *uirgini.* **sita erat** here presumably 'had been laid out', though the normal meaning would be 'had been buried'. The corpse was customarily laid out on the *lectus funebris* in the *atrium* with the feet towards the door. **exaduorsum,** 'facing the street'.

98. The reading *uicinus* is strongly supported by Donatus: A and one branch of minuscule MSS. read *cognatus.* **extra,** 'except'; cf. Pl. *Amph.* 833, *extra unum te.* As this use is found in Cicero and Livy, it is not simply colloquial (so Ashmore). **anicula,** again the diminutive.

99. **adiutaret,** strictly a potential Subj., 'no one who might help', Eng. 'no one to help'. **miseritumst,** sc. *me,* 'I felt sorry'.

100. **uirgo ipsa.** 'As for the girl herself (as opposed to her unhappy predicament)'. **facie egregia,** abl. of description, sc. *erat.*

101. **commorat** = *commouerat.* The pluperfect, marking completion in past time, seems a slightly more graphic equivalent of *commouit.* **ibi** (temporal), 'thereupon', 'then', as often in Plautus and Terence. **Antipho,** sc. *dixit* or *inquit*; cf. 80n.

102. **uoltisne eamus,** 'Shall we go?' originates from *uoltisne? eamus?* where *eamus* is simplest regarded as deliberative subjunctive ('D'you want? Are we to go?'). **eamus uisere,** infinitive of purpose; cf. *Hec.* 189, 345. **alius,** another of the group, not Phaedria, who is indifferent (cf. 110) and would be referred to as *alter.*

102–3. **censeo: eamus,** 'I vote, let's go.'

103. **sodes** = *si audes*; like *sis* (59n.) mostly appended to an imperative. It is slightly more formal than *sis,* which is often untranslated in English. **imus, uenimus, uidemus,** asyndeton of rapid narration, as *ueni, uidi, uici*: the change of tense (*uēnimus*) seems to be due to metrical convenience; cf. 135.

104. **diceres,** subject is the indefinite 'you'—'and, to make you say so all the more.' For the imperfect cf. *An.* 135, *tum illa, ut consuetum facile amorem cerneres, reiecit se.*

106. **capillus passus.** See note on *adulescens lacrumans* (92).

107. **uis boni,** 'a power of good'.

107–8. **ut, ni . . . inesset forma, haec formam exstinguerent.**

In Plautus and Terence the rules for mood and tense in conditional clauses are less rigid than in classical Latin. The imperfect Subj. may be used of a past condition without any emphasis on continuous action, e.g. *Ad.* 106–7, *nam si esset unde id fieret, faceremus. Ph.* 119, *non, si redisset, ei pater ueniam daret?* In the present passage there is the further complication that the apodosis is itself in a subordinate clause. A close parallel is *Hec.* 128–9, *ibi demum ita aegre tulit ut ipsam Bacchidem, si adesset, ibi eius commisereceret.* **forma . . . formam,** note change of meaning (1) her figure, (2) the beauty of her figure.

109. Scan *ĭll' quĭ ĭll–* (*quĭ* by prosodic hiatus, *ĭll–* by B–B; for *ill',* cf. Introduction, p. 30). **tantum modo,** cf. 142 (same position in the line).

110. **noster uero . . .** Don. ἀποσιώπησις (aposiopesis), *quae succurrit, quotiens uerba rebus minora sunt.* **iam scio,** 'don't tell me'.

111. **scin quam,** sc. *amare coepit* (*quam = quantum*), 'And how!' **euadat.** The subjunctive, the normal mood in an Ind. Question in classical Latin, requires notice here, for Terence after an imperative of a verb of saying or thinking generally keeps the indicative of the *Oratio Recta* (contrast 346 and 358).

112. **recta,** sc. *uia.*

113. **eius copiam,** 'access to her'. Scan *ĕĭŭ'* with B–B and final '*s*' dropped. **enim,** in Plautus and Terence, is usually affirmative or corroborative, 'indeed', 'certainly', 'to be sure', *nam* usually causal, 'for'. **se negat,** sc. *eius copiam facturam esse.*

114. **neque =** *et non*; the negative belongs to *facere,* not *ait.* **ait.** Scan *a͡it* (but *a͡in*). **ciuem . . . Atticam,** although the bigamous marriage of Chremes took place at Lemnos. From 286 to 279 B.C. Lemnos was in the hands of Lysimachus, and it is improbable that an Athenian could have visited the island between these years. Now for some reason Chremes did not visit Lemnos for so long a time that his wife and daughter set out from there for Athens to look for him (569–70). Perhaps this suggests a date soon after 279 for Apollodorus' play; anyhow a date between 286 and 279 looks unlikely.

115. **si uxorem uelit,** sc. *eam*; the pronoun as object is frequently omitted.

117. **nescire.** The historic Inf. can have a primary or historic sequence. **quid ageret,** indirect deliberative, 'what (he was) to do'. O.R., *quid agam?* **et . . . et,** 'both . . . and'.

119. **si,** almost = *cum.* **non,** probably for *nonne,* which Plautus

never, Terence rarely, uses before a word beginning with a consonant. **daret,** 'would he not have given?' For tense, cf. 108n.

120–1. ille . . . daret?, colloquially 'What? Him let his son marry . . . ? Not (never) on your life!' This use of the subjunctive, in a 'repudiating' or 'indignant' question, is explained in the note on line 304. **numquam faceret,** for tense, cf. *daret* (119) and 108n. **quid fit denique?,** lit. 'What happens eventually?'; trans. 'What's the outcome of it all?' **denique,** 'finally'; cf. 325 where it has the same position and the same force.

122. quid fiat? Geta echoes Davos' words with change of mood: equivalent in English to 'What happens? Well may you ask!' But the mood of *fiat* is better explained, not as Ind. Question dependent on an elliptical verb of asking, but as an independent subjunctive in a 'repudiating' or 'indignant' question. **est,** note the initial position: *est* is existential 'there is'. **homo confidens,** 'impudent fellow'; *confidens,* 'self-assured', frequently from the context has the pejorative sense 'brazenly self-assured'.

123. qui, expressing a wish in Latin is rare and archaic, and is only used in formulae; a pronoun, the object of the verb, immediately follows *qui* and the wish is almost always a curse, e.g. Pl. *Men.* 451, *qui illum di omnes perduint. Qui* is an indeclinable instrumental-ablative and may be interrogative ('in what way?'), exclamatory ('in what way!'), or indefinite ('in some/any way'), as well as relative ('with which, whereby'). **perduint,** an archaic form of the subjunctive (as is *duint* 519 etc.), used by Terence *metri gratia* at verse ends (exc. *Hec.* 134). Like a few other Subjj. in -*i*- (*sim, uelim, edim*), the form is really a pure optative, and, consistently with that origin, *perduint* is used by T. only in imprecations, *duint* mostly in wishes.

125–6. These lines may be a Roman addition, in which Terence summarizes the provisions of the Attic law for the benefit of his Roman audience. Diodorus Siculus XII. 18. 3 forms an interesting commentary: 'A third law to be revised (by Charondas, putative lawgiver of Thurii) was that concerning heiresses, which is also found in Solon's legislation. Charondas ordered that the next of kin be assigned to an heiress and that likewise an heiress be assigned to her nearest relative (ἐπιδικάζεσθαι τῷ ἀγχιστεῖ), who was required to marry her or contribute 500 drachmas for her dowry if she were poor.' Cf. *Ad.* 650–2. **qui . . . is,** inverted rel. cl. *is* for *iis.* **sint,** probably Subj. by attraction **proxumi,** orthography 28n.

127. dīcam . . . dĭcam, paronomasia (play on words); *dīcam* =

Gk. δίϰην, only here and 329, 439 (*dicas* 668) in Terence, rarely in Plautus; it is used by Cicero *in Verr.* II. ii. 37 of Sicilian legal procedure.

128. **paternum amicum** = *patris amicum*; cf. 39, *erilem filium.* **adsimulo,** mostly ante-classical. **me,** for the omission of *esse*, cf. *Ht.* 888, *gnatus . . . se adsimulat laetum.*

129. **qui.** The classical distinction between *quis* (pronoun) and *qui* (adjective) does not obtain in Pl. and Ter. who for the most part use as the pronominal form *quis* before a vowel and *qui* before a consonant.

130. **qui,** indeclinable interrogative 'how' or 'why'; cf. 123n.

130-1. 'who her father was, who her mother, how she is related to you, all this—I'll make up what will be fine and advantageous to me'. In this translation *quod . . . commodum* is taken as the direct object of *confingam*, and a slight anacoluthon is assumed after *omnia haec* (cf. *Hec.* 286-7).

133. **paratae lites.** 'I'm in for it'. *lites*, metaphorically 'a row'; the same phrase *Ad.* 792: for the omission of *sunt*, cf. 238n. **quid mea,** sc. *refert*; for the full expression, cf. 723, but in interrogative sentences Terence usu. omits *refert.*

134. **iocularem audaciam.** 'What cheek!' (the adj. *iocularis* can scarcely be translated in English). The acc. of exclamation, with or without interjections, is common in Terence 'owing to the liveliness of colloquial speech' (Allardice, p. 14).

135. Note asyndeton, cf. 867f.

136. **quid narras.** 'What's that you say?', expressing unbelief. **hoc, quod audis.** 'You heard me!' Lit. 'I say (sc. *narro*) this which you hear.'

137. **quid te futurumst?,** *te* abl. of instrument. This is the common colloquial construction, esp. in interrogative sentences with *facere, fieri, esse*; cf. *An.* 709, *quid me fiet?* Less commonly a dative or *de* + abl. is found. **nescio hercle,** *hercle* emphasizing a negative, 'I really don't know'; **hoc scio,** *hoc* refers to what follows.

138. **quod fors feret, feremus,** note alliteration and word play (*ferre* = (1) bring, (2) bear). The best parallel is *Ph.* 429-30, *quin quod est ferundum fers? tuis dignum factis feceris.* Donatus notes the mock-heroism of Geta's grandiloquence, *hae graues sententiae ex persona seruorum cum dicuntur, ridiculae sunt*—perhaps even more so if *quod fors feret* is a reminiscence of the noble passage spoken by Pyrrhus in Ennius' *Annals* (quoted by Cicero *de off.* I. 12. 38) *quidue ferat Fors/uirtute experiamur.* **placet,** 'Good!'

139. **em istuc.** (There! That's) 'Spoken like a man!'

140. **laudo.** 'Good for you', 'Bravo!' **credo,** parenthetic and ironi-

cal 'I suppose'. **adeam.** The nature of the Subj. is disputed; trans. 'I suppose I'm to go and get someone to plead for me'. **mihi** = *pro me.* **oret.** The Subj. may be final or consecutive-generic. **amitte,** 'let him off'; classical Latin *dimittere.* **quaeso,** parenthetic.

142. **si quicquam,** sc. *fecerit.* **quicquam.** *Quisquam* and *ullus* (adj.) are used, even in classical authors, in conditional clauses, after *dum, donec, quam,* and in relative clauses, as well as in negative sentences and in interrogative sentences implying a negative.

142-3. **tantummodo non** = μόνον οὐ, meaning, 'he as good as adds'. Because Geta knows that he is bound to get into mischief again soon, the intercessor's 'If ever he does wrong again, punish him' is virtually equivalent to 'Punish him the moment I leave you'. **uel,** probably in origin a second person sing. imperative from *uelle,* meaning 'If you will'; with another imperative 'You can (for all I care) . . .' *uel ŏccid-ŏc-* by B-B. For a similar use of the future imperative in *-to,* cf. *Eun.* 853, *si aliam* (sc. *noxiam*) *admisero umquam, occidito.*

144. **quid paedagogus,** sc. *agit* (uel sim.); trans. 'What about . . . ?' **paedagogus ille** (παιδαγωγός). Phaedria is sarcastically so called because he escorts the girl to and from her music school (cf. 86). **qui citharistriam,** sc. *sectatur* or *amat.*

145. **quid rei gerit?** 'How's he getting on?' **sic** is accompanied by a gesture of despair (or some such emotion). **non multum habet?** Was Davos asleep at line 84?

146. **fortasse,** hiatus at change of speaker. **immo.** Instead of the pompous 'nay rather' the corrective effect of *immo* can be got by 'Not much? Why, he's nothing but hope, pure and simple.'

148. **quoad,** 'up to what time', 'when', 'how soon . . . ?'

149. **ab eo adlatam,** 'from him' (not 'by him').

150. **portitores,** the custom-house officials, who, to prevent evasion of import and export dues, had the right to open all foreign mail.

151. **numquid . . . aliud me uis?,** common formula of leave-taking, 'Anything (else) I can do for you?' Sometimes *aliud* or *me* or *uis* is omitted; still shorter, *numquid aliud?* or *numquid uis?* may be used. **aliud me uis,** two accusatives after *uelle* on the analogy of verbs of asking. **ut bene sit tibi.** 'Look after yourself' politely declines the offer of help.

Davos, his function of 'ideal listener' fulfilled, departs towards the forum.

152. Geta moves towards the door of Demipho's house and calls forth a boy to whom he gives the money with instructions to hand it

over to Dorcium, his 'wife'. **nemon hoc prodit?** This kind of
formula for ordering servants is common, e.g. Horace, *Serm.* II. 7, 34,
nemon oleum fert ocius? **hoc** (adverb = *huc*), an archaic form which is
already rare in Plautus and Terence, though it continues officially at least
till the first century A.D. **da hoc,** *hoc* (pronoun) is deictic and refers to
the bag of money. **Dorcio.** The neuter ending in -*ium* is often used for
women's names, e.g. *Phanium.* Dorcium is probably the *contubernalis* of
Geta (strictly speaking 'concubine', as slaves could not contract a legal
marriage, but normally translatable as 'wife').

After handing over the money to the boy, Geta leaves, as he
expressed his intention of doing (150), to go to the harbour.

ACT I. SCENE 3

Antipho and Phaedria enter, (probably) from Demipho's house. Each
complains that his position as a lover is more wretched than the other's.
Antipho enjoys his wife's company but dreads his father's return:
Phaedria, while he has no such fear for the future, is denied the present
enjoyment of his love.

153. **Adeon rem redisse.** 'To think that things have come to such
a pass that . . .' The exclamatory or interrogative infinitive, often expressing indignation or surprise, is used with or without an acc. subject,
and with or without the particle *n(e)*. The negative form is introduced
by *non* or *nec* (*neque*), e.g. 232–3. **qui uelit,** inverted rel. cl. with
patrem as inverted antecedent. Sloman takes the Subj. as concessive; more
probably it is Subj. by attraction. **consultum esse,** impersonal
passive. **ut,** repeated, cf. *An.* 828–30.

154. *Phaedria.* The final -*a* is long in Greek; here metre allows either
-*ā pătr(em) ŭt* or -*ă pătr(em) ŭt.* **aduenti,** -*i* is the commonest form of the
4th decl. gen. sing. in Pl. and Ter. Cf. *An.* 365, *nil ornati, nil tumulti*; a gen.
in -*uis* occurs at *Ht.* 287. **in mentem . . . uenit.** The impersonal
use + gen. is common in Cicero, and is found in Pl. *Rud.* 685 f. Elsewhere the personal construction, with the thing remembered in the nom.
is much commoner, e.g. *Ph.* 77, 652. Scan *ŭb(i) ĭn* | *mēnt(em) eius* | *āduēn* |
tī uĕ | *nīt* (*ĭn* by B–B, *eius* by synizesis).

155. **quod,** 'but' (cf. 9n.), most often followed by a protasis (*si, ni,
nisi*); it is followed by a wish in 157, Cic. *ad fam.* XIV. 4. 1 (*quod utinam*),
Virg. *Aen.* X. 361 (*quod ut*). **ita ut par fuit,** 'as was right', 'as I
should have'.

156. trochaic octonarius; first foot scans *quĭd ĭstūc* (*ĭst–* by B–B).
conscius sis. The Subj. is concessive; *qui* is translatable idiomatically in English as 'when'.

157. **utinam ne** and *utinam non* are both found introducing negative wishes. **id . . . eo** are better taken as referring back to *audacis facinoris* than as antecedents of *quod . . . principiumst mali.*

159. **illos aliquot dies,** 'the next few days' starting from a past time, just as *aliquot hos . . . dies* (832) means 'the next few days' starting from the present time. **fuisset . . . aegre,** cf. 162; *esse +* advb. is common in colloquial speech.

160. Scan either *angerēt anim–* with original long vowel (cf. 250, *accidēt animo* and 9n.) or *angerĕt anim–*. **audio.** 'Quite!' ironically agreeing with Antipho.

161. **consuetudinem,** used of cohabitation both with wives and concubines.

162. **aliis . . . tibi,** adversative asyndeton. More usual than *defit* would be *deest*. **quod amant,** 'the object of their affection' is the subject of *defit*: from it is understood the subject of *superest* (*quod amas*). **dolet,** impersonal + dative, cf. Caecilius 241, *tibi dolebit*; Cic. *pro Murena* 20. 42, *cui placet obliuiscitur, cui dolet meminit*. Scan *quĭă sŭ | pĕrēst | dŏlēt.*

164. **quidem hercle uero,** note accumulation of particles; more commonly *certe hercle*, as 523.

165. **ita me di bene ament,** a frequent oath in Pl. and Ter. It is either inserted inside the statement it emphasizes (e.g. 883, 954) or precedes it; in the latter case the correlative *ut* (= 'as') often introduces the main clause. Here the main clause is *iam . . . cupio* ('So help me, I'm eager'); in the clause *ut . . . liceat* it is simplest to take *ut =* 'on condition that', 'if only'. Alternatively, *ut . . . liceat . . . frui* may be a noun clause dependent on *depecisci*. **quod amo** serves as object of *frui*.

166. **morte,** abl. of price. **conicito cetera,** cf. *Cas.* 94, *dehinc conicito ceterum.*

167. **inopia . . . copia,** 'lack', 'plenty'; cf. *Trin.* 671, *quom inopiast, cupias, quando eiius copiast, tum non uelis.*

168. **ut ne addam.** *Ut ne* in a neg. final cl., though not in Caesar, is still fairly common in Cicero, but disappears in the Augustan period.

170. **ni . . . desit,** 'but for one thing'. **istaec.** For the nom. and acc. neut. pl. Terence also uses, though less commonly, *ista*.

171. **quo** A: *quocum* Σ. The preposition is normally repeated in Latin, but where the verb, expressed or understood, of the rel. cl. is the same

as that of the main clause the preposition is sts. omitted by Pl. and Terence, e.g. *Cas.* 317 f., *quicum litigas, Olympio?—cum eadem, qua tu semper.*

172. plerique . . . omnes, 'almost all', as *An.* 55, etc. **nosmet,** 280n. **nostri,** emphatic, 'our *own* lot makes us discontented': *nostri* might be the gen. neut. sing. of *noster,* but is probably gen. of *nos,* 'we are sorry for ourselves'.

173. uidere, *-re* is the normal form of the 2nd sing. passive in present stem tenses in Pl. and Ter. In Terence the form in *-ris* is quite uncommon.

174. etiam, temporal 'still'. **quid uelis** (not *utrum*) seems to imply more than two alternatives; these are given in the next line *retinere, amare, amittere* (the reading of all MSS.), even if stricter logic would require *retinere atque amare an amittere.*

Because of 176, where only two alternatives are stated, many editors have tried by emendation to eliminate *amare* in 175, thus reducing 175 also to two alternatives, *retinere, amittere.* Bentley suggested *an mittere* for *amittere.*

176. With the printed text the syntax is straightforward, though the scansion requires *mihī.* But most of the *Σ* MSS. read *mihi eius sit amittendi . . . copia.* With this reading the feminine genitive *eius* is apparently governed by the gerunds *amittendi* and *retinendi.* The construction of the gerund apparently followed by an objective genitive is rare but not unparalleled, e.g. *Ht.* 29, *nouarum* (sc. *fabularum) qui spectandi faciunt copiam:* however, in all the literary exx. the gerund is itself genitive and dependent upon some such word as *copia,* and it is better to take both the gen. noun (pronoun) and the gen. gerund as dependent on *copia* than to assume that the gerund governs the gen. noun. So in *Ht.* 29, 'the chance of new plays, of viewing', and here 'power over her, of letting go'.

177. Antipho, looking along the street in the direction of the harbour, sees Geta in the distance running towards him. The *seruos currens* was a stock device of the *palliata,* cf. *Ht.* 37, *Ph.* 841 f. and Duckworth (*op. cit.,* pp. 106–7). **uideon Getam . . . aduenire,** cf. 50, *uideon Getam.*

178. ipsus, an alternative form in Pl. and Ter, for *ipse;* here *metri gratia,* avoiding hiatus. **ei,** an exclamation of distress, mostly confined in the dramatists to men (women use *heu*—used by men also, cf. 187) and almost always followed either by a pronoun (e.g. 797, *ei mihi*) or some explanatory statement, often a *uerbum timendi;* it stands alone in Pl. *Most.* 739. **miser,** 96n.

ACT I. SCENE 4

Geta appears from the direction of the harbour in some agitation. At first he does not see the two young men, who have moved to the back of the stage, and his expressions of disquiet increase still further Antipho's apprehensions. He calls Geta over and learns the worst—his father has landed. Phaedria and Geta persuade Antipho to try to put a bold front on his actions. Antipho has just succeeded in assuming a look of confidence, when the sight of his father approaching from the harbour sends him in hurried flight in the opposite direction. Phaedria and Geta remain to face the situation as best they can.

179. The function of the *seruus currens* episode is well described by Donatus: *in hac scaena serui currentis officium est tendens ad perturbationem Antiphonis, quem oportet abesse conspectui patris usque ad cognitionem rerum et* κατaστροφὴν (dénouement) *fabulae.* **nullus,** a colloquial usage, 'You're done for'. **celere** is here, according to Donatus, neuter adj., but *Curc.* 283, *ita nunc subito, propere et celere obiectumst mihi negotium,* suggests that it is an adverb.

180. **ita,** 'all unprepared' (lit. 'unprepared like this, as I am'). **te inpendent,** *inpendere* is normally used absolutely, or with a dative, or with *in* + acc. For the acc., cf. Lucilius 1227 (Marx), *quae res me inpendet* and Lucr. I. 326.

181. **uti,** 'how'. **deuitem . . . extraham,** indirect deliberatives. **modo.** The adverb always scans *mŏdŏ*, but the noun, as here, *mŏdō*.

181a. This verse (= *An.* 208) can be omitted without any loss to the sense; it is probably an interpolation.

183. This is the first example in the *Phormio* of a most common stage convention in Plautus and Terence, the use of eavesdropping and the aside. Geta does not see Antipho and Phaedria, but they can both overhear his remarks and make comments upon them audible to each other and the audience, but not to Geta. All Antipho's and Phaedria's words in this scene are asides of this nature until Antipho's *sta ilico* (195).

Occasionally an intriguing character (usually a slave) learns by eavesdropping facts that will enable him to devise a plan to outwit his opponents (e.g. Pl. *Pseud.* 594 f.). An instance of this occurs off stage in the *Phormio* (described by Geta, 862 f.), but in Terence the device of eavesdropping with attendant asides is more often used for other purposes, e.g. the creation of suspense (whether fear, as here and in 606 f., or joy, as in 841 f.), or simply for the humour of the asides themselves (see Geta's remarks in lines 231–78). So traditional a device is it that characters on the stage may, by pretending that they are not aware that they are being overheard, cause the eavesdropper to believe a fictitious account of the situation; so in *Ph.* 351 f.

illic, nom. masc. sing., i.e. *ille-ce*.

184. **tum** here has no temporal significance and is almost equivalent to *praeterea* ('besides'), with which it is joined in 518. **temporis . . . punctum**, here only in Terence, not in Plautus. **ad hanc rem.** Don. *ad deliberandum, quod ago.* **illuc**, adverb.

185. **quod**, i.e. Antipho's marriage, hinted at in *nostra . . . audacia* (182). **quod eius.** Scan *quŏd ĕiŭ'* (*ĕi-* by B-B).

186. The rhetorical device of asking and answering one's own questions is technically designated as *subiectio* (ὑποφορά); cf. Cic. *Or.* 223 (quoting *pro Scauro* 45); cf. Ter. *Eun.* 549 f. **laterem lauem**, a Greek proverb, also with alliteration πλίνθον πλύνεις, of useless labour; cf. *actum . . . ne agas.* **loquarne . . . instigem . . . lauem**, so-called 'deliberative' subjunctives.

187. **heu**, 178n. **me miserum**, acc. of exclamation, 134n. **quom . . . tum**, 'both . . . and'. **excruciat animi**, cf. Pl. *M.G.* 1068. **animi** has been interpreted as locative, but is better taken as gen. of respect, as in Pl. *Ep.* 138, *desipiebam mentis* and *Trin.* 454, *satin tu's sanus mentis aut animi tui?*

188. **eius . . . ei . . . is**, triple anaphora (repetition); scan *eīus* and *eī* by synizesis. **absque eo esset**, *absque* + abl. pronoun + *esset/ foret*, meaning, 'if (it were) apart from (him etc.)', is found only in Pl. and Ter. The origin of this construction is uncertain; trans. 'but for him'.

189. **uidissem** = *prouidissem*.

190. **conuasassem**, here only in ante-classical, and never in classical Latin. **protinam.** All MSS. have *protinus* (*prŏ-*), but metre requires *prŏ-*, which is given by *protinam*; cf. *Bacch.* 374, *contuli protinam in pedes.*

193. **nescioquod.** Scan *nēscĭŏquŏd*, similarly *nēscĭŏ* (775). **ah**, an interjection capable of many shades of meaning, among which one of reproof is perhaps the commonest. Terence frequently has a mono-syllable at the end of a line, belonging in sense to the next verse.

194-6. The metre and scansion of these lines is disputed.

195. **reuocemus hominem.** It was a traditional joke of the *palliata* to call back a *seruos currens* without any reason. So it is only when Geta is called by name in the next line that he stops and turns round. **hem**, 52n.

196. **pro imperio.** Don. *imperiose.* Cf. Livy III. 49. 5, *iam pro imperio Valerius discedere a priuato lictores iubebat.* **ipsest quem uolui**

obuiam. 'It's the very person I wanted to meet.' The Latin is probably to be construed as *ipse est quem uolui ⟨mihi esse⟩ obuiam.*

197. **cedo quid portas.** 'Come! What's your news?' *Cedo* is used (1) + acc., e.g. 321. (2) + question, as here, (3) absolutely, e.g. 692. Its etymology is uncertain, though *ce* is probably the deictic particle (elsewhere enclitic) found in *hos-ce*, etc. **uerbo expedi,** cf. Pl. *Rud.* 1102, *tu paucis* (sc. *uerbis*) *expedi quid postulas.*

198. **meumne,** sc. *patrem uidisti?* **intellexti.** Terence, much more than Plautus, with verbs having perfects in *-si* or *-xi* favours the syncopated form (omitting *-is-*) of the 2nd sing. perf. indic. active and, occasionally, the perf. inf. active (e.g. *Ad.* 561, *produxe*). The rapid change of speakers here is most striking. **hem . . . quid ais?** both spoken by Phaedria, cf. 1004, 1040. Antipho is nearer to Geta than Phaedria, who, failing to catch exactly what is said by Geta, interposes *hem*, then, receiving no immediate answer, *quid ais?* The punctuation indicates that *hem . . . quid ais?* should be taken together, 'What? What's that you say?'

199. **quid ais.** The three meanings of this phrase are well summarized by Sloman (1) 'What d'you say?' asking for information, (2) 'What d'you say!' 'What!' exclamation of incredulous surprise or anger, (3) not unlike *quid?* introducing a further question. 'Tell me (now)'.

huius, monosyllable by synizesis—*huĩus.* **huius patrem . . . et patruom tuom** though omitted by some MSS. *et* (almost 'who at the same time is') is clearly right; other exx. in Ashmore 199n. (Appendix).

200. **nam quod.** In interrogative sentences *nam* enclitic upon interrogative *quis* (*qui*) or *ubi* lends insistence to the question (Eng. 'whoever', 'wherever'): in the comedians it may be separated from the interrogative word by one word (e.g. *Eun.* 656, *quod istuc nam monstrum fuit?*) or more (*Amph.* 592–3) and, apparently, precede it, as here and elsewhere (e.g. 732). **remedium inueniam,** cf. 185. **subito,** presumably adverb, as 180, though Terence does use the adjective *subitus* at *Ad.* 985.

201. **redeunt.** The present tense in a protasis (as in English), where the future or the fut. perf. would be more exact, is common in colloquial speech (often in Cicero's letters). **Phanium,** Antipho's wife (who does not appear in the play): it should be remembered that the social conventions of Greek New Comedy restricted the appearance of young women on the stage. **abs te ut.** Construe *ut abs te.* **abs,** an archaic form, confined almost entirely to the phrase *abs te*; it begins to disappear from Cicero's writings about 54 B.C.

202. **nullast mihi uita expetenda,** cf. 164; *nulla* = *omnino non.*
quom . . . sunt. *Quom* causal does not in itself require the Subj. in early Latin.

203. **fortis fortuna adiuuat,** the emphatic word first 'fortune favours the *brave*'. The idea is already found in Greek (Soph. *fr.* 927 (Pearson) οὐ τοῖς ἀθύμοις ἡ τύχη ξυλλαμβάνει), but only in Latin is the alliteration possible. Cf. Cic. *Tusc.* II. 11, *fortis . . . fortuna adiuuat, ut est in uetere prouerbio.*

204. **non sum apud me.** 'I'm not myself': a colloquialism paralleled by the Greek ἐν ἐμαυτῷ εἰμί. **nunc quom maxume,** 'now especially', perhaps originating from the ellipse *nunc ⟨est⟩ quom maxume* ('now is (the time) when most . . .').

204. **opus est . . . ut sis.** *Ut* with subjunctive is not a classical construction with *opus est*; normal constructions are:

(i) the thing needed is in the ablative, e.g. *enimuero uoce est opus* (985). This construction must be used when the phrase is qualified by *quid* or *nihil*, e.g. *quid uerbis opust?* (75). If the thing needed is the doing of an action, the neuter abl. sing. of the perf. participle passive is used, e.g. *non opus est dicto* (1003) 'there's no need to say'.

(ii) the thing needed stands as subject nominative, e.g. *quantum opus est tibi argenti* (557), 'how much money you need'.

(iii) infinitive or acc. and infinitive, e.g. *opus est mihi Phormionem . . . adiutorem dari* (560), 'I need Phormio (to be given) as a helper.'

ut sis, sc. *apud te.*

206. **commeruisse culpam.** In Ter. *commerere,* usu. of deserving blame, *promerere* of credit, *merere* of either.

208. **quom . . . possum,** causal *quom* + indic., 202n. **hoc nil est,** 'this is no good', cf. *nil agere.* **ilicet** (= *ire licet*), Don. *semper ilicet finem rei significat, ut actum est.*

209. **quin abeo?,** lit. 'Why don't I go off?' may be translated 'I'm off'. **et quidem ego,** 'me too'; cf. Gk. καὶ ἔγωγε, Pl. *Mil.* 259, *abeo—et quidem ego ibo domum.*

210. **garris.** 'Don't be absurd!' lit. 'You're talking nonsense'.

211. This passage might seem to show that masks were not used at the time of the composition of the play, but Beare (*Roman Stage*, p. 183) points out that there are 'similar references (to facial expressions) in Greek drama, which certainly was performed by masked actors'. On the other hand there is nothing to prove that masks *were* worn in Terence's time.

212. **par pari ut respondeas.** The phrase is proverbial, cf. *Pers.*

223, *par pari respondes dicto*, Cic. *ad Att.* XVI. vii. 6, *ut sit unde par pari respondeatur*; *par pari* are here to be taken as nouns, but by omitting the comma after *uerbo* it would be possible to take them as adjectives agreeing with *uerbum* and *uerbo*. **ut respondeas,** for syntax of *ut*, cf. 38n.

213. **saeuidicis,** ἅπαξ εἰρημένον on the analogy of *maledicus*. Plautus also has *blandidicus, magnidicus, spurcidicus, uanidicus*; Lucretius alone has *suauidicus*. **protelet** clearly means 'drive forth, forward': it may be connected with the straight line in which a team of oxen (*protelum*) was driven. **scio.** Don. *apparet . . . absenti animo esse eum qui loquitur.*

214. **ui coactum . . . inuitum,** for the pleonasm, cf. Cic. *pro Quinct.* 51, *ui ac necessitate coacti inuiti.* **tenes.** 'Have you got it?' 'Do you understand?' Cf. *Ht.* 700, *tenes quid dicam?*

215. **hic** (adverb), scans short by B-B. **ipsus,** sc. Demipho. **ultima platea,** 'at the far end of the street'. *Platea* from Gk. πλατεῖα (ἡ πλατεῖα ὁδός); for the shortening of an original long Gk. quantity, cf. *balineum* (339) from Gk. βαλανεῖον.

216. The metre changes to senarii. *quŏ abis*, prosodic hiatus.

217. **inquam,** in addition to its normal use with quoted words has two other uses; (1) it emphasizes affirmations, e.g. *Hec.* 847, *itanest factum?* PAR. *ita, inquam* ('It is, I tell you'), (2) it is used with imperatives, as here ('I say!' 'Look here!'), and exclamations (987).

218. **et uitam meam.** For life without Phanium is not worth living! Cf. 201–2. Exit Antipho in haste towards the forum.

220. **plectar pendens,** already metaphorically, of the tortures of love, in *Trin.* 247. **nisi quid me fefellerit,** *quid* adverbial acc. 'in any way': 'If I don't prove mistaken' (such is the force of the fut. perfect here): *fallit* impersonal.

221–2. **quod . . . id,** inverted rel. cl.

223. **quin** (for *qui-ne* 'why not') is originally interrogative, but since *quin taces?*, 'Why don't you shut up?', is equivalent to a command, *quin* comes to be used as a particle emphasizing imperatives, as here and often; cf. 350, 857. There is a contrast between *oportet* and *impera*, 'no need to talk of duty: just give the word what I'm to do'. The freeborn *adulescens* puts himself in the hands of the slave, who becomes, as it were, *imperator*. Putting a scheme of trickery into effect is often described in military terms; cf. 229–30, 321, 346–7 and Pl. *Pseud.* 383 f. **faciam,** indirect deliberative.

224. **olim,** construe inside the *ut* clause; **ut** = 'how', almost = *qualis*, 'what your tale was like'. **uostra,** not *tua*, i.e. 'the tale you and Antipho were going to tell'.

225. **in re incipiunda**, 'at the beginning of the business'. **defen-dundam**. For the form, cf. 22n.

226. **iustam . . . causam**. sc. *esse*; the acc. and inf. explains *ut fuerit . . . oratio*. **illam**, sc. *Phormionis*. **uincibilem**. Don. *quae facile uincat*; so *placabilius* (961) is active; cf. the well-known *Boreae penetrabile frigus* (Virg. G. I. 93) and *dissociabilis Oceanus* (Hor. C. I. 3. 22). Other forms in -*bilis* in Terence are passive, e.g. *incredibile* (239).

227. **siquid**, *quid* adverbial acc. 'if it is at all possible'. **potest**, impersonal and absolute.

228. **meliore et callidiore**, sc. *oratione*.

229. Scan *ădī | tō t(u)*, *ĕg(o)*, i.e. *tu* is elided in spite of its emphasis in adversative asyndeton.

229-30. **in insidiis . . . succenturiatus**, for military metaphors, cf. 223n. For *insidiis* some MSS. read *subsidiis*.

230. **age**, used absolutely is uncommon; here it seems to mean 'get on with it!', 'hurry!' More often *age* is used with an imperative or a jussive Subj. As Demipho approaches, Geta and Phaedria withdraw to the rear of the stage, where they can hear, but are not seen by, the old man. It should be noted that, though Donatus marks the end of Act I here, the stage is not empty.

ACT II. SCENE 1

Demipho enters from the harbour and expresses his indignation at Antipho's marriage during his absence. He does not see Phaedria and Geta who stand up-stage. During Demipho's monologue Geta keeps up a running commentary upon it for the amusement of Phaedria and the audience. Later, when Phaedria steps forward to greet his uncle and defend Antipho's conduct, Geta continues his asides, praising Phaedria for the success with which he affects an air of injured innocence. Finally, Geta too steps forward to greet his master. He defends himself against Demipho's reproaches with the plea that as a slave he had been powerless to assist Antipho in his lawsuit against Phormio. Demipho's anger is thus diverted to Phormio, whom Geta promises to bring to see Demipho. Demipho asks Phaedria to go and find Antipho. He himself intends, after calling at his home, to go to the forum to enlist the help of some legal friends for his forthcoming interview with Phormio.

231. **itane tandem**, *itane* = 'like this?', 'really?' *tandem* in questions adds a note of impatience or exasperation. It is common in classical prose, e.g. Cic. *Cat*. I. 1, *quousque tandem abutere, Catilina, patientia nostra?*

232. **nec meum imperium,** sc. *eum reuereri*; the acc. subject of the acc. and inf. of exclamation is easily understood, because Antipho has already stood as subject of *duxit* in the previous line. **imperium,** the authority which he had over his son by virtue of his *patria potestas*. **mitto** = *omittere*, 'to leave (the question of my authority) out of it'. **non . . . saltem,** almost = *ne . . . quidem*.

234. **uix tandem,** 'you've been a long time getting to me', sarcastically equivalent to 'I thought you'd forgotten me'. All Geta's remarks till line 286 are spoken aside, first to Phaedria (to 252) and then in soliloquy.

235. **aliud cura,** 'don't worry about *that*!' **an** is often used in single direct questions with almost the same sense as *num*. **dicet** followed by quoted words is not uncommon.

236. **inuitus feci: lex coegit?** cf. 214, *ui coactum te esse inuitum*. PH. *lege, iudicio*. **audio, fateor.** 'Quite! I grant that.' **places** for *placet*, 'Good'. The personal construction with this meaning only here in Terence.

237. **uerum . . . causam tradere,** sc. *te*. The acc. + inf. is picked up by *id* (238), which is the direct object of *coegit*.

238. **illud durum.** The apparent omission of *est* or *sunt* is in fact an example of a 'nominal sentence', consisting usually of a subject (sts. suppressed) and a predicate. The 'omission' of *esse* is particularly frequent in proverbs (e.g. 454, *quot homines tot sententiae*; Cic. *Off.* I. 10. 33, *summum ius summa iniuria*), exclamations (e.g. 492 f. *fabulae—logi— somnium*) and comments, as here (cf. *factum* 524, *male/bene factum*, 751, 883). **ego expediam: sine.** 'I'll get out of it: leave it to me!' (lit. 'I'll clear up that difficulty').

239. **quid agam,** in O.R. would still be *quid agam*? 'What am I to do?' Here indirect deliberative subjunctive, 'I'm undecided what to do'. **incredibile,** a predicative adj. 'this has happened to me as an unexpected thing'; trans. as an adverb, 'unexpectedly'. Note that Demipho's wrath is already changing to sorrow.

240. **animum,** direct object of *instituere*.

241f. The thought of these lines corresponds very closely to a passage from Euripides' *Theseus* (Nauck *fr.* 392), translated by Cic. *Tusc.* III. 29 (Cicero goes on to quote *Phormio* 241–6—with some minor differences in the text).

242. **ferant,** indirect deliberative, cf. 239n.

243. **rediens,** virtually a noun ('the homecomer'), but *pater* can easily be understood from the context; *exsilia* refers to the departure of

a son to serve as a mercenary—a ready way out in the unsettled times
after the death of Alexander for a young man, who could not, because
of some *peccatum* (244), face his father's wrath; cf. *Ht.* 111 f., *Ad.* 385.

244. Solicitude for a wife's health is not a characteristic of the men of
New Comedy. As a marriage usually involved a settlement (cf. *uxor
dotata*), perhaps the concern was rather for any financial loss that a wife's
death might involve.

246. **spem,** here = 'fear (for the worst)', not 'hope (for the best)'.
This is not a common meaning of the noun. The verb *sperare* is
somewhat more often used to mean 'apprehend', but is still unusual.
eueniat. Contrast the Subj. here (hypothetical) with the assertive force
of the Indic. *eueniet* in 251. **deputare** presumably depends on *oportet* (242),
though one would have expected it to be co-ordinate with *cogitet* (243).

247. **ante eo,** 'outstrip'. **incredibile quantum,** like *nescioquis*,
coheres virtually as a single word and consequently, again like *nescioquis*,
does not affect the mood of the following verb; cf. *mirum quantum*
(*quam*) and Gk. θαυμαστὸν ὅσον; for *nimium quantum*, cf. 643n.

248. **meditata,** picks up *meditari* (242). Geta mockingly parodies
Demipho's words (241–6). The parallelism is particularly close between
lines 245–6 and 250–1. Terence is fond of employing parody,
especially on the lips of meaner characters. So in *Ad.* 425–9 the *senex*
Demea reflects on the need to exercise care in choosing models of conduct. The slave Syrus, parodying the words, remarks that just the same
care is needed in choosing fish! **meditata** is one of a number of
deponent verbs whose perf. participle may have a passive meaning.
mihi, probably dative of agent. **omnia,** *syllaba anceps* at diaeresis
(scan *omniā*). **si,** almost = 'when', as in Cat. 14, 17, *nam si luxerit*
and elsewhere.

249. **molendum esse** (acc. + inf.) can stand only if it is separated
from *habendae compedes* by a semi-colon after *uapulandum*: with *molendum
usque*, suggested by Donatus, sc. *est*. For slave punishments, cf. Pl. *Men.*
976–7, *uerbera, compedes, molae; An.* 199, *uerberibus caesum te in pistrinum,
Daue, dedam usque ad necem.*

250. **accidet,** *-ēt*, probably with retention of original long vowel, cf.
9n. The tasks of the country slave were particularly unwelcome to the
town-bred slave.

252. **quid cessas.** 'Why don't you . . . ?' **hominem,** almost =
eum. Phaedria steps forward to greet his uncle; Geta remains out of
Demipho's sight and makes humorous comment on the interview
between uncle and nephew.

255. **saluom uenire**, sc. *te gaudeo*, cf. 286; the usual formula for greeting a returned traveller. **credo** is spoken to cut short the formal exchange of greetings and thus = 'let's take that as said', 'Quite!' A close parallel is Pl. *Trin.* 1073– STAS., *saluom te . . .* CHAR. *scio et credo tibi: set omitte alia; hoc mihi responde..* **hoc** refers to *sed ubist Antipho?* (254). 'But answer my question.'

256. **hic**, adverb = 'in town', 'in Athens', not 'in the house (Demipho's) here', as *foris* in 308 shows.

257. **uellem quidem**. 'I (only) wish it were.'

258. **bonas**, sarcastically (and ironically), 'a fine marriage'.

259. **id**, an adverbial accusative best described as Acc. of Inner Object, 'about that'. Allardice, p. 8, 'With Verbs of emotion this Acc. signifies the ground of emotion'. **eho**, with (e.g. 384) or without a vocative is followed by (i) a question (as here), = 'What?' (ii) an imperative (748) = 'Here!', 'Look here!'

261. **sua culpa**. Note emphatic position of *suus* before its noun, 'by his own fault'.

262. **illum** = 'that (that used to be)'; trans. 'that I, that kind-hearted father (sc. that once was), have become . . .'

263. **atqui**, *at* + indefinite *qui* (123n.), often translatable as 'and yet'.

264. **ecce autem**, a common collocation sts. standing independently, e.g. *Ad.* 722, *ecce autem*, 'Here it comes!' **congruont**, orthography, 14n.

265. **quom noris**. 'Know one, know them all.' In both cases *noris* is fut. perf. indic. Cf. *An.* 10, *qui utramuis recte norit ambas nouerit.*

266. **hic**. The nom. masc. sing. pronoun in Pl. and Ter. scans *hĭc*, the adverb ('here') *hīc*; *hoc* (nom. and acc. neut. sing., really *hocc* for *hod-ce*) is long unless shortened by B-B.

267. **tradunt operas mutuas**, cf. the proverbial *mutuum muli scabunt*, 'Mules scratch each others' backs'.

268. **probe horum facta . . . depinxit**, cf. Pl. *Poen.* 1114, *formam quidem hercle uerbis depinxti probe*; Cic. *pro Sex Roscio* 74. **inprudens** 'without knowing it'.

269. **cum illo . . . stares** more commonly, in classical prose, *ab aliquo stare*.

270. **si est . . . ut**, cf. 925. 'If it is a fact that' periphrasis for 'if he really has'.

culpam . . . in se admiserit, cf. 415; *Mil.* 103, *quod in me tantum facinus admisi?*

271. **ex qua re,** 'as a result of which'. **minus,** 'too little' almost = *non*. **foret,** subjunct. because the rel. cl. has a consecutive force.

rei ... famae, *rei* = 'fortune, property', cf. 120, *indotatam ... ignobilem. rei* and *famae* are probably genitives; cf. Tac. *Ann.* XIII. 46, *potestatis temperantior.*

272. **quin,** its origin *qui* + *ne*, 'why not?' is apparent here (as it is in *non recuso quin*). **ferat,** 'get (what he deserves)'.

273. mentioning no names, but implying Phormio.

274. **insidias fecit,** cf. *Bacch.* 299, *quoniam uidemus auro insidias fieri.*

275. **nostra.** The omission of *utrum* or *-ne* with the first member of a disjunctive question is quite common; *nostran*, read by several MSS., is also possible.

276-7. The partiality of the law-courts was a trait rather of Athenian democracy than of Roman law.

278. **nossem ... crederem,** unreal condition referring to present time; 'did I not know, I could believe'.

279. **iudex,** not 'judge', but 'jury man'; cf. the plurals in 129, 282, 400.

280. **possit** is potential subjunctive in a generic relative clause after a virtually negative antecedent (Allardice, p. 151), *respondeas* subjunctive by attraction. **iusta,** neut. pl. adj. used as noun, and qualified by an adj., 'your rights'. **tute,** *-tě* (2nd person only), *-mět, -ptě* (usu. emphasizing possessive adjj.), are intensifying pronominal suffixes.

281. **fecit,** 'as he did' = *non respondit* in the previous line.

281-2. **functus ... (e)st ... officium.** The construction of those verbs that in classical Latin take the ablative is, at the time of Plautus and Terence, still fluid. In Terence *abutor, fungor* (abl. only *Ad.* 603), *potior* (abl. only *Ph.* 830) usually take the accusative; *fruor*, usu. has ablative, *utor*, usu. ablative (but acc. of neuter pronouns). **cogitata proloqui,** 'get out (deliver) the speech he'd thought up'.

284. **timidum,** 'being of a timid nature', 'in his bashfulness'. **obstupefecit.** The *-e-* before *facere* in verbs such as *calefacere, patefacere* must originally have been long; normally, however, the *-e-* is shortened. Occasionally, as here, the original long vowel was retained; cf. Lucr. IV. 345.

285. **hunc.** Phaedria. **sed cesso.** Geta advances to greet Demipho.

286. For the formula of greeting, cf. 255.

287. **columen,** used already as a metaphor in Pl. *Cas.* 536, *senati columen, praesidium popli*; cf. Cic. *Verr.* II. 3. 176, *Timarchides autem, columen familiae uestrae.*

290. **horunc** for *horum-ce*; cf. 442n. **inmeritissimo,** ἅπαξ

εἰρημένον; the coinage is made easier by the presence of *inmerito* at the beginning of the line.

291. **tibi,** dative of advantage, 'for you'.

292. **seruom hominem,** 'a man (one) who is a slave'. Plautus has many exx. of *seruos* and *homo* in apposition: cf. also Cic. *pro Tullio* 43 *homines seruos* and *Verr.* II. 3. 91, *seruos homines.* **leges non sinunt.** Neither in Greece nor in Rome was it legally permissible for a slave either to act as *aduocatus* (συνήγορος) or to give evidence; in both countries information might, under certain circumstances, be extracted from a slave under torture.

293. **dictiost,** *est* with the verbal noun in *-io* here has the force of 'is allowed'. **mitto . . . do . . . sino.** Demipho mentions the excuses in promising to pass them over (the rhetorical device of *praeteritio*).

294. **inprudens,** 'from lack of experience'.

295. **'tu seruo's'** (= *seruos es*) is not a strict quotation which would have needed the first person (as in 236), *ego seruos sum.* **si . . . maxume,** lit. 'if in the highest degree', so 'however much'.

297. **daretis, quaereret.** sc. Antipho. These subjunctives are better classed as 'past jussive' (= you ought to have done so-and-so) than as 'past potential' (= you might have done); Cf. 299, 468; Virg. *Aen.* VIII. 643, *at tu dictis Albane, maneres.*

298-9. **qua ratione . . . non ratio.** To keep the play on the two meanings of *ratio* ('reason', 'financial account') Sloman suggests 'on what account'.

299. **argentum,** 'ready cash'. **deerat** is probably to be scanned as *dēerat* (with synizesis). **sumeret,** past jussive 297n.

301. **fenore,** sc. *sumeret.*

302. **hui,** an exclamation of astonishment, here used sarcastically, 'Ha! Ha!' ('Don't make me laugh!') **pulchre,** sarcastic, 258n. 'Splendid idea *if . . .*' **siquidem,** for scansion of *si-,* cf. Intro., p. 30. Trans. '*If* anyone would have lent us money with you alive.' **crederet** 'would have (lent us money)'; for the imperfect where classical Latin would use pluperfect cf. 119n. In Pl. *Pseud.* 303, there is a specifically Roman reference to the *lex quina uicenaria* (*Lex Plaetoria*) which forbade loans to young men under twenty-five; but young men in the *palliata* did manage to borrow money (e.g. Philolaches in the *Mostellaria*), and it is probable that the reference here is not to Roman legal restrictions but to the reluctance of Greek moneylenders to advance loans to sons whose fathers were likely to repudiate the debt.

303. **non, non,** emphatic. **non futurumst; non potest.** 'It shan't be; it can't be.'

304. **egon . . . ut patiar?** 'Am I to allow etc.?' This independent interrogative subjunctive, sts. loosely classified as deliberative, is best described as a Subjunctive in Repudiating or Indignant Questions (Bennett I. 186; Handford, p. 66–). The speaker rejects or expresses indignation at some suggestion. It may be used with or without particles (*-ne, ut, -ne ut, utin*); the negative is usually *non*.

305. **nil suaue meritumst.** From other passages (e.g. 1051) *meritum* appears to be a neuter substantive. In this passage, therefore, sc. *eorum* (or *eius*) and construe 'Nothing pleasant is their (his/her) desert'. This is more likely than that *meritum* is perfect participle passive.

conmonstrarier . . . demonstrarier, for the forms in *-ier*, cf. 92n. Assonance, frequent in Terence only in the prologues, is most unusual between line-ends.

307. **nempe.** 'You mean?' scans *nemp'*: Intro., p. 30.   **istum,** etc. We should insert 'Yes . . .' at the beginning of Demipho's reply.

308. **iam,** 'before you can say Jack Robinson'.   **faxo.** In Greek the commonest way of forming the future is by inserting σ between verbal stem and personal ending λύ-ω (pres.) λύ-σ-ω (fut.). Early Latin *capso faxo* are simple futures formed in the same way; the forms *faxim*, etc., are their subjunctives, formed with the optative suffix found in *sim, uelim, edim*. In Ter. *faxo* is construed with fut. indic. (as here), acc. + perf. participle passive (1028), or, when the verb precedes *faxo*, pres. Subj. (*Ad* 209, 847).   **foris,** 'out of doors' (place where) and *foras* (motion towards) are abl. and acc. respectively from **fora*, an obsolete by-form of 3rd decl. *foris* (usu. pl. *fores*).

310. **recta uia quidem—illuc.** Exit Phaedria in the direction of the forum; at the word *illuc* he points, unseen by Demipho, to Dorio's house, where as Geta comments, Pamphila is. At the end of the line Geta too moves off to the forum to fetch Phormio.

311. **deos Penatis** is a Roman allusion. Its introduction adds a slight complication to the staging of the play. Demipho goes inside his house at 314 to greet the Penates. Though we do not see him come out of the house, his next entrance (348) is from the forum (with the *aduocati*). In the Greek original Demipho would greet the altar of Apollo Agyieus on the stage and leave (R.H. exit) at 314 for the forum.

313. **aduocabo,** hence *aduocatus*.   **adsient.** In addition to the classical forms Ter. uses, esp. at line ends *metri gratia*, the archaic pres.

subj. forms *siem, sies, siet, sient*. These are closely related to the Gk. optatives εἴην (for *ἐσιην), etc.

314. Exit Demipho into his own house.

ACT II. SCENE 2

Geta returns with Phormio from the forum: they enter conversing about the new situation that has arisen with the return of Demipho. Phormio undertakes to see that Antipho shall keep Phanium as his wife and that Demipho's wrath shall be diverted upon himself; since he is an indigent parasite, there is no legal reprisal against him from which Demipho can derive any satisfaction. He is discoursing on the advantage of the parasite's life when Geta, looking back towards the forum, sees Demipho approaching with three friends whom he has brought along to give him legal advice.

So much are the machinations of Phormio the mainspring of the plot that it comes as a surprise to realize that this is his first appearance. It is even more surprising that after two scenes (315–440) he does not appear again for almost 400 lines (829). Yet even when he is off the stage almost every scene testifies to his resourcefulness and activity.

315. **itane . . . ais.** 'D'you really mean to say?' Cf. 231n. As there is no evidence for a long *i* in *ais*, *conspectum* (making *ais* long by position) is more probable than *aduentum*. **admodum,** 'just so'.

317. **oppido.** 'Absolutely'; etymology uncertain, but the second half (*-pido*) may be cognate with Gk ἔμπεδος. **ad te.** All Phormio's remarks till *cedo senem* (321) are addressed to himself.

318. **tute hoc intristi,** Don. παροιμία ('proverb') *apta parasito, quia de cibo est*; 'you've got us into the mess, you get us out of it'. Eng. 'mess' corresponds exactly to the idea of *intristi* (for *intriuisti*), but Latin *exedendum* continues the metaphor, whereas Eng. 'get us out' does not. **accingere,** middle, 'prepare for action!'

319–20. **eccere,** probably a strengthened form of *ecce*. 'Look here'. The subject of *reddet* as of the preceding *rogabit* is Demipho; with *reddet*, therefore, understand *responsum*. **sic, opinor,** 'That's it, I think' (*sic* = 'I'll get out of the mess like that').

321. **iam instructa,** for the military metaphor, cf. 223 n. **cor** is widely used both as the seat of emotions and, as here, of the intelligence.

323. **deriuem,** metaphor from diverting a stream; cf. Cic. *pro Mil.* 29. *deriuandi criminis causa*.

324. **o . . . amicus.** Exclamation with *amicus* nom. for voc. The O.T. (*forti's* = *fortis es*) makes the sentence a statement.

325. **in neruom erumpat denique,** 'land you up in gaol (the stocks)'.

326. Phormio explains the parasite's philosophy of life. Since he has no means of his own, he can give offence without fear of retribution. The patron worries whether the meal he offers his guests will be a success: the parasite can eat it without a care in the world. **periclum** here used in its original sense of 'trial'; 'I've tried the road and I know where to put my feet'.

327. **usque ad necem,** a humorous exaggeration on the part of Phormio.

328. Supply *cum* before *hospites*; *cum . . . tum,* 'both . . . and'. **noui.** Supply the object (? *uiam*) from the context. **tanto saepius,** sc. *id facio.*

329. **cedo dum,** *dum* as an enclitic particle may be translated as '. . . now'. *Agedum* (784 cf. Gk. ἄγε δή) is perhaps its commonest use. **enumquam,** 'have you ever . . . ?' confidently expects a negative answer. **iniuriarum,** 'an action for damages': the genitive as Gk. αἰκίας δίκη.

330. **qui istuc.** 'How's that?' For *qui,* cf. 123n. **tennitur,** so most editors after Donatus: the MSS. have *tenditur.*

331. **qui nil faciunt,** sc. *nobis male.*

332. **in illis . . . in illis.** The use of the same pronoun for contrasted groups of people is not uncommon in colloquial language. **opera luditur,** 'their efforts are wasted'.

333. **aliis aliunde,** cf. Livy XLIV. xii. 3, *alii aliunde coibant* and L & S, s.v. *aliunde* II. C. 'Different people from whom something can be squeezed are in danger from different sources: everyone knows *I*'ve got nothing.' **unde** = *a quibus.*

dices 'ducent damnatum domum', note the alliteration, cf. 347, 998. In Athens enslavement for debt was abolished by Solon (τὸ μὴ δανείζειν ἐπὶ τοῖς σώμασιν Arist. *Pol.* IX), though Demosthenes XXXIII, 1 implies that imprisonment was retained for some forms of commercial debt. In Rome a judgement-debtor (*addictus*) might be kept in custody by his creditor till the debt was paid, but he did not lose his public or private rights, i.e. did not legally become a *seruus.*

335. **edacem,** the stock epithet of the parasite, cf. *Ht.* 38, *Eun.* 38 (both good passages for stock epithets of other characters as well).

337. **potest,** -*ĕst* by B-B. **ab illo,** sc. *Antiphone.*

338. **regi,** of the parasite's patron, cf. 70n. Notice that this passage does not fit properly because Antipho is not the *rex* of Phormio; see Intro., p. 13.

339. **asymbolum,** Greek ἀσύμβολος, Latin *immunis,* one who makes no contribution (συμβολή Latin *collecta*) to a joint meal. For the custom, cf. *An.* 88–9, *symbolam dedit, cenauit.*

balineis, from *balineae*; for the form, from Gk. βαλανεῖον, cf. 215n.

339–41. The whole of Donatus' note here is worth transcribing: *haec non ab Apollodoro sed ⟨de Enn. sat (?)⟩ translata sunt omnia: 'quippe sine cura laetus lautus cum aduenis infertis malis, expedito bracchio, alacer celsus, lupino exspectans impetu, mox cum alterius ablingas bona: quid censes domino esse animi? pro diuum fidem! ille tristis est dum cibum seruat, tu ridens uoras.'* Though there is a fairly close general resemblance between the two passages, it is an exaggeration to say that *Ph.* 339 f. is derived entirely from the passage quoted.

340. **otiosum ab animo,** 'easy in mind': for this use of *ab* cf. Pl. *Ep.* 129, *ab animo aeger fui*; *Truc.* 833, *ab ingenio inprobust.* **quom,** with an adversative sense may have Indic. or Subj. in Terence.

341. **ringitur.** Don. *ringi est stomachari tacitum; est enim translatio a canibus latratoriis,* i.e. '(curl the lips back in a) snarl'.

rideas . . . bibas . . . decumbas, 'you may, are free to . . .' The subjunctives are potential, but are often classified as subjunctive of indefinite 2nd person.

342. **prior decumbas.** Sloman and Ashmore 'have a better place at table', but as *prior* with *bibas* is used of priority of time, it is likely that it is similarly used with *decumbas.* **cena dubia.** The phrase is also used by Hor. *Sat.* II. 2. 77 with *dubius = uarius.*

343. **ubi dubites,** mood 341n. **sumas,** indirect deliberative 'what you are to take'.

344. **haec quom . . . ineas quam sint,** etc. 'When you consider how attractive and expensive these things are, won't you count the man who provides them a very god indeed?' The structure is complicated by the fact that the rel. cl. (*qui praebet*) is inverted (standing immediately before the main cl.), and that the subject of the Ind. Quest. (*haec*) and the object of the rel. cl. (*ea*) stand in anticipation outside the clause to which each belongs.

345. **non . . . habeas,** mood 341n. **praesentem,** here, as often when used of gods, means more than merely 'present'; 'present with powerful aid'.

346. Geta looks round and sees Demipho approaching from the forum, accompanied by three *aduocati*. **senex adest,** -*ἔx* by B-B. **quid agas,** indirect deliberative. **coitio.** Don. *translatio a proelio, nam et congredi milites et coire dicuntur.*

347. **postilla,** *ante, inter, post, praeter, propter* are compounded with demonstrative adverbs whose form is identical with the abl. fem. sing. (*illa*(*c*), *hac, ea*). *Postilla* is not in classical prose and only ante-Augustan. **ut lubet ludas licet,** note the alliteration; the play on *lubet . . . licet* is a common one: *licet* + subj., only here in Terence (elsewhere + inf.). **lubet,** orthography 28n.

ACT II. SCENE 3

Enter Demipho from the forum with his three legal advisers. At first they do not see Phormio and Geta, who, aware of their presence, stage an altercation in a loud voice so that Demipho cannot avoid overhearing what they say. Phormio attacks Demipho's character and conduct in seeking to get Phanium's marriage annulled: Geta pretends to make a heated defence of his master's integrity. Eventually Demipho calls on Geta to stop the argument so that he can himself question Phormio about the alleged kinship between Phanium and Demipho's family. Phormio proves more than a match for Demipho and reminds him that the case has already been settled by a verdict of the court. Demipho now seeks to effect a compromise by offering to pay Phormio the statutory dowry of five minae for the girl, if the parasite will take her off their hands. Phormio indignantly rejects this suggestion and counsels Demipho to accept the *fait accompli*, knowing that this suggestion will infuriate Demipho still more. The scene ends with Demipho threatening to eject Phanium if Phormio doesn't remove her, while Phormio in reply threatens to have the law on Demipho if he dares to lay a finger on the girl. With this ultimatum Phormio sweeps from the stage.

348. Demipho's remarks are addressed to the three *aduocati* who accompany him.

350. At *pro deum immortalium* Geta and Phormio raise their voices in such a way that Demipho thinks he is overhearing a private conversation. **hoc age.** *Hoc age* is originally a religious formula, whose significance is explained by Plutarch, *Coriolanus* XXV, 2, 'When magistrates or priests perform any religious function, they are preceded by a herald, crying in a loud voice "*Hoc age*", which means "Do this" (*κῆρυξ πρόεισι μεγάλῃ φωνῇ βοῶν· "Ὀx ἄγε." σημαίνει δ' ἡ φωνή, τοῦτο πρᾶττε*), warning

the people to give heed to the sacred rites and to allow no task or claim of business to stand in their way.' The phrase is then widely used in colloquial language meaning either 'Get on with the job in hand' (e.g. *Capt.* 444) or 'Just ⟨be quiet and⟩ watch (pay attention to) this' (e.g. *Asin.* 1); the latter is the meaning here: Don. *annuit ut taceat.*

351. **iam** + fut. = 'soon' 'before you can tell', cf. 308n. **pro,** an exclamatory interjection which does not affect the case of the word it precedes.

deum, this form of the gen. plural, usually retained in words for coins and measures and in a number of stereotyped phrases (e.g. *duumuirum*), corresponds exactly to the 2nd. decl. Gk. gen. pl. in -ων (e.g. θεῶν). The usual Latin *-orum* is by analogy from 1st decl. *-arum.*

The gen. depends on *fidem* understood; the full phrase in Caecilius (R. 211–12), *pro deum popularium omnium omnium adulescentium | clamo postulo obsecro oro ploro atque inploro fidem.*

352. **hanc,** construe with Phanium.

353. **hanc ... cognatam,** repeats the previous line almost verbatim, but with *negat ... hanc* inverted; the repetition emphasizes Phormio's (feigned) indignation.

353–6. **negat ... negat ... negat.** Geta, too, playing his part, answers Phormio with an unvaried stolidity.

354. **neque eius patrem se scire qui fuerit.** The 'proleptic accusative' (imitated by Milton, e.g. *P.L.* II. 990, 'I know thee, stranger, who thou art'), in which the logical subject of the subordinate clause stands grammatically as object of the verb in the main clause, is common in all kinds of Greek literature, but in Latin is a phenomenon of colloquial speech originating from parataxis (e.g. Pl. *Most.* 855, *quin tu illam aspice ut placide accubat* from *quin tu illam aspice! ut placide accubat!*). It is commonest after verbs such as *scire, nosse, uidere, facere,* but is apparently avoided when the subordinate verb is passive.

355. Demipho addresses the *aduocati* in an aside. **de quo agebam,** sc. *uobiscum,* 'whom I was talking to you about'.

356. Though Demipho overhears the name 'Stilpo', in 385 f. he pretends not to know it; otherwise he would reveal that he had been eavesdropping.

357. **egens relictast misera,** *egens* complement of *relictast,* 'left in want'; *misera* agrees with the subject understood of *relictast,* 'she, poor girl'. **ignoratur** 'is disowned'.

358. **uide quid auaritia facit.** The mood in Ind. Questions in Terence varies. Where original parataxis would have indic. the indic. is

commonly retained after imperatives or their equivalents (e.g. *uide*, *uiden*), esp. of *uerba dicendi*. In all other cases the subj. is the usual mood (and the invariable mood where the subj. would have stood in parataxis). The difference is well shown by comparing 446 and 473.

359. **malitiae**, gen. of charge after *insimulabis*. **male audies**, cf. 20n. Note the word-play *malitiae—male*. Geta, playing his part, sticks up for his master against Phormio.

360. **o audaciam**, acc. of exclamation. Scan ŏ *aŭd-* (prosodic hiatus and B-B). **etiam . . . ultro**, reinforce each other 'even/actually'. *Ultro* is often used of an action that takes the wind out of another's sails —'so far from waiting for *me* to accuse *him*, *he* is actually coming to accuse *me*'.

361. **nam iam**. Donatus takes *iam* to imply that there was a time when Phormio *was* annoyed with Antipho: more probably *iam* is expletive 'As regards the young man, now, I've no reason.' **nil est quod** + subj. as in classical Latin.

363. **pauper**, not of abject poverty, but of limited means, cf. *Eun.* 486, *seruom . . . domini pauperis*. **quoi opera**, scanning *quŏi*. Don. takes *opera* as instrumental abl., *uita* as nom. (= *uictus*) 'whose livelihood was by manual labour'; elsewhere *uita* is rather 'manner of living' than 'means of living'. *Opera* may also be nom. 'whose life was toil', and the nom. is perhaps supported by parallels such as Eur. *Suppl.* 550, παλαίσμαθ' ἡμῶν ὁ βίος ('Our life is a struggle'); Sen. *Ep.* 96, 5, *uiuere . . . militare est*; Plin. *N.H. praef.* 18, *uita uigilia est*.

364-5. **agrum. . . colendum habebat**, the acc. gerundive is found as the complement after *do* and a small number of verbs in Plautus. To these Terence adds *habere*, *curare* (*An.* 865), *propinare* (*Eun.* 1087).

365. **interea**, 'during those days', cf. 347n.

366. **se**, is acc. object, **hunc . . . cognatum** acc. subj. of *neglegere*.

367. **at quem uirum!** The use of the interrogative pronoun in the acc. of exclamation is very rare; cf. *Eun.* 590 *at quem deum!* **quem . . . uiderim in uita** qualifies *optimum*. The Subj. *uiderim* is difficult; possibly it has a restricting force 'the best that I (at least) have ever seen'. *in uita* is equivalent to *umquam*.

368. **uideas . . . narras**. The correct interpretation of this passage is quite uncertain; it had been lost before the time of Donatus. *Ut narras* means 'according to your tale' and implies disbelief in the tale; *atque* might be a comparative conjunction 'like', 'as', even though no adj. or advb. of equation precedes (e.g. Pl *Bacch.* 549, *quem esse amicum ratus sum atque ipsus sum mihi*). In this case take *uideas* as optative and trans.

'May you see yourself like him (i.e. *optumum*)—*if* we can believe your tale.' If *atque* is taken as a simple co-ordinating 'and', take *uideas* as jussive and trans. 'You ought to look at yourself and him (i.e. note the contrast between your villainy and his excellence)—*if* etc.' **in' malam crucem,** *in'* = *isne*, 'Won't you go?' **malam crucem,** adverbial acc. or acc. of motion without a prep. as *Eun.* 536, *malam rem hinc ibis?* Much commoner are expressions with a verb (*i, abi, in', abin'*) followed by *in* (prep.) *malam rem; malam crucem* occurs only here in Terence, but is common in Plautus. All are equivalent to 'Go to the devil!' Cf. Gk. ἔρρ᾽ ἐς κόρακας.

369. **grauis,** for the position of the adj. separated from its noun, cf. 24.

370. **hanc,** Phanium. **ob hanc inim-,** *hănc* by B-B.

371. **quam,** antecedent *hanc*, not *familiam*. **inliberaliter,** 'unworthily', i.e. in a manner quite unbecoming a gentleman (*liberalis*): a strong phrase, cf. *Ad.* 662-4.

372. **pergin** = *pergisne*; *pergere* + inf. is commonly used colloquially as a periphrasis for the future tense ('are you going to . . . ?'), sts. with continuative force ('are you going to go on . . . -ing?'). Cf. *Truc.* 265, *pergin male loqui, mulier, mihi?*

ero, dative after *male loqui* (= *male dicere*).

373. **hoc,** sc. *male loqui.* 'Abuse is just what the fellow deserves'. **ain tandem** (*ain* = *aisne*) expresses a threatening question, 'You don't say?' For *tandem*, cf. 231n., *uero* is sometimes used in the same way, e.g. *Eun.* 803, *ain uero, canis?* **carcer,** 'jail-bird': place for person; the metonymy is Greek, cf. Menander, *Epitr.* 149, ἐργαστήριον; Lucilius (Warm. 1176), *carcer uix carcere dignus*; Ter. *Ph.* 526n. (*sterculinum*). As the argument threatens to become more acrimonious, Demipho calls on Geta to stop. At first Geta pretends not to hear him.

374. **extortor . . . contortor,** the latter is ἅπαξ εἰρημένον, the former not in classical Latin. Terence departs from his usual purity of speech (i) when a slave is speaking, (ii) to mark a climax. Some attempt must be made in translation to convey the assonance and word-play (? 'property-stealing, double-dealing rogue').

Geta. Demipho calls Geta's name more loudly: Geta still pays no attention till Phormio, in an aside, bids him answer. Geta turns round and affects an air of astonishment at seeing his master. Geta explains, as though he were not aware that Demipho had overheard the whole argument, that he has been defending his master against Phormio's unworthy insults.

375. **ehem,** scans *ĕhĕm*; for its use cf. 52n.

376. **te indignas seque dignas,** word-play.

377. **hodie** is often used, esp. with negatives, merely to add emphasis ('never' or 'never . . . at all'?).

Demipho finally silences Geta: for the rest of the scene the argument is carried on between Demipho and Phormio, but Geta makes inter-jections—aloud, in encouragement of Demipho, and aside, in support of Phormio.

378-9. **bona uenia . . . si tibi placere potis est,** the sarcasm of excessive politeness, 'by your leave, if you don't mind'. **potis,** in early Latin may refer to a subject of either number and any gender. In Ter. it is used only before vocalic forms of *esse*; elsewhere the alternative form *pote* (also indeclinable) is used, e.g. 535.

380. **quem . . . ais fuisse . . . explana mihi** is ·a pleonasm for *quis . . . fuerit, explana.* Pleonasms of this kind are frequent with *uerba dicendi et sentiendi* in colloquial speech, though the verb in the relative clause is usually subjunctive. Here the indicative *ais* may be explained by the original parataxis, *quem . . . ais fuisse istum? explana mihi.*

382. **proinde . . . quasi,** 'just as if'. **expiscare,** exactly the Eng-lish metaphor 'you're fishing for it': Don. *expiscari est diligentissime quaerere, ubinam pisces lateant. ergo tractum uerbum a piscatoribus.* But *expiscari* is not common in this metaphorical sense (cf. Cic. *in Pis.* 69; *ad Att.* II. 17, 3).

383. **ego me nego,** sc. *nosse.* **tu** 'The 2nd Pers. Pron. with the Imper. is a feature of Comedy' (Allardice, p. 82). **tu qui ais,** sc. *me nosse,* 'you who say I do'.

384. **eho tu.** 'What?' ('Come off it!'), cf. 259n. **noras** = *noueras*; the latter form is found, at the line end, in 390.

enicas, lit. 'you're torturing me (to death)', colloquially expressing impatience ('put me out of my misery'): 'Quick man, out with it!'

385. After *maxume* Phormio halts: Demipho is immediately sus-picious.

386. Phormio, in an exclamatory aside to the audience, explains why he has suddenly lapsed into silence.

quid ais? Cf. 199n. 'What's that?' Demipho knows that Phormio has just made a remark, but has failed to catch it.

386-7. **Geta . . . subice,** aside to Geta. **olim,** presumably when Phormio and his allies were making up their story to take before the court. Since Stilpo is the name Chremes used at his Lemnian establishment (cf. 740), it is best to assume that Phormio or one of his allies got the name from Phanium or her nurse.

388. **non dico.** 'I'm not saying' ('I won't say'); Allardice, pp. 63–4, 'With some common verbs like *do, dico, audio,* the Pres. negative gives an emphatic denial to a request.' **temptatum,** supine, 'put to the test', with, possibly, the implication 'try to catch me out'.

389. **ego autem tempto?** *autem* adds indignation to the question; colloquially 'Me catch you out?' **Stilpo,** aside to Phormio. **atque adeo.** Besides its normal adverbial meaning of 'so far' [of space (55), time (589), and degree (497)] *adeo* has two further uses, (1) meaning 'besides' (= *praeterea*), esp. with *atque, neque*; (2) as an emphasizing enclitic, 'indeed', most frequently with pronouns. In the present passage *atque* seems to have an adversative force, 'and yet' (= *atqui*). Trans., 'And yet (after all) why shouldn't I tell you? (His name's) Stilpo.' **quid mea,** sc. *refert.*

392. **horum,** probably masc., sc. *aduocatorum,* 'before these gentlemen'.

393. **talentum,** gen. pl., cf. 351n. A talent = 60 minae; for some indication of its purchasing power, cf. 557n. **rem,** 'property', 'an estate' (in its legal sense).

394. **malefaciant,** *mălĕfăcĭ-,* proceleusmatic.

394–5. **esses . . . proferens,** cf. An. 508, 775 (both *ut sis sciens*). The use of the participle and *sum* as a periphrastic present is simplest when the participle is virtually an adjective. The present example is a bold one, not paralleled in Pl. or Terence. **memoriter,** cf. *Eun.* 915; almost = 'in detail'.

396. **ita ut dicis.** 'Just as you say', 'I agree'. **quom aduenissem.** Subj. because it is an unreal supposition relating to past time (the hypothesis of 393 *si reliquisset* still holds); *quom,* almost 'if ever', *aduenissem,* 'I had come (before the court)'.

398. **cedo,** 197n. **eu noster, recte.** Geta pretends to express his admiration for the brilliant way in which his master tackles Phormio's arguments. **eu** = Gk. εὖ, 'Well done!' 'Splendid'; cf. *Eun.* 154, *eu noster, laudo.* **heus,** followed or, rarely, preceded by a vocative summons attention, 'Ho there!' Sometimes it is used, without a vocative expressed (e.g. 819, 903), to draw attention to the following remark, 'Look here!' 'Look you!'

399. **quibus me oportuit,** sc. *expedire.*

400. **falsum fuerat, filius,** note alliteration. **fuerat.** The Indic.

leaves open the question of the truth or falsehood of Phormio's contention. *Fuerat* is pluperfect because the assumption is prior in time to the time of *refellit*; trans. 'If what I said was untrue . . .'

401. filium ñarras mihi? Eng. 'Don't talk to me about my son'.

402. quoius, connecting rel., 'Words fail me to express his stupidity'.

403. tu qui sapiens es. Phormio sarcastically contrasts with the son's stupidity his father's wisdom. Trans. 'you who are so wise'. **adi,** 'appear before (and ask them to)' hence *ut +* subj.

404. Demosth. *Lept.* 147 states explicitly the principle of Athenian law that it is illegal to make a second legal investigation upon the same charge against the same person. Roman law did allow *in integrum restitutio,* though it did not normally offer much prospect of securing a reversal of a *res iudicata.* It was, in fact, an *auxilium extraordinarium* whose operation was restricted within narrow limits.

405. solus regnas. The allusion is here to *regnum* literally, 'unconstitutional tyranny' (the Greek equivalent is τυραννίς), not, as in 338, to *rex* in the benevolent sense of *patronus.* **soli,** sc. *tibi.*

406. iudicium adipiscier, -*dĭcĭ(um)* | *ădĭ-.* **hic,** 'here' (at Athens).

408. secter . . . audiam, for Subj. after *potius quam* (almost = *ne*), cf. *Eun.* 173–4, *uerum tamen potius quam litis sequar.*

409. itidem ut . . . si, cf. 413 *itidem ut . . . ubi.*

410. dotis, partitive genitive depending on *id.* **abduc.** In his excitement Demipho says, 'Take her away' before, instead of after, 'take five minae.' **minas quinque.** For the law and its provisions, see 125n. Five minae = 500 drachmae. *Mina* (Gk. μνᾶ) has an enthetic vowel, so too *drachuma* (from δραχμή), *Alcumena* ('Αλκμήνη), *Aesculapius* ('Ασκληπιός).

411. Scan *hăhăhæ* (with hiatus before) *hŏmŏ* (-*mŏ* by B-B), *ĕst* (B-B) and *nŭm* (prosodic hiatus). **homo suauis,** sarcastically 'fine fellow!'

413. meretricem, for case cf. 281n. **abusus sis,** 'have had your pleasure of'.

415. ut ne, 168n. 'Or was it to prevent a (female) citizen doing anything unworthy of herself because of poverty that the law enacted that she should be given in marriage to her nearest relative to live with him alone?'

416. quod, connecting relative.

418. ita . . . unde? *quidem* emphasizes the preceding word 'Yes, to his *nearest* relative. But how do we come to be his nearest relatives (sc. *proxumi sumus* after *unde*)?' **ohe** (pyrrhic in Terence), 'Hold on',

'Hold hard' indicates an impatient interruption or objection; often *ohe iam*, 'Hold on now'. Cf. Hor. *Sat.* II. v. 96 and I. v. 12 *ohe* (with long first syllable) | *iam satis est.*

419. **actum . . . ne agas,** proverb derived from the sphere of the law courts. 'Don't take to law what's already been settled'. An effective translation must reproduce the pithiness of the Latin and its word-play (*actum . . . agas*), even at the cost of losing the reference to the law courts. Perhaps 'What's done can't be undone': *non agam* is then 'Can't be undone?' **aiunt.** Don. *dicimus cum prouerbium significamus*; cf. 506, 768.

419. **immo.** The contradicting force of immo is clearly shown here. Instead of the archaic 'nay rather', trans. (here) 'Why!' or. 'Heavens!'

420. **ineptis.** 'You're talking nonsense'. **sine modo,** *modo* adds an expression of impatience to the imperative, 'only' 'just': cf. 496. But does *sine modo* mean 'Leave me alone (let me be)!' or 'Just wait (and I'll show you)!'? Here the latter interpretation is more to the point. DE. 'I'll never stop till I achieve my aim.' PH. '(You're talking) nonsense.' DE. 'Just you wait and see.'

424. The imperative in *-to*, the formality of *illum quae ego dico dicere* convey Demipho's earnestness.

425. **aut quidem.** For *quidem* emphasizing the preceding word, cf. 418, 'Or else . . .' 'If not, . . .' **hac,** pejorative: 'with that wife of his'.

426. **iratus est,** spoken aside by Geta to Phormio. **tu te idem . . . feceris.** 'You'd better do the same to yourself'; *te* (*tĕ* by prosodic hiatus) is abl. after *feceris* (137n.), *idem* is neut. acc. sing. Less probably *ĭdem* might be nom. masc. sing. (shortened by B-B) and *tute* (280n.) the emphatic form of *tu*. **feceris** fut. pfct. almost = imperative, as in 430.

428-9. **metuit . . . principia.** Phormio and Geta exchange asides.

428. **infelix,** 'wretch', 'poor fool'.

429. **bene habent,** for *habere* without *se*, cf. *Ad.* 364-5; for the more usual *se habent*, cf. 479, 820.

430. **ferundum fers . . . factis feceris,** alliteration and *figura etymologica* (twice), 'bear what must be borne, and do what it's best for you to do, namely, let us be friends'.

431-2. **egon . . . expetam? . . . aut . . . uelim?,** subj. of indignant repudiation. **te uisum aut auditum uelim,** *uelle*, *nolle* are frequently used with acc. + pple. (without *esse*).

435. **te . . . tibi,** anaphora, 'Let her look after you. Keep her (for) yourself!' **hoc age.** 'To the point (matter-in-hand)': cf. 350n.

436. nisi tu properas, for the tense of *properas*, cf. 850n.

436–9. Note the parallelism of the final threats of Demipho and Phormio. For *dixi* at the end of a formal pronouncement cf. 452.

439. dicam (*dĭc-*), cf. 127n. **inpingam.** 'I'll bring an action against you that will cripple you.' For *inpingere* with the meaning of 'forcing something upon an unwilling recipient', cf. Cic. *ad Att.* VI. i. 6, *impingit mihi epistulam*.

440. As Phormio leaves the stage he attracts Geta's attention to impart his final aside. Geta's reply also is made aside. **domo me,** *domo* abl. of separation, ellipse of verb of summoning, e.g. *arcesse*.

ACT II. SCENE 4

After instructing Geta to go home to see if Antipho has returned yet, Demipho turns and asks his legal friends whether they consider he will be able to get the court's verdict reversed. In a brief, but delightful, scene of caricature the *aduocati* give their opinions. Cratinus believes that the verdict can be reversed, Hegio thinks that it cannot. The casting vote rests with Crito, who replies that the matter is a difficult one, which requires further consideration. Demipho declines the offer of their further help with ironical politeness. The *aduocati* depart; Demipho declares himself even more undecided than he was. Geta returns to say that Antipho has not yet returned. Demipho announces his intention of deferring his decision till he has consulted with his brother Chremes on his return from abroad; he goes off towards the harbour to find out when he is expected. Geta starts to move off towards the forum to find Antipho, when the latter, who had fled at the sight of his father (218), is seen coming towards him.

441. Demipho soliloquizes; as earlier, his chief anxiety is to set eyes on his son.

442. hisce, *huiusce, hosce, hasce, horunc, harunc* (?) *hisce* (dat. and abl. pl.) are used by Terence only before a vowel or '*h*'. The nom. masc. pl. form *hisce* found in Plautus before a vowel occurs in Terence only at *Eun.* 249.

444. sententiae partitive gen. dependent on *quid*.

447. quid ago? The Indic. is frequently used in Pl. and Ter. to express a deliberative question; cf. 1007. Bennett (I. 23) summarizes the researches of Sjögren as follows: ' "quid agam" is used only in soliloquy, in true deliberatives, or else in dialogue in questions of helplessness or despair, whereas 'quid ago' (barring *Ph.* 736) is not used in soliloquy at all, and in dialogue is confined to questions asking for advice.' **Crati-num censeo**, sc. *dicere debere* (*vel sim.*).

449. **quae . . . sint, ea,** inverted rel. cl. **in rem tuam,** 'to your advantage'.

450. **sic,** 'as follows'. **hic,** adverb.

451. **restitui in integrum,** 'rendered null and void' ('the judgement should be quashed'); cf. 404n.

452. **dixi,** of formal pronouncement, cf. 437, 439.

453. **uerum itast.** 'But the truth is' (lit. 'but it is like this').

454. **quot homines tot sententiae,** quoted by Cic. *de fin.* I. 5. 15; for absence of *sunt*, cf. 238n.

456. **turpe inceptu est,** 'it is shameful to try'. For the supine *inceptu* cf. *Ad.* 275, *turpe dictu; turpe inceptumst*, 'the attempt is shameful' (taking *inceptum* as a neuter noun) is also possible.

457. **amplius** may be a reference to the Roman legal usage of *ampliatio*, technically a 'renewal of the case' after the jury had returned a verdict of *non liquet*. So ps-Asc. on Cic. *Verr.* II. i. 9, 26, *amplius pronuntiabatur . . . cum dixissent iudices non liquet*.

458. **res magnast.** 'It is a weighty matter'. **fecistis probe,** with polite irony. After these words the *aduocati* depart; they must have left before Demipho's next remark *incertior . . . dudum*.

459. **incertior sum multo.** Don. *ex tribus enim* (sc. *aduocatis*) *unus suasit, alter dissuasit, tertius nihil dixit.* **dudum,** 'previously', cf. 786n. Geta now returns from Demipho's house.

459–60. **negant redisse,** sc. *Antiphonem*.

461. **quod . . . consilium, id sequar,** inverted rel. cl.

462. **percontatum ibo,** the supine is the commonest way of expressing purpose after verbs of motion: after *ire* is also found the inf. of purpose (102n.) and a final clause (*Ad.* 632). **percontari** lit. 'to probe with a pole (*contus*) to see how deep water is'. **se recipiat,** Subj. of Ind. Quest. Exit Demipho to the harbour, thus missing Antipho, who, three lines later, returns from the direction of the market-place.

463. **quae acta . . . sint,** Subj. by attraction, standing inside the final cl. *ut . . . sciat.*

464. **eccum** is a compound of *ecc*(*e*) and (*h*)*um* (i.e. *hunc* without deictic -*ce*); Terence also has *eccam, eccos. Eccum* is used (1) absolutely (*An.* 957), (2) with a second acc. (*Ph.* 600), (3) with the person referred to as the subject or object of a verb (464, 484). **in tempore,** 'opportunely'; trans. 'Splendid! I see him coming towards me.'

ACT III. SCENE 1

Antipho, who fled towards the forum as soon as he saw his father approaching from the port, returns from the city. In soliloquy he reproaches himself for running away and leaving Phaedria and Geta to look after Phanium's interests. Geta goes up to him and reassures him that his interests have been well upheld during his absence. He tells him also that there is a lull in affairs because Demipho has decided to wait for Chremes' return before taking any action.

465. Antipho enters from the forum (R.H.) soliloquizing. He is separated by the whole length of the stage from Geta, whom he does not see. **multimodis** almost = 'very' as in *Ht*. 320, *multimodis iniurius*, | *Clitipho, es.* **cum istoc animo,** *cum* may indicate cause as well as accompaniment, especially in imprecations; trans. 'you and your . . .'

467. **tuam rem,** 'your interests'. **tete,** 280n.

468. **utut,** 'always takes the Indic. It is associated with some part of *esse* or its equivalent (e.g. *se habere, Ph*. 820)' (Allardice, p. 120). Trans. 'how(so)ever', 'no matter how'. **consuleres,** past jussive, 'you ought to have thought of her'.

469. **tuam fidem,** 'her trust in you'; cf. 1016 for pronominal adj. = objective genitive. *Ad*. 621, *tua nos frustratast fides* ('our trust in you'). **poteretur** is the only form of the imperf. subj. in Plautus and Terence; for acc. after *potior*, cf. 281n.

471. Geta steps forward and interrupts Antipho's soliloquy. **et quidem . . . nos,** cf. 209 'we too'. **qui abieris,** causal subj.

472. Antipho does not see Geta until he speaks.

473. See 358n. for mood of *sunt*.

474. **numquid patri subolet?** *subolet*, impersonal or with neuter pronoun subject 'give off a smell', only in Plautus and Terence. **nil etiam,** *etiam* is temporal here, 'still' 'as yet'.

475. **nisi** preceded by *nescio* = 'only', 'but' (originating from 'I don't know anything except that . . .'); cf. 952–3. **cessauit** with inf. is virtually confined to interrogative and negative sentences. In the former it always means 'hesitate', 'lose time in doing'; in the negative (e.g. 376–7) the sense may be 'never stopped'.

476. **praebuit.** For *praebuit* without *se*, cf. Apul. *Met*. X, 28, *talem parentem praebuit qualem exhibuerat uxorem*; but there may be a difference between *strenuom hominem se praebuit* 'showed himself an untiring friend' and *strenuom hominem praebuit* 'played (the part of) the untiring friend'.

477. **confutauit,** generally a synonym for *conuincere, redarguere*; literally it seems to mean 'keep the pot from boiling over'. Trans., 'The old man was quite worked up, but he sat on him nicely'. **admodum,** qualifies *iratum,* 'quite' 'very'.

478. **ego . . . porro,** sc. *feci.* 'I too did what I could'; **porro,** 'going further (with the story)', 'too'. **omnis uos amo,** 'my thanks to you all'.

480. **mansurusque patruom . . . est,** *manere* is often used transitively (= *exspectare*) in Plautus and Terence; it is sometimes so used in classical prose, but not by Cicero, who however quotes from M. Antonius (*Phil.* XIII, 45), *me aliud fatum manet.* **dum . . . adueniat,** prospective subjunctive. **quid eum?**, sc. *mansurus est.* **aibat,** 4th conj. verbs and *aio,* in addition to the classical forms, have imperfect forms in *-ibam* and archaic future in *-ibo,* e.g. *scibam* (582), *scibat* (529), *scibit* (765). **ut aibat . . . sese uelle facere,** a conflated construction: either *ut aibat, . . . uolebat facere* or *aibat . . . sese uelle facere* would have been logical. For a similar conflation, cf. *Ad.* 648, *ut opinor eas non nosse te.* **de eius consilio,** 'in accordance with his advice'.

482. **metus,** 4th decl. gen. sing. in Terence is normally *-i* (154n.): *-us,* though not certainly found in Plautus, is attested in Ennius and Lucilius. If *metus* (partitive gen. dependent on *quantum*) is read here, it must scan short by B-B: *quantus* is read by Σ (*metus* is then nom. sing.). **uidere.** Inf. after *metus est* on the analogy of the infinitive after *uereor.*

483. **per eius unam . . . sententiam.** For the separation of *unam* from its noun, cf. 505, *huius modi . . . malo*; 621–2, *bona . . . gratia.*

484. **ubinam,** *nam* as an enclitic upon interrogative words lends eagerness to the question; cf. 200n. **ab sua palaestra.** Young Greeks were accustomed to take exercise in the *palaestra* (wrestling school): Phaedria comes from 'his own playground', where he has been taking exercise of another kind.

Geta, who during his conversation with Antipho has been facing towards the R.H. exit, announces the approach of Phaedria, whom he sees coming from Dorio's house. With Phaedria's appearance a new impetus is given to the plot. Phormio and his followers had intended to await Demipho's next move: now a new complication in Phaedria's love affair makes it necessary for them to take the initiative.

ACT III. SCENE 2

Phaedria and Dorio enter from the latter's house, arguing. At first they do not see Antipho and Geta. It transpires that Dorio has threatened to foreclose Phaedria's option on the music-girl, Pamphila; he intends to accept a cash offer from a soldier, who has promised to bring the money tomorrow morning. Eventually, under combined pressure from Phaedria, Antipho, and Geta, he agrees to let Phaedria have the girl, if he can produce the money before the soldier does. With these words Dorio retires to his own house.

485–. Till 503 Phaedria and Dorio are unaware of the presence of Antipho and Geta, whose remarks to each other are made aside.

487. quod dicam, future 'what I'm going to say'.   **at enim.** Here *enim* merely strengthens the adversative *at*, 'but indeed'.   **iam,** lit. 'by now'; omit in translation.   **miliens.** The adverbial suffix -*iens*, which some ancient grammarians would restrict to the forms *totiens, quotiens* (otherwise writing -*ies*) seems to be the older form; *miliens* is found with two '*ll*'s as well as one. For its use as an indefinitely large numeral, cf. *Eun.* 422, *plus miliens audiui.*

488. loquere, audio. 'Out with it, I'm listening'.

489. triduom hoc, 'these next three days', cf. 159n.

490. mirabar si ... adferres. 'I wondered if you could be bringing forward ...' The adverbial *si* clause approximates to an Ind. Question. As such it is commonest after verbs of waiting, wondering, and striving. The transition from conditional to noun clause is perhaps most clearly seen in exx. where the Indic. is used in the *si* clause, e.g. 553, 898; *Eun.* 545, *uisam si domist.*

490–1. Whatever the correct division of line 491 (*vid. infra*), the comments of Antipho and Geta are made aside to each other.

491. metuo lenonem ne ... suat, for the proleptic acc., cf. 354n. All MSS. make Geta begin at *idem*, but Sloman, Ashmore, and O.T. follow Bentley (though Bentley's suggestion is bound up with a complete rewriting of the line) in marking GE. before *suo.* **suo ... capiti,** cf. Cic. *ad Att.* VIII. 5. 1 '*suo capiti*' *ut aiunt*; Eng. 'bring it on his own head'.   **suat,** *suere* ('sew') metaphorically here only; perhaps used for the word-play on *suo suat.*   **idem ego uereor.** Geta, with conscious sarcasm.

492. non mihi credis? O.T. reads *nondum*, 'not yet', but it is difficult to give a meaning to 'yet' in this context.   **hariolare** is often taken to mean 'You're talking nonsense', but *hariolari, hariolus* never have this meaning in Pl. or Ter. or in classical literature. In the present passage *hariolare* should be taken sarcastically 'You must have second sight' ('However did you guess?'), exactly as in Pl. *Rud.* 347. In *Ad.* 202 *hariolor* means 'I make this prediction'; cf. Knapp (*C.R.* XXI, 46–7).

493. **feneratum,** passive from *fenerare*, as *Ad.* 219. Normally *fenerare* (classical *fenerari*) = 'lend at interest'; cf. Sen. *de ben.* I. 1. 9 *demus beneficia, non feneremus.* But at *Ad.* 219 it certainly means 'repay with interest'; Eng. 'it was a splendid investment' suits either interpretation. **logi,** Gk. λόγοι, 'mere words', only here in Terence, several times in Plautus, who more readily admitted foreign words. Where Terence does allow foreign words, it is often in the mouths of slaves or parasites; cf. *phaleratis* (500).

494. **uerum,** adj. **somnium,** cf. 874; Eng. 'You're dreaming'.

495. **cantilenam,** Don. *uetus et uulgata cantio,* 'the same old song'. **cantilenam . . . canis,** *figura etymologica.*

496. **tu . . . tu . . . tu . . . tu.** Note the emphatic repetition (anaphora); the form and thought of the sentence recall (? intentionally) Andromache's pathetic appeal to Hector (*Il.* VI. 429–30). **garri modo.** 'Just talk away!' Dorio goads Phaedria on; he has no intention of listening to what he has to say.

499–500. Dorio mocks Phaedria by mimicking the form of words he used in 497–8. So Phormio (438–9) mocks Demipho (436–7).

500. **ducas dictis . . . ductes,** *ducere* = 'lead by the nose', cf. *An.* 644, *etiam nunc me ducere istis dictis postulas? ductare* of taking a mistress, e.g. Pl. *Men.* 694, *nisi feres argentum, frustra me ductare non potes.* **phaleratis,** 'decked out with trappings (fine words)': cf. Fulgentius *serm. ant.* (Helm 111. 5), *non faleratis sermonum studentes spumis quam rerum manifestationibus dantes operam lucidandis.* **gratiis,** three syllables.

501. Antipho and Geta comment to each other aside. **miseritumst.** Editors interpret *me Phaedriae miseret,* 'I feel sorry for him', but this ignores the perfect tense (Latin has no parallel to the Gk. instantaneous aorist, e.g. ξυνῆκα, 'I understand') and Donatus' comment εἰρωνεία ('sarcasm'). Interpret *lenonem Phaedriae miseritumst* 'Dorio has shown him pity' (Phaedria had asked for it in 498 *misericordia*) meaning, sarcastically, that Dorio has shown the pity that *lenones* usually show, namely none. **ei, ueris uincor,** 'I can't deny the truth'; note the alliteration. **uterque.** Dorio and Phaedria rather than Antipho and Phaedria; Geta is contrasting Phaedria's tearful weakness with the pander's immovable hardness.

502–3. **neque . . . malum.** This passage has troubled ancient and modern editors alike. A satisfactory interpretation must be consistent with *fortunatissime* (504) and, possibly, should account for the subjunctive *occupatus esset*—for Terence does not necessarily follow the classical usage of having the subj. in subordinate clauses in Oratio Obliqua. Four solutions may be considered:

(i) 'And then to think that this blow shouldn't have befallen me when A. had some love trouble on hand too.'—R. C. Jebb (*alia* = 'another similar'; accounts for *esset* and *fortunatissime*).

(ii) emend *neque* to *atque* (Wagner, Dziatzko-Hauler). 'To think that this trouble should have befallen me when A. was already bothered' (seems to ignore *fortunat.* and does not explain *esset*; *alia*, as in (i) = 'another similar').

(iii) *alia* = *minore* (so Don., i.e. *alia* = 'another less engrossing'; explains *esset*, but not, apparently, *fortunat*).

(iv) *neque . . . alia* = *eadem* [Stallbaum, Sloman; liable to the same objections as (ii)].

The first interpretation thus seems the least objectionable in syntax, but the thought 'I wish A. had been in similar trouble now that I'm in this mess' is a most remarkable one; the alleged parallels quoted by Ashmore are in no way comparable. In spite, therefore, of some illogic-ality (iii) (*alia* = 'less engrossing') seems best. Phaedria regrets that Antipho is too busy with his own troubles to be able to help him; at the same time he regards Antipho's position as enviable in comparison with the hopeless state of his own love affair.

503. Antipho steps forward and addresses Phaedria. **autem.** Omit in translation.

504. **fortunatissime,** cf. 173 and the whole of that scene. **quoi quod amas domist.** The rel. cl. explains **fortunatissime,** 'since (yes, for) you have your love at home'. **quod amas** 'the object of your love'.

505. **cum huius modi . . . malo.** For collocation of words, cf. 483n. **conflictares.** *Conflictare* active and intrans. (= *pugnare*) only here; the passive *aliqua re conflictari* (= *uexari*) is common. **neque . . . usus uenit ut,** 'nor did you ever have the experience of . . .'

506. **id quod aiunt,** 419n. **auribus teneo lupum.** Donatus *Graecum prouerbium*: τῶν ὤτων ἔχω τὸν λύκον · οὔτε γὰρ ἔχειν οὔτ᾽ ἀφεῖναι δύναμαι. The comparable English proverb 'to catch a Tartar' is quoted from the end of the seventeenth century (Butler, Dryden).

507. **amittam . . . retineam,** cf. 175-6. The subjj. are indirect deliberative. **uti,** 'how'.

508. **in hoc,** sc. *homine,* i.e. Phaedria. 'That's exactly my case with him.' **heia,** from Gk. εἶα but in Plautus and Terence usu. with initial aspirate; here of ironical reproach, 'Oh! Come now!' ('Come! That's no

way to go on.') It is quite 'out of character' for a *leno* to confess himself at a loss what to do.

509. hic. As Antipho turns to Phaedria, *hic* refers to Dorio.   **numquid hic confecit?** 'Has he been up to anything?'   **homo inhumanissimus,** oxymoron: *inhumanus* lacking the feelings of a human being.

510–11. The quadruple repetition of *uendidit* helps to stress the incredulity of Phaedria's friends at Dorio's 'inhumanity'. Dorio, who, as a *leno*, is used to being abused, can see the humour of being blamed for exercising his legal right.

510. uendidit. For scansion of the second *uendidit* (-*īt*), cf. 528n.

511. suo. Donatus comments *belle 'suo' quasi de tertia persona.*

512. illo, the other fellow mentioned in 522.   **mutet fidem,** 'cancel his bargain', 'break his word'.

513. dum . . . aufero, pres. indic. in colloquial speech where we might expect prospective subj. or at least fut. (pfct.) indic. With *dum* the idiom is helped by the confusion of 'while' and 'until', cf. Pl. *Bacch* 737, *mane dum scribit,* which may be interpreted either way. North Country idiom similarly uses 'while' for 'until' ('Wait while I come back').

514. praeterea with numeral *unam* = 'a single hour longer'.   **ne oppertus sies.** *ně ŏpp-* by prosodic hiatus and B-B. A 2nd person prohibition may be expressed in Pl. and Ter., as in classical Latin, by *noli(te)* + Inf. or, less often, by *ne* + perf. subjunctive. But much more frequently than those two constructions Pl. and Ter. use (1) *ne* + pres. imperative (e.g. 664, *ne clama;* 803, *ne nega*) and (2) *ne* + pres. subjunctive (e.g. 419, *actum ne agas;* 508, *heia ne . . . sies*).

515. optunde, *optundere* is, literally, 'to blunt a tool or weapon by excessive use', metaphorically 'to dull the keenness of the hearing by an excess of words', e.g. *Ht.* 879, *ohe iam desine deos, uxor, gratulando obtundere.* Here the imperative is to be taken sarcastically, 'Keep on at it (I don't care)!'

516. idem hic (both masc. nom.) trans. as emphatic 'he' (viz. this same Phaedria to whom you are asked to make a concession). Reading *idem hoc* (O.T.), *hoc* is antecedent of *quod, idem* 'Phaedria himself'.   **promeritus fueris.** For periphrastic fut. perfect of a deponent cf. *Ad.* 603, *fueris functus.*   **conduplicauerit,** note fut. perfect. Sometimes it implies speed and certainly of fulfilment, whereas the fut. simple implies only fulfilment at an indefinite future date. Often, however, metrical convenience, esp. at a line end (e.g. 681), may be a factor.

517. uerba, cf. Dorio's vocabulary 492–6.

518. horunc = *horum-ce*; cf. 442n. **poterin** = *poterisne*. Note delayed position of *-ne* attached to verb; cf. 612, *Ht.* 884.

519. neque ego neque tu, sc. *poterimus id pati.* Dorio, who is about to sell the music-girl, unctuously professes that there is nothing that either he or Antipho can do about it. The words *di . . . duint* are best given to Phaedria (some MSS. give them to Antipho or Geta); he has not addressed Dorio directly since *ei ueris uincor* (501), but the pander's callous indifference now rouses him to utter this imprecation. **quod es dignus.** For *dignus es* (= (*con-*) *meruisti*) followed by an acc. neut. pronoun, cf. Pl. *Capt.* 969. **duint,** 123n. **di . . . dignus . . . duint** alliteration.

520–1. te . . . tuli . . . flentem. Acc. + participle instead of acc. + Inf. is common with some verbs (e.g. *uidere, audire*), but not with *ferre*; cf. Virg. *Aen.* IX. 621–2, *talia iactantem dictis ac dira canentem non tulit Ascanius.* **ferentem, flentem** rhyme (and asyndeton).

521. contra omnia. *Contra* in Ter. is mostly an adverb; but it is certainly found as a preposition in Plautus, and it is better taken so in the present passage; *omnia haec* has thus its natural reference back to all the procrastinating of Phaedria, contrasting with the swift deal the new customer is prepared to do.

522. det neque lacrumet, consecutive-generic subjunctives, 'I've found a man to pay up and no tears.' **da locum melioribus,** I know of no evidence for Sloman's assertion 'said to have been a formula used by the consul's lictors in clearing the way.' The normal formula was *animaduerte.*

523. Antipho turns to address Phaedria.

524. quam ad. Examples of a polysyllabic preposition after its noun are found in Terence (e.g. 427, *me aduorsum*), but this is the only case with a monosyllabic preposition. However, cf. Pl. *Vid.* 90, *quam ad . . . diem,* Cic. N.D. II. 4. 10, *senatus quos ad soleret referendum censuit.* **dares,** 'by which you were to pay' (past jussive). **factum,** 238n., 'Yes, there was.'

525. haec ei antecessit. 'This date has come first'; *haec dies* the day on which the other client promised to pay, *ei* that fixed for Phaedria.

526. dum ob rem, sc. *sit,* 'provided it's to my advantage'. **sterculinum,** only here in Terence; cf. 373 for another example of abuse by metonymy. Terence showed much more restraint than Plautus and puts the coarser abuse only in the mouths of the commoner characters. The *leno* is the most common butt of such abuse; so Dordalus (Pl. *Persa,* 406–) is greeted with a string of abuse beginning *oh, lutum lenonium, commixtum caeno sterculinum publicum . . .*

527. **sic sum.** 'That's my nature'; *sic* almost = *talis*; cf. *Amph.* 604, *sic sum ut uides.*

528. **decipis,** scan *-īs*; either syllaba anceps at change of speaker or retention of original long vowel. **decipis . . . decipit,** Dorio is the equal of the younger men in debate, and with great verbal dexterity turns Antipho's argument upon him. **sicin hunc** *hŭnc* by B-B; *sicin(e)* is for *sice*, archaic form of *sic*, + *ne*. **enimuero** should perhaps be printed as two words; *enim* here emphasizes the adversative force of *immo, uero* = 'indeed', 'in truth'. 'On the contrary, indeed, Antipho, it's he who's cheating me'.

529-30. **hic . . . ego . . .   iste . . . ego,** adversative asyndeton (twice). **aliter** with *esse* is virtually an indeclinable adj.

532. **dare** where classical prose would have *daturum esse.* As the pres. indic. may colloquially be used for the fut. indic. (388n), so the pres. inf. may be used for the fut. inf. (e.g. 720, 837 *et saepe*). Here the adverb *cras* makes the reference to future time unmistakable.

533. **uale.** Exit Dorio to his own house.

ACT III. SCENE 3

Phaedria is in despair at the necessity of finding thirty minae at such short notice. Antipho urges Geta to think of some way of getting the money and suggests that Geta might try his father, Demipho. When Geta refuses, Antipho declares that he will follow Phanium to the ends of the earth—or take his own life. To avert this threat Geta, though still fearful of the punishment that he will be bringing upon himself, undertakes to procure the money, provided that he can have Phormio to assist him. Antipho is sent home to comfort Phanium: Phaedria and Geta move off towards the forum to find Phormio. Geta promises to tell Phaedria his plan for getting the money as they go.

This is Phaedria's final appearance in the play. His problem can be simply settled by the finding of the money; he has no part to play in the deception that secures that money. But he is not forgotten in the final settling of accounts; in the last scene, at Phormio's instance, Nausistrata not only pardons Phaedria's own relationship with Pamphila, but also appoints him to sit in judgement on his father, Chremes.

534. Phaedria, standing slightly apart from Antipho and Geta, expresses his despair.

535. **quoi** = *quom mihi.*   **minus nihilost,** Don. ὑπερβολή ('hyperbole').   **pote,** 379n.   **quod,** sc. *argentum.*

535–6. triduom hoc, either retained accusative (in the active *si potuissem hunc hoc triduom exorare*; for two accusatives, cf. *An.* 901 *sine te hoc exorem*) or acc. of duration of time (cf. 489). **exorarier,** 'be persuaded to wait'. **si pote fuisset** is not the protasis of *quod . . . promissum fuerat*, but a parenthetic unfulfilled wish 'The money—if only he could have been persuaded to wait three days—had been promised'.

536. promissum fuerat, for the composite tense, cf. 516. Antipho and Geta discuss Phaedria's predicament together. **itane,** 231n., 'shall we really . . . ?' **patiemur,** future indicative with a function indistinguishable from that of the deliberative subjunctive.

537. adiuerit, for *adiuuerit*; scan *adiŭerit*, as *Rud.* 305 and Catullus 66. 18. The reason for the subjunctive is uncertain, as it is in line 60 (q.v.).

538. quin . . . experiemur seems to be a conflation of *quin experimur?* 'Why don't we try?' and *experiemur?* 'Shall we try?'

539. equidem, a strengthened form of *quidem* (cf. *e-castor*), mostly used with the first person, as though it was for *ego quidem*.

540. cupio, 'I'm willing enough'.

541. hic, 'back home' (from abroad). **dictum sapienti sat est,** for other exx. of this proverb, cf. Otto, p. 112.

542. itane? ita, hiatus at change of speaker; 'You don't mean?' 'I do'. Antipho says nothing inconsistent with his *pietas* towards his father, but Geta is left in no doubt as to what is expected of him. **pulchre,** sarcastic, as in 302. **etiam tu hinc abis?** 'Get away with you!' *Etiam* with interrogatived pres. indic. expresses an impatient imperative (e.g. *Ad.* 550, *etiam taces?* 'do shut up!').

543. non triumpho + explanatory clause (*si nanciscor*) + *ni* + subj. and *parumne est* + explanatory clause (*quod suscenset*) + *ni* + subj. correspond closely in form. Trans. 'Isn't it success enough for me to avoid getting into trouble over your marriage, without your bidding me further now (*etiam nunc*) get into still deeper water for your cousin's sake?' 'Isn't it enough that the old man's angry with the lot of us now, without our goading him further (*etiam* lit. "still") till (lit. "so that") there's no room left to ask for mercy?'

544. quaerere in malo crucem, 'go looking for trouble' ('stick one's neck out'); *quaerere crucem* as a variant for *malum quaerere* is common in Plautus.

545. When Geta declares that he is afraid to try to help Phaedria, Phaedria, who has been silent since line 536, makes an earnest appeal to him for assistance. **uobis.** *Vos* may be used when a single person is apostrophized, but perhaps only when the single person is one of a group; cf. Cic. *ad fam.* XIV. 5. 2, *uos, mea suauissima et optatissima Terentia.* Virg. *Aen.* IX. 525, *uos, o Calliope, precor.* Here *uobis* is justified because Antipho is with Geta.

546. parumne, *-ŭmne* by B-B.

547. preci. This and *An.* 601 are the only exx. of the dative sing. No case of the singular is common at any period of Latin; *prece* (abl.) is the least uncommon.

551. quoquo, relative adverb. *terrarum* partitive genitive: *quoquo* is used as an indefinite adverb in Tac. *Ann.* XIV. 1, *ituram quoquo terrarum.* **persequi,** with no idea of hostile pursuit; Don. *perseuerationem sequentis ostendens.* **certumst** (or *certa res est*) + inf., where we should use personal 'I am resolved to . . .'

552. aut perire. Perhaps there is a slight hesitation after *persequi* before Phaedria adds his pathetic alternative: with Geta this pathos cuts no ice—he has little fear that Phaedria will die for thwarted love. **pedetemptim tamen,** 'but not too fast'; Don. *pedetemptim: caute, a pedibus et temptando.*

553. si quid? quid? ' "Any help?" Yes, but what help?' **quaere,** 'try to find'—here almost 'think'.

554. nequid, *ne =* 'for fear lest'. **faxit.** Subj. of *faxo,* for which see 308n. **plus minusue,** a vague phrase for the sake of euphemism, 'something or other'.

555. quaero. After this word Geta pauses. Then, as inspiration dawns, he continues *saluos,* etc. *uerum enim metuo malum* is added as an afterthought. The idea is a good one—but he fears the consequences.

556. una, adverb. **bona mala,** asyndeton with antonyms: similarly with synonyms, e.g. 757, *forte temere.*

557. argenti, partitive genitive dependent on *quantum.* **triginta minae.** Ramsay on Most. 300, 'The price of an accomplished and attractive female slave seems to have varied from 20 to 60 minae'.

559. age age. Repeated *age* indicates unwilling or impatient assent, 'All right, all right'. **inuentas reddam.** 'I'll see you have them'; cf. 856, *delibutum reddo, An.* 684, *inuentum tibi curabo.* **o lepidum,** sc. *hominem;* acc. of exclamation. **aufer te hinc.** Most editors take this to mean 'Get away from here', an anticipation of *modo te hinc amoue* (566). Another interpretation is possible; with the preceding words (*o lepidum!*) Phaedria shows his gratitude by embracing Geta (or some such action). Geta pushes Phaedria away from him saying 'Get away with you!' *aufer te hinc* is then equivalent to *abin hinc* (542n.); for *aufer,* 'Cut (it) out!' cf. 223, 857. **iam opust,** *iam* here of the immediate future, 'at once': for the whole passage, cf. *An.* 703-4, DA. *hoc ego tibi profecto effectum reddam.* PA. *iam hoc opus est.* DA. *quin iam habeo.*

561. **praestost**, 'He's at hand'. *Praesto est*, besides meaning 'he's here before your eyes' (51), can mean 'he's at hand to help.' Both meanings are combined at 267. **oneris quiduis inpone et feret.** 'Put any burden you like on him and he'll bear it.' English can say 'Ask and it shall be done' or, less usually, 'Ask: it shall be done'. Latin too can say either *roga, et fiet* or *roga: fiet*, but the form without *et* is the more usual, e.g. Pl. *As.* 723, *exopta id quod uis maxume tibi euenire: fiet.* The O.T. *ecferet*, which has little manuscript support, eliminates *et*, but involves taking *ecferre* in the sense of the simple verb *ferre*, whereas it normally means 'carry forth' (*exportare*).

563. **numquid est quod . . . opus sit?**, a variant on the common formula for leave-taking, *numquid uis* (151n.), 'Is there anything you need my help for?' *Quod* is probably adverbial acc. ('with respect to which', 'for which'); *opera mea* may be nom. or abl. with *opus sit.* **opera . . . opus** play on words, cf. 760-1, *opere . . . operam.*

564. **illam.** Phanium.

565. **aeque.** Construe with *lubens.* Exit Antipho to Demipho's house.

566. **modo te hinc amoue,** *modo* expresses Geta's impatience. Geta and Phaedria move off towards the marketplace.

ACT IV. SCENE 1

Demipho enters with Chremes from the harbour. Chremes has just returned from the Aegean island of Lemnos, and from their conversation it transpires that the purpose of his visit was to bring back to Athens a grown-up daughter, his child by a bigamous marriage with a Lemnian wife. He has however returned empty-handed, for the girl and her mother, wearying of his delay, had already sailed to Athens to look for him. To keep the secret of the girl's parentage Demipho had earlier agreed to her marriage with his son, Antipho. But the latter's marriage to Phanium during Demipho's absence abroad now seems to have rendered this solution impossible, and Chremes fears that the secret of his Lemnian marriage cannot be kept from the ears of his Athenian wife. Demipho too expresses concern at the situation, but assures Chremes that he still hopes to implement their original plan.

567. **Quid? qua profectus causa hinc es.** Postpone the rel. clause in English and translate, 'Tell me! Have you brought your daughter with you, as you set out to Lemnos to do, Chremes?'

568. This is the first we hear of Chremes' double life. **quid ita non?** 'Why not (so)?'

569. **postquam uidet ... manebat,** *uidet* is historic present; the imperfect after *postquam* is rare in early Latin.

570. **manebat,** transitive, cf. 48on.

571. **cum omni familia,** *familia* = 'the household'; this seems to contradict the information of 97f. and 733f.

572. **aibant,** scan *ai̯-*.   **illi,** adverb.

574. **pol.** According to Aulus Gellius XI. 6, 'In our early writings neither do Roman women swear by Hercules nor the men by Castor ... but the oath by Pollux is common to both sexes.' The whole subject is elaborately analysed by Nicolson (*H.S.C.P.* IV. 99), who shows that in Terence *pol* is much more of a woman's oath than a man's.

575. **senectus ipsast morbus.** Cf. Sen. *Ep.* 108. 28, *senectus enim insanabilis morbus est.* Sargeaunt notes that it was dramatically necessary for Chremes to be detained in Lemnos to allow time for the development of the relationship between Antipho and Phanium.

578. **quod quidem,** -*ĕm* by B-B.   **consili incertum.** Cf. *Hec.* 121, *animi ... incertus*; Pl. *Rud.* 213, *incerta sum consili.* Livy XXXVI. 42. 6 has *incertus consilii*, Tacitus *Hist.* II. 46. 1, *consilii certus.*

580. **quo pacto aut unde** virtually synonymous, cf. 952.   **dicundum ordinest,** cf. *Most.* 552, *dixi, inquam, ordine omnia.*

585. **aliqua,** sc. *uia*, used as adverb.

586. **me excutiam,** perhaps only a colourful synonym for *egrediar*, 'clear out'. But *excutere aliquem* or *aliquid* is used of searching someone for stolen goods (by shaking them); and in view of 587 ('I haven't a thing in the world to call my own except myself') the meaning here may be literally 'turn out my pockets and get out'.

586-7. **ut me excutiam ... id restat** for impersonal *restat*, cf. 85n.

588. **sollicitudini,** predicative dative.

590. Demipho and Chremes remain on the stage, but, being engrossed in their own conversation, fail to notice the arrival of Geta from the direction of the forum.

ACT IV. SCENE 2

Geta enters from the direction of the forum. He gives an account of his interview with Phormio, who has readily fallen in with the suggested plan for getting money out of Demipho. Geta now catches sight of

Demipho talking to Chremes. For a moment the sight of Chremes disconcerts him, but he quickly recovers his confidence with the reflection that, if now he has two old men to tackle, he has a double chance of getting the money.

591 f. Demipho and Chremes fail to notice the presence of Geta till he greets them in line 609. Similarly Geta, though he is walking in their direction, fails at first to see the old men; during these nine lines he soliloquises, presumably in a normal voice, without being overheard. After catching sight of Demipho and, beyond him, Chremes (600) he continues to address the audience in an aside until *adibo* (609).

591. **hominem . . . neminem,** pleonasm, since **nemo** = *ne-homo*; similarly *nemo homo* in *Eun.* 549 and several times in Cicero.

592. **uenio . . . ut dicerem,** historic tense after historic present: cf. 117n.

593. **argentum opus esse.** *argentum* is the acc. subject of the acc. and inf. For constructions with *opus est*, cf. 204n. **fieret.** The first syllable here scans long (contrast 760). *Fieri* here almost = *confici* or *effici*; it is indirect deliberative subjunctive, 'how it was to be found'.

597. **ostenderet** in O.R. would still be subjunctive—*tempus mihi datur ubi . . . ostendam.*

598. **hominem,** sc. Phormio. **ad forum,** for *in foro*, a not uncommon colloquial usage.

599. **senem,** sc. Demipho. Geta does not yet know of Chremes' return.

600. Geta, who has been facing the audience as he delivers his soliloquy, turns to go along the street to Demipho's house. As he does so, he sees Demipho and, beyond him, Chremes. **attat,** scan *attāt*; a strong exclamation of surprise, often of fear or confusion, frequently occasioned by the unexpected and unwelcome arrival of some character.

601. **belua,** as a term of remonstrance or abuse rather like Eng. 'ass'; Latin *asinus* is also used, e.g. *Ad.* 935.

603. **duplici spe utier,** 'to have two strings to my bow'; Greek uses variants on the proverb ἐπὶ δυοῖν ἀγκύραιν ὁρμεῖν, 'moor with two anchors'; so also Latin, e.g. Prop. II. 22. 41, *nam melius duo defendunt retinacula nauim.*

604. **petam,** sc. *argentum.* **a primo,** *primum* used as a neuter noun; cf. 642.

605. **si . . . nil fiet,** 'if there's nothing forthcoming'; **eo,** Demipho. **hospitem,** 'new-comer', viz. Chremes.

ACT IV. SCENE 3

The door of Demipho's house opens and Antipho comes out to look for Geta; catching sight of his uncle and his father he remains unseen in the back of the stage and listens with mounting anxiety to what is said. Geta goes up to Demipho and Chremes and tells them that he has had a private talk with Phormio, who is willing, for a consideration, to marry Phanium himself. Demipho is inclined to refuse his demand of thirty minae as excessive, but Chremes, whose plans are well suited by Phormio's proposal, agrees to pay the money from the rent he is just bringing back from his (Athenian) wife's property in Lemnos.

606. Antipho re-enters from Demipho's house, where he had gone at line 565. As he knows that Geta has gone to see Phormio, he turns to look for him in the direction of the forum; instead he sees his uncle and father talking together. Since his one idea is to avoid meeting his father, he stays at the back of the stage, where he is able to overhear and comment on the conversation unobserved.

607. **ei mihi,** 178n.

610. **uenire saluom,** for formula of greeting, cf. 254 f. **uolup est,** *uolup,* an adverbial neuter **uolupe* from *uolupis,* is found only here and *Hec.* 857 in Terence; it is commoner in Plautus. **quid agitur?** 'How goes it?' Cf. *Ad.* 885, *quid fit? quid agitur?*

611. **compluria.** Don. *sic ueteres, quod nostri dempta syllaba complura dicunt.*

612. **audistin,** for delayed position of *n(e),* cf. 518n. **quae facta,** for omission of auxiliary verb in subordinate clause, cf. 46n.

613–14. **facinus indignum . . . sic circumiri!** *facinus indignum* is an accusative of exclamation, *circumiri* an explanatory infinitive; cf. Pl. *Men.* 1004, *o facinus indignum et malum . . . erum | meum deripier.* It would be possible to punctuate *facinus indignum, Chreme! sic circumiri!* taking *circumiri* as an independent exclamatory infinitive.

614. **commodum,** neuter adj., used adverbially in colloquial Latin, first = 'opportunely', then, most commonly, = 'just now' (as *modo*). Cicero uses it several times in his letters, once (*Verr.* II. 3, 61) in his speeches.

615. **nam hercle,** *hercle* emphasizing asseverative *nam;* cf. 113n. **id . . . agitans mecum.** Cf. Hor. *Sat.* I. 4. 137–8, *haec ego mecum | compressis agito labris;* Pl. *Truc.* 451, *eam rem in corde agito.*

616. **remedium huic rei.** Cf. 200; in 185 too *iracundiae* is probably dative.

618. qui Phormio, 129n.

619. uisumst mihi ut ... temptarem. $Ut +$ Subj. after impersonal *uidetur* is unusual.

620-2. 'Why don't you see to it that we settle this business ... ?' The imperative *uide* (and its equivalents) is followed by $ut +$ Subj. with the sense of *cura ut*, 'see to it that'. **cum bona ... gratia quam cum mala.** For separation of adjective from noun, cf. 505.

623. fugitans litium, the objective genitive after the participle *fugitans* here only until post-classical Latin, though Caesar has *fugiens laboris* (B.C. I. 69. 3). The genitive follows participles in *-ans* and *-ens* when used adjectivally.

624. modo, 'just now'.

624-5. omnes ... uno ore. Cf. *An.* 96; Cic. *de am.* 86.

625. auctores fuere ut ... daret. Cf. Pl. *Merc.* 312, *auctor sum ut me amando—enices. Auctor ut* is common in Plautus and Cicero.

626. Antipho, aside. He has not been told what the plan is for getting the thirty minae out of Demipho and is at a loss to understand what Geta is up to. **hic,** hĭc by B-B. 'What's he up to or whatever will be the outcome?' **hodie** intensifies the interrogative *quo*; 377n.

628. iam id exploratumst. 'That's all been thought out'. **sudabis.** The metaphorical use of *sudare* is rare but classical.

629. ea eloquentiast, *ea = tali.*

630. tandem, 'after all', 'when all's said and done'.

631. capitis, *caput* has a broader connotation than our 'capital' (charge, offence, etc.), and refers to the civil rights enjoyed by a free person.

633. soli sumus nunc hic, cf. Pl. *Poen.* 891, *loquere (locus occasioque est) libere: hic soli sumus.*

633-4. dari ... in manum, 'to be given in cash'. According to Donatus the phrase is used of an underhand transaction; we might say 'to be put in your hand (or pocket)'.

635. facessat, intransitive, 'take herself off'.

636. Antipho, aside, in some alarm; he continues to take Geta's narrative at its face value. **satin illi di sunt propitii?** = *satin sanus est?* Elsewhere *di propitii* and its opposite *di irati* are generally used of good and bad luck. **illi,** (dat. sing.) Geta.

638. ut est, '(inasmuch) as'; cf. 774n.

638-9. tria non commutabitis uerba. According to Donatus, *uerba commutare = altercari,* 'quarrel': if so, trans. 'You'll not say three wrong words to each other'. Alternatively, since *tria uerba* is used proverbially of a very brief speech, 'You'll not exchange even three words' might mean 'You'll settle the matter in a jiffy'.

639–41. We see here a clear indication of the difference in character between Chremes and Demipho; the former eager to preserve his secret at any cost, the latter proud of his reputation as a man of business and determined not to pay through the nose. The failings of both old men have their own reward. Demipho's elaborate precautions fail to safeguard the money and Chremes' guilty secret becomes known to his wife.

641. Antipho, aside; he is now convinced that Geta has betrayed him and that he will really have to surrender Phanium.

643. quid? nimium; quantum libuit. 'How much? Too much; whatever came into his head'. It is also possible to punctuate *nimium quantum libuit*, taking *nimium quantum* together as *incredible quantum* in 247 (q.v.), 'How much? (He wanted) Far too much'.

644. talentum magnum, the Attic talent containing sixty minae. The purchasing price for a young female slave was normally from about twenty to sixty minae (cf. 557n.). The amount that a freeborn girl would bring as her dowry seems to have varied enormously: on the one hand orphan girls had to be given a minimum of five minae by their nearest of kin (125n.), on the other hand ten talents are spoken of as *dos summa* (*An.* 101, 951), while two talents are spoken of as an ordinary amount (*Ht.* 838, 940). See the remarks on Demipho's character in note on 639–41. **immo malum hercle,** sc. *magnum dabo*, 'A good hiding, more likely!'; cf. *Merc.* 643, *malum magnum*, *Cas.* 729, *dabo tibi μέγα κακόν*. **ut nil pudet,** *ut*, exclamatory, 'how'.

645. quod dixi adeo ei. '(That's) What I said to him': *adeo* (cf. 389n.) is used as an enclitic to emphasize the preceding word ('I *told* him so').

645–6. quaeso, quid si . . . locaret? *quaeso*, initially, like *quid?*, merely anticipates the following question; but whereas the question following *quid* usually asks for information, the question following *quaeso* may express surprise or indignation: so here 'Why? What if . . . ?' and 935 *quaeso, quid narras?* 'What? What's that you say?' **quid si . . . locaret?** 'What (more could he do) if he were dowering . . . ?' **locaret,** sc. *nuptum* or *in matrimonium*.

646. retulit, from *rēfert*, 'Little advantage he's got from not bringing up a daughter of his own.' The sense is made clear by Donatus' comment: *in Graeca fabula senex hoc dicit, 'quid interest me non suscepisse filiam, si modo dos dabitur alienae?'*

647. suscepisse. An Athenian father was free to expose his child at birth; if he wished to rear it, he indicated this by taking the child in his arms (hence *suscipere* or, more commonly, *tollere*). In a society where the father had to provide a dowry for his daughter on marriage, the father might be reluctant to acknowledge female children. The parsimonious Demipho is just the sort of person who would have exposed a female child. At times *suscipere* means no more than 'beget' or 'bear a child'.

648. **mittam** = *omittam*. **ineptias** 'impertinences'.

651. **fuerat.** The pluperfect is strictly correct, as it is prior in time to the perfect *uolui*; cf. *Ad*. 686, *uirginem uitiasti quam te non ius fuerat tangere*. In both cases the pluperfect is used in an impersonal phrase; cf. Allardice, p. 68.

653. **in seruitutem . . . dari.** Phormio consciously alters the expected *in matrimonium dari*.

654. **sed mi opus erat,** sc. *uxore*. **erat** scan *erāt*. Laidlaw, p. 61, 'Syllaba anceps at pause?'

655. **quae adferret,** *quăe ădf-*, prosodic hiatus followed by B-B. **qui,** ablative, cf. 123n.

659–60. Antipho, still aside. **dicam,** indirect deliberative subjunctive.

661. **quid si animam debet?** Don. *Graecum prouerbium spreuit*, εἰ δὲ ὤφειλε τὰς χεῖρας; Eng. 'What if he's up to the eyes in debt?' **pignori,** final dative (dative of purpose), cf. *Pseud*. 87, *si me opponam pignori*.

662. **age age,** to express impatience; cf. 559n.

663. **oiei,** a cry of anguish, trisyllabic (*ōĭĕĭ*) in Terence, disyllabic in Plautus.

664. **ne clama.** See 514n. where the ways of expressing a 2nd person prohibition are discussed.

665. **pluscula,** like *maiuscula* and *meliuscula*, is a diminutive formed by adding -*culus* to a comparative; other wheedling diminutives in Phormio's proposals are *aliquantulum* (655), *aediculae* (663), *ancillula* (665).

667. **sane** with the imperative = 'if you will'; trans. 'let's say'.

668. **sescentas** used as an indefinite large number, e.g. Pl. *Aul*. 320, *sescenta sunt quae memorem, si sit otium. Mille centum* and *trecenti* are similarly used. **perinde** (-*ĭnd*- by B-B), a comparative particle 'in like manner', may be translated as 'He may just as well . . .' *proinde*, read by some MSS., may either be a comparative particle like *perinde*, or lend insistence to the imperative, '(Well then) just . . .' **dicas,** 127n.

669. **nil do,** for present tense, cf. 388n. **inpuratus** used as a substantive, cf. 962. **ille ut . . . inrideat!** indignant (repudiating) subjunctive. Demipho, in disgust, now withdraws from the conversation except for an interjected imprecation at 678.

670-1. **filium fac ut . . . ducat,** proleptic accusative, 354n.

671. Antipho, aside, in despair.

673. **mea,** abl. sing., *mĕă* by B-B or *me͡a* by synizesis. **eicitur,** sc. *Phanium.* **me hoc,** *mĕ hŏc* prosodic hiatus and B-B.

674. **quantum potest,** impersonal, 'as quickly as possible'.

675. **illam,** sc. *Phanium.* **hanc,** cf. 657, *ab hac quae sponsast mihi.*

676-7. **illi . . . illis,** the relations of Phormio's intended bride.

677. **accipiat,** sc. *argentum* or, possibly, *Phanium*; in view of *hanc ducat,* the former is preferable. *Accipiat* is jussive subjunctive: *accipiet* has less MS. support but may be right, 'he shall have it at once'; cf. 559, *iam feres.* **repudium renuntiet,** cf. *repudium remittere* (928); the same two phrases occur at *Aul.* 783, 799.

678. **quae quidem illi res uortat male,** modelled on the expression of good wishes, *quae res bene uortat.* English can say, sarcastically, 'And much good may it do him!'

679. **opportune adeo.** Enclitic *adeo* emphasizes the preceding word. **argentum,** 'ready money'.

680. **Lemni,** locative; contrast 873, 1004 *in Lemno.*

681. **inde,** scan *ind*'; cf. Introduction, p. 30. **dixero.** The future perfect is often used in Plautus and Terence (esp. at line ends *metri gratia*) with the same sense as the future simple.

Exeunt Demipho and Chremes to the latter's house; they do not notice Antipho outside Demipho's house. Geta remains on the stage (front centre).

ACT IV. SCENE 4

Antipho comes forward and bitterly reproaches Geta with treachery; Geta is eventually able to persuade him that the suggested divorce of Phanium is merely a device to raise the money that Phaedria needs. Phormio will subsequently find some pretext—possibly the occurrence of bad omens—to repudiate his agreement to marry Phanium. As Demipho and Chremes re-enter from Chremes' house, Geta sends Antipho off towards the forum to tell Phaedria that the money he needs will be forthcoming.

682. **Geta.** Antipho calls out to Geta from behind. **hem,** in answer

to someone calling one by name has the force of 'Yes? What is it?'
emunxi, Gk. ἀπομύττειν, lit. 'wipe the nose', metaphorically 'clean
someone out of something'; the abl. *argento* is an abl. of separation on the
analogy of *exuo*, etc.

683. **satin est id?** 'It's enough, isn't it?' Antipho means, 'Isn't
arranging that I must divorce Phanium enough?' Geta, always ready to
tease the apprehensive Antipho, deliberately misunderstands him to mean
'Isn't the sum of money enough?' **tantum iussus sum,** 'That's all
[lit. '(only) so much] I was ordered (sc. to find)'.

684. **uerbero,** only here and 850 in Terence: common in Plautus.

685. **quid ergo narras?** 'What d'you mean, then?' **quid ego
narrem,** indignant subjunctive in sentence-echo, cf. 122n.

686. **ad restim . . . res redit,** the same phrase in Caecilius 215;
cf. *Ht.* 931, *mihi illaec uere ad rastros res redit.*

687. Note *tĕquidem* (as *mĭquidem* in 686; cf. Introduction, p. 30),
d͡eaeque (synizesis), *superī* (hiatus before *inferi*).

688. **malis exemplis.** *Exemplum* is often used of 'signal (condign)
punishment'; cf. *Most.* 192, *di deaeque omnes me pessumis exemplis inter-
ficiant.*

689. **mandes,** jussive subjunctive; a weakly attested variant *h.m. qui
te ad scopulum e tranquillo auferat* ('to land you on the rocks') may have
arisen because it was not realized that *quod . . . uelis* is spoken ironically.

690. **utibile,** 226n. Both here and elsewhere, e.g. *Pl. M.G.* 613, *ad
rem utibile,* *utibilis* may be active, 'conferring advantage', but is more
probably passive, 'that can be used,' 'useful'. **ulcus tangere.** Don.
prouerbiale.

692. **cedo nunc porro.** 'Besides, another point'; *cedo nunc* 'come/
listen now'.

693. **uxor ducendast domum,** also *ducere* without *domum,* 694,
700.

694. **non enim ducet.** 'Why, he won't marry her'. For *enim* see
113n. **noui,** sarcastically 'of course'; so too *scilicet* in 695. **ceterum,**
in origin an adverbial accusative, 'as for the rest'; both here and in 141
it is well on the way to becoming an adversative conjunction, 'but'.

696. **in neruom,** cf. 325. **potius,** 'will choose to'.

699. **iam si.** Ashmore translates 'the moment he receives', giving *iam*
a temporal sense (= *statim*). Another interpretation is more probable;
iam si (more often *si iam*) may mean 'granting for the sake of argument';
cf. Munro on Lucr. I, 968. So here, 'Granting he takes the money, he
must marry her, as you say, I admit'.

701. **spatium . . . apparandi nuptias,** cf. *Hec.* 684, *quam longum spatium amandi amicam tibi dedi!*   **tandem,** 'after all'.

702. **uocandi,** sc. *amicos*, 'inviting (the) guests'.   **paullulum,** adj. as in *Ad.* 779; it is also used as a noun, e.g. *An.* 360.

705. **monstra,** 'portents'; Festus (Linds. 122) *monstrum, ut Aelius Stilo interpretatur, a monendo dictum est, uelut monestrum.*

707. **inpluuium** may be either the rain-water basin that receives the water through the skylight in the *atrium* or the skylight itself, whereas *compluuium* is used only of the aperture; cf. Pl. *Amph.* 1108, *deuolant angues . . . deorsum in impluuium duo.*

708. **gallina cecinit.** 'Midwives believe this to be an omen that the wife will outlive the husband' (Donatus).

708–9. **hariolus . . . haruspex.** *Hariolus* is used generally as a soothsayer, whereas *haruspex* is always retained as a technical term describing a member of that professionally organized band who made their divinations according to the *Etrusca disciplina*.

709. **brumam,** contraction from *breuima (for *breuissima*).   **ante brumam . . . incipere!** is an independent sentence in which *incipere* is exclamatory infinitive and *autem* emphasizes the absurdity of the idea (389n.). The partitive genitive after *incipere* is remarkable. Löfstedt (*Syntactica* I. 116) compares Pl. *Poen.* 640–1 and *Most.* 1016, but the present passage is even more difficult, because the unattached *negoti* is not preceded, as *boni* and *negoti* in the examples from Plautus are, by the same partitive genitive dependent, in the normal manner, on a neuter pronoun.

710. **quae,** connecting relative, '—and that's the best excuse'.

711. **ut modo,** for particles with optative subjunctive cf. 773 (*modo ut*) and Allardice, p. 77.   **me uide.** 'Trust me!' Cf. Pl. *Rud.* 680, *tace ac bono animo es. me uide.*

712. **pater exit,** sc. from Chremes' house.   **abi . . . Phaedriae.** Geta despatches Antipho in the direction of the forum, the direction in which Phaedria had gone when he left the stage with Phormio at 566.

ACT IV. SCENE 5

Demipho and Chremes reappear from the latter's house. Demipho, who is carrying in a bag the thirty minae promised to Phormio, assures Chremes that he will see that the transaction with Phormio takes place in the presence of witnesses; Phormio will have no chance of cheating him. Chremes suggests that Demipho, after seeing Phormio, should ask

Nausistrata to visit Phanium to inform her of her impending transfer to Phormio, so that she will not later be able to complain that she has been forcibly ejected. Demipho offers to do this job himself, but eventually agrees that the task is better performed by another woman. Demipho departs towards the forum for his meeting with Phormio: Chremes remains on the stage and wonders where to look for his Lemnian wife and daughter.

713. **quietus esto.** 'Don't worry (about that)': cf. 670 (*quiesce*); *Curc.* 492, *de istoc quietus esto.* **inquam.** 'I tell you': for *inquam* emphasizing imperatives cf. 217n. **uerba dare,** 'to cheat': the person deceived is put in the dative case. **duit,** 123n.

714. **hoc,** the money he is carrying. **quin,** after a negative main clause equivalent to Eng. 'without' + verbal noun in -ing: in origin it is a negative relative clause of result, e.g. *Haut.* 67, *numquam tam mane egredior . . . quin te . . . conspicer* (= 'so early that . . . not').

715. **quoi dem** is an Ind. Question co-ordinate with *quam ob rem dem*: with the better attested *quom dem* (O.T.) *quom* is temporal and *et* = 'also', 'as well', but the reason for the subjunctive is obscure. **commemorabo** hiatus at change of speaker. Though Demipho and Chremes are by now standing close to Geta, stage convention allows Geta to address asides to the audience.

716. **et.** Contrast *An.* 956 si., *age fiat.* PA. *at matura.* In both cases English says 'but': Latin uses *at* where there is a change of speaker, but *et* where the same speaker continues.

717. **forsitan** (= *fors sit an,* 'there may be a chance whether/that') is normally followed by the Subj. It first occurs with the Indic. in Lucretius.

718. **rem ipsam putasti.** 'You've hit the nail on the head'; spoken by Geta aside. **duc me ad eum ergo.** Demipho addresses Geta. **eum,** sc. Phormio. **non moror.** Geta, whose previous remarks in this scene have been delivered aside, replies in a normal voice to Demipho, and turns to go towards the forum. **egeris,** sc. Demipho. Chremes detains his brother to give him further instructions, as Demipho turns to follow Geta.

719. **conueniat,** transitive. **hanc,** Phanium. **prius quam . . . abit,** *priusquam* + pres. indic. referring to future time is common in colloquial Latin (e.g. 898, 1036; so also *dum* 982); but when the main clause is negative, the fut. perf. indic. is more usual (e.g. 1045). *Donec,* on the other hand, usually has a future tense, whether the main clause is positive or negative.

720. **dare . . . nuptum,** cf. 752, *nuptum locaui.* **ne suscenseat,** negative final clause depending on *dicat,* not on *nuptum.*

721. **qui . . . sit** is Subj. in causal rel. clause (trans. 'since he'), not the common Subj. after *dignus/idoneus est qui.*

722. **officio . . . digressos esse,** apart from here and *Culex* 223, in this metaphorical sense only in post-classical Latin.

723. **dotis,** partitive genitive dependent on *quantum* (722). Once again the difference in character between Demipho and Chremes asserts itself. **malum** is frequently used as a colloquial imprecation standing second or third word after an interrogative pronoun (cf. Eng. 'the devil' (et sim.) after an interrogative, e.g. 'What the devil . . . ?'). It is occasionally used by Cicero in his speeches; apart from one instance in the *pro Scauro* all the exx. are from the early speeches (*pro Q. Roscio, Verrines*) or the *Philippics.*

724. **non sat est,** *ěst* by B-B.

725. **uoluntate** (*-ǔnt* by B-B); for the first foot possibly *uǒl(o)ǐpsī-* (*ǐps-* by B-B).

726. **idem . . . possum.** 'I can do that (just) as well'. *Idem* may be nom. masc. (*ī-*) or acc. neut. sing. (*ĭ-*). **mulier mulieri conuenit.** Dziatzko-Hauler compare Eur. *Hel.* 830, σὸν ἔργον, ὡς γυναικὶ πρόσφορον γυνή.

727. Exit Demipho towards the forum. Chremes remains on the stage, probably towards the back, where, without being seen, he overhears the soliloquy of the nurse who now comes out of Demipho's house. **ubi . . . reperire possim cogito.** *Possim* may represent a Subj. in Oratio Recta, cf. 827, *ubinam . . . inuenire possim?* 'Where might I find?' **illas** refers to the Lemnian mother and daughter.

ACT V. SCENE 1

Sophrona, Phanium's nurse, enters from Demipho's house. She comes forward without seeing Chremes and soliloquizes on the wretchedness of her mistress's position. Chremes is astonished to recognize her as the nurse of his Lemnian daughter, and after some hesitation calls her by name. When Sophrona turns round, she greets him as 'Stilpo'. He explains that this was a fictitious name which he had used to prevent his Athenian wife finding out about his double life. Somewhat obtusely he does not at first comprehend that Antipho's wife and his Lemnian daughter are one and the same person, but suspects that Antipho, like himself, has two wives! When the truth dawns on him, he expresses his thanks to the gods and hurries in with Sophrona to Demipho's house to talk over things in greater detail.

728. misera, 96n. Here best translated by an exclamation 'Whom, alas!' **consilia haec,** those referred to 733f. **referam** here used, as in *ad senatum referre*, of bringing a matter before an appropriate authority.

732. All Chremes' remarks till *Sophrona* in 739 are delivered aside. *nam quae = quaenam;* 200n. **exanimata** belongs to the relative clause. **a fratre,** 'The idiomatic *ab aliquo*, "from the house of", is quite a feature of colloquial Latin' (Allardice, p. 101).

733. quod, connecting relative referring to 730 (Sophrona's advice to Phanium to marry Antipho). **inpulit** is completed by two noun clauses (i) *quod ut facerem,* (ii) *ut id consulerem; id* in the second clause is explained by the following *ut* clause. **quom scirem,** *quom* is concessive; the clause depends on *ut facerem,* not *inpulit,* and continues its mood and tense.

735. nisi me animus fallit. The impersonal *fallit* (220n.) is much commoner, especially in classical Latin.

736–7. For the indicatives in deliberative questions, see 447n. and contrast 728. **adeo, maneo,** note asyndeton for the alternative questions. **haec,** nom. fem. sing., sc. Sophrona.

739. conloquar, spoken aside by Chremes, but the sound of his voice carries to Sophrona. **Sophrona,** spoken aloud.

740–1. Sophrona is standing at the front of the stage before Demipho's house, Chremes up stage by the door of his own house. When Chremes calls to her, she turns round and moves towards him; Chremes, for the reason given in 744, then tells her to move away in the direction of Demipho's house. **respice ad me.** When *respicere* is used literally, the direction in which the gaze is turned is expressed by preposition (*ad*) or adverb (*huc,* etc.): contrast the use of the accusative without preposition in 434, 817, where the meaning is 'have regard for'. **Stilpo;** cf. 389, 390. Though Phormio, when he had appeared in court, had invented a fictitious relationship between Phanium and Demipho's family, he had used the real name of Phanium's father. This he could have got from either Phanium or her nurse.

741. concede, etc. A similar bit of stage play occurs in *Men.* 158–61. **istorsum =** *isto* (adverb) + *uorsum.*

742. ne . . . appellassis, prohibition expressed by *ne* + Subj. (514n.). The origin of *-ss-* forms like *amasso* (Indic.) and *amassim* (Subj.) is uncertain, but, like *faxo, faxim,* etc., they have nothing to do with the perfect stem tenses, as is shown by forms such as passive *faxitur* and infinitive *impetrassere*. **obsecro,** often parenthetically with imperatives or questions (= enclitic 'pray', 'please'), sts. equivalent to an exclamation of astonishment; best translated here by emphasizing 'not'—'What? You're *not* . . . ?'

743. **semper dictitasti,** note the pleonasm of *semper* with a frequentative verb; Cicero and Livy have similar examples. **st,** occupies one long syllable; interjection calling for silence.

745. **eo,** adverb, anticipates the *ne* clause. **perperam,** etymology uncertain: the adjective *perperus* occurs once in Accius. **foris** 308n.

746. **effuttiretis,** 'blurt out'; the basic root is *fundo*; for the rest of the line, cf. 585.

747. **istoc,** causal, 'for that reason', as *eo* frequently and *hoc* occasionally (804).

750. **ex aegritudine,** for *ex* denoting source or origin and hence, (virtually) cause, cf. *An.* 268, *laborat e dolore*. **hac** because they could not find 'Stilpo'. **mors consecutast,** for *mors* as subject of a trans. verb, cf. *An.* 297, *mors continuo ipsam occupat.*

751. **male factum,** 238n. Ashmore translates 'bad job!' 'too bad!' and Sloman says 'a very cool expression of grief'. But cf. Cic. *ad Att.* XV. 1. 1 (on the recent death of Alexio), *o factum male de Alexione! incredibile est quanta me molestia affecerit.* Catull. III. 16, *o factum male! o miselle passer!* **quae essem.** 'Causal Cls. take both Indic. and Subj. —the latter, however, much more frequently' (Allardice, p. 148).

752. **nuptum uirginem locaui,** cf. Caes. *B.G.* I. 18. 7, *sororem ex matre et propinquas suas nuptum in alias ciuitates conlocasse.*

753. **dominus.** Strictly speaking, Demipho is the *dominus*, but no doubt during his absence Antipho acted as if he were.

754. **duasne is uxores?** The humour of the bigamist Chremes expressing concern at the thought of his nephew having two wives is apparent; cf. 1041. **au obsecro,** *aŭ* by prosodic hiatus; Don. (on *Eun.* 899) '*au* interiectio est perturbatae mulieris. It is often conjoined with *obsecro*, e.g. 803.

755. **quid illam alteram.** 'What about that other one?' The construction of the accusative is obscure. Allardice (p. 16) calls it an Accusative of Limitation. **haec ergost.** 'Why! That's her!' **quid ais?** here expresses surprise; 199n.

756. **composito,** abl. noun used as adverb; Don., *sic ueteres, non 'ex composito'.* The latter expression is common in Livy. **quo modo . . . posset,** final rel. clause. **amans,** participle used as noun, cf. 243.

757. **di uostram fidem,** sc. *obsecro (uel sim.)*; a common oath, e.g.

808. **quam saepe.** The thought is a commonplace; parallels are collected by Otto, p. 330. **forte temere,** a fairly common combination, found also in Cicero and often in Livy.

758. **quae non audeas,** for the 2nd person potential subj., cf. 341n. **offendi,** literally 'dash against', frequently 'come across someone', e.g. *Eun.* 1064, *si te in platea offendero hac post umquam . . . periisti.*

759. **quicum,** *qui* is indeclinable ablative (123n.): some MSS. read *quocum.* **amari** must depend on *offendi* (= *inueni,* lit. 'I have found her loved, (being) married to whom and how I wanted'), though there is no parallel to an infinitive after *offendere.* From *filiam* (Σ), which interrupts the sequence of iambic septenarii, Faernus conjectured *gnatam* for *amari.*

760. **fieret,** *fíeret*; contrast 593, *fíeret.*

761. **haec sola,** sc. Sophrona: *solus* (A and O.T.) would refer to Antipho, but the contrast is between the unaided effort of a helpless woman and the combined exertions of the two *senes.*

762. **sit** in spite of the general tendency to retain the Indic. in Ind. Questions after imperatives of *uerba dicendi, sentiendi* etc. (358n.); some MSS. read *est.*

764. Scan $\widehat{deos}$ āt | qu(e) hŏmĭnēs | mĕ(am) ēs | s(e). **caue resciscat quisquam,** 'mind no one finds out'; *caue* + Subj. (less often with *ne* + Subj.), like *uide ne* + Subj. (803), is almost equivalent to a prohibition.

765. **scibit,** for the form, cf. 480n. **cetera,** sc. *audies; audies* is in fact the manuscript reading, but must either be omitted to make an iambic senarius, or expanded to *audiemus* or *audietis* to make an iambic septenarius. Chremes, followed by Sophrona, retires into Demipho's house.

ACT V. SCENE 2

Demipho returns with Geta from the forum, where he has paid over the thirty minae to Phormio. Demipho's reflections on the unwisdom of encouraging Phormio's villainy by paying him money are interrupted by Geta, who expresses anxiety that even now Phormio may change his mind. To forestall this possibility Demipho hurries off to Chremes' house to get Nausistrata to go and tell Phanium of the arrangements that have been made about her future. Geta, after a short soliloquy on the purely temporary nature of the solution that has so far been discovered to their problems, goes into Demipho's house to acquaint Phanium with their plan, so that she will not be dismayed at Phormio's proposals.

766. **nostrapte**, for -*pte*, cf. 280n. **malis expediat esse.** Understand *hominibus*; *malis* is complement of *esse*.

768. **ita fugias ne praeter casam**, an obscure proverb. If, as Donatus suggests, *casa* is *tutissimum receptaculum*, the meaning would be 'Run away in such a way that you don't overshoot your place of refuge', perhaps equivalent to 'Don't jump out of the frying pan into the fire'. **ita . . . ne**, sc. *fugias* (*curras, uel sim.*); Latin sometimes has a neg. final clause where English uses a consecutive clause, e.g. *Capt.* 737, *atque hunc me uelle dicite ita curarier ne qui deterius huic sit quam quoi pessume est.*

769. **etiam . . . ultro**, 360n.

772. **ut . . . gesserimus**, consecutive clause continuing Demipho's sentence in 771. **illi**, adverb. **gesserimus**, note -*īmus*. Norden (on Aen. VI. 514) '*egerĭmus*: first certain example of ĭ in Perfect Subjunctive'.

773. **modo ut**, 711n. **discedi.** Here impersonal passive; *discedere* means 'come out of it', 'come off', cf. 1047. **hoc consilio** is explained by *ut istam ducat.*

774. **haud scio . . . an**, virtually = 'perhaps'. **ut homost.** Sloman says 'being human' (*ut* = 'seeing that'): rather *homo* = 'the fellow' (Phormio) and *ut* = *cum talis*, 'such being the fellow's nature'. Cf. *Cist.* 194, *ut sunt humana, nihil est perpetuom datum; Phorm.* 55 *ut nunc sunt mores.*

775. **si forte**, sc. *animum mutet/mutauerit.*

776. **ita** is correlative with *ut* (. . . *censuit*); cf. 795, *faciam ut iubes*: *ut . . . adducam* is a noun clause explanatory of the whole. **censuit**, ĭt, syllaba anceps at diaeresis. **ut uxorem eius**, ŭt ŭxōr(em) eius; ŭx- by B-B.

777. **cum ista . . . hanc**, sc. *Phanio . . . Nausistratam.* **abi prae, nuntia.** As English can say 'Go on! Do it!' or 'Go on and do it!' so Latin can say *abi prae, curre* (*Eun.* 499) or *abi prae strenue ac fores aperi* (*Ad.* 167). Exit Demipho to Chremes' house to fetch Nausistrata.

778. **siletur**, impersonal passive, cf. Allardice, p. 54.

779. **prouisumst ne** (this construction not in Plautus and here only in Terence), cf. *Hec.* 729, *uidendumst ne minus . . . impetrem.* **haec**, sc. Phanium.

780. **in eodem luto haesitas.** Cf. Lactantius *inst.* VII. 2. 3, *et in eodem luto, sicut comicus ait, haesitauerunt.* **uorsuram solues.** *Vorsura* is, in essence, borrowing from a second creditor to pay a first, or the money so borrowed. Normal phrases are *uorsuram facere*, 'raise a (further)

loan' and *uorsura soluere*, 'pay by (a further) borrowing'; Bentley accordingly here reads (after Guyet) *uorsura soluis*, 'you're paying one debt by incurring another'. But *quid fiet* supports the future *solues*; *uorsuram solues* is then 'you'll be repaying (or "you'll have to repay") a new loan'. The money for Phaedria's music girl has been raised by 'borrowing' from Demipho and Chremes. But when Phormio goes back on his offer to marry Phanium (650 f.), the 'borrowed' money will have to be repaid; Geta and his party will be no better off than before.

781. **in diem abiit.** Does *in diem* mean 'for the present' (i.e. *in hunc diem*) or 'until another day' (i.e. *in alium diem*)? Either interpretation is possible, but the similarity between Pl. *M.G.* 861, *in diem extollam* and *Poen.* 500, *extollo . . . in alium diem* perhaps suggests that here *in diem* means 'until another day'.

783. **eius,** must (in spite of Sloman, who says 'sc. *Nausistrata*') refer to Phormio. Exit Geta to Demipho's house to warn Phanium not to be alarmed when she is told of the proposal to marry her to Phormio instead of Antipho.

ACT V. SCENE 3

Demipho reappears from Chremes' house with Nausistrata, who has agreed to inform Phanium of the plan to marry her to Phormio. Demipho's deference encourages Nausistrata to expatiate on the inferiority of Chremes as compared with her father in managing her Lemnian estates. As she moves towards Demipho's house she halts on seeing Chremes coming out from there.

784. **agedum,** for *dum*, cf. 329n. **ut soles,** flattery, which Chremes would not endorse. **Nausistrata,** *-tā*|*făc ĭll-* (B-B), with syllaba anceps at diaeresis, rather than *Nausistrătă, făc*|*ĭlla*; cf. Laidlaw 85.

785. **sua uoluntate,** note emphatic position of *sua*; cf. 725.

786. **pariter . . . ac,** 'just as', cf. 31 *simili . . . atque*, 581-2, *aeque atque*, 684, *aliud . . . ac*, 1028, *tali . . . atque*; Allardice, p. 116. **dudum,** in Plautus and Terence mostly refers to time recently past, during the action of the play or within the same day (e.g. 459, 838). It is best, therefore, to refer *re . . . opitulata es* to 681 rather than to some unspecified event in the more remote past.

788. **quid autem?** *autem* (389n.) here expresses surprise rather than indignation; 'Why, what do you mean?'

790. **statim,** 'regularly'; Don. *perpetuo, aequaliter et quasi uno statu,*

capiebat, sc. *pater meus.* **uir uiro quid praestat,** cf. *Eun.* 232, *di inmortales, homini homo quid praestat!*

791. **rebus uilioribus,** Abl. absolute with concessive force. There is a proceleusmatic in the 6th foot, *tămĕn dŭŏ* (*-ĕn d-* by B-B).

792. **quid haec uidentur.** 'What do you think of this?' **scilicet,** indicating assent, 'Quite', 'Of course'.

792-3. **uellem ... ostenderem** are both probably unreal past potentials; for the tense, cf. 107-8n.

793. **ostenderem,** *ŏst-* by B-B. **quo pacto ...** Nausistrata is only too ready to hold forth on her husband's shortcomings, but is recalled by Demipho to the business in hand.

794. **cum illa,** sc. (*con-*)*loqui.*

795. Nausistrata begins to move towards Demipho's house, but halts as she sees her husband hurrying out from there. **abs te,** *ex te* in the Oxford Text is a misprint; all MSS. have *abs te*; 732n. **ehem Demipho.** 'Ah! Demipho'. Terence is particularly fond of using *ehem* with a vocative.

ACT V. SCENE 3 *continued* (line 796)

A (before *faciam*) and D give *notae personarum* here, indicating the beginning of a new scene: the other MSS. make the scene continuous from 784. The Oxford Text compromises by printing the *notae personarum* afresh, but treating lines 784-819 as one scene.

Chremes rushes excitedly out of Demipho's house, eager to tell his brother that his daughter is found and is the girl whom Antipho has married. Failing at first to see his wife he nearly says too much. For the rest of the scene he tries ineffectually, without letting Nausistrata into the secret, to convey to Demipho why it is no longer necessary for Phanium to be divorced from Antipho. Though made suspicious by Chremes' incoherence, Nausistrata is persuaded to return to her own house. Even then, fearful that his wife may overhear their conversation, Chremes delays his explanations to Demipho till they are inside the latter's house.

796. **illi,** Phormio. **nollem datum.** 'I wish (lit. 'could have wished') you hadn't.'

797. **paene plus quam sat erat,** cf. *Cist.* 122, *plus loquimur quam sat est.*

798. **iam recte.** Chremes tries to cover up his confusion by professing that all is well; *iam* indicates that he has now altered his view from

that expressed by *nollem datum*. **quid tu?** 'What about *you*? Have you . . . ?' *Quid tu?* merely anticipates the following question; *tu* has the case it is going to have in the succeeding question. **istac . . . hanc,** sc. *Phanio . . . Nausistratam*, cf. 777.

799. **quid ait tandem?** *tandem* adds urgency to the question, 'What does she say then?' **qui,** interrogative, 'How/Why'?

800. **uterque utrique** for the reciprocal force ('each to the other') of the doubled pronoun, cf. *Ht.* 394, *utrique ab utrisque . . . deuincimini.* **cordi,** predicative dative.

801. **deliras** *lira* is the ridge between two furrows, *delirare* is thus 'to stray from the straight path'. **sic erit.** 'Thus it will prove to be', 'You'll find I'm not talking nonsense'.

802. **non temere dico.** Cf. *non temere est*, 'it's not by accident'. **redii mecum in memoriam,** elsewhere *in memoriam redeo* (without *mecum*). **satin sanus es?** 'Are you in your right mind?'—a common formula.

803. **in cognatam pecces,** *in* = 'against', cf. *Ad.* 725, *hoc peccatum in uirginemst ciuem.* **non est,** sc. *cognata.*

804. **hoc,** 747n.

805. **quor aliud dixit?** Demipho, unaware that Phanium is Chremes' daughter, attempts to discredit Phanium's story—much to Chremes' embarrassment. **hodie** merely emphasizes *numquam*; cf. 377n.

806. **nil narras.** As *aliquid* can mean 'something sensible', so *nil* = 'nonsense'. **perdis,** lit. 'You're killing me (by talking like this)', equivalent to an impatient 'For Heaven's sake, shut up!' **hoc,** *hŏc s-* by B-B.

807. **at** emphasizes the oath by protesting against Demipho's unbelief; cf. *Poen.* 1258–9 *at me(d) ita di seruent | ut hic pater est uoster.* For *ita me seruet . . . ut*, cf. 165n.

809. Demipho, convinced by Chremes' earnestness that Phanium really is a relation of the family, suggests that all three of them should visit Phanium to learn the truth. As Nausistrata's presence would be fatal to the preservation of Chremes' secret, he implores Demipho to trust him for the time being; Demipho, without professing to understand what is afoot, agrees and tells Nausistrata that she may return home, as it is no longer necessary for her to visit Phanium.

811. 'D'you want me to stop asking you questions?' lit. 'Do you want that subject to have been adequately investigated by me?' with emphasis on the perfect tense, 'a sufficient investigation concluded'. **mi,** dative

of agent. **age,** here, as *age age* at 559, indicates impatient assent, 'All right', 'Very well'.

811–12. quid illa filia . . . ? 'What about that daughter . . . ?' *Filia* is ablative, anticipating the case it would have had, if it had stood in the clause *quid futurumst?* For abl. with *futurumst,* cf. 137n.

812. amici nostri, 'that friend of ours'; Demipho is, of course, referring to Chremes himself, but uses this allusive manner to deceive Nausistrata. **hanc** refers to Chremes' daughter, just alluded to as *illa filia amici nostri.* In the next line, however, *illa* means 'that other one' (Antipho's wife, Phanium), for Demipho still believes that Chremes' daughter and Phanium are different people. **hanc igitur mittimus?** probably deliberative question, cf. 447n. The deliberative indicative without interrogative pronoun or particle is rare, but cf. *M.G.* 613, *eodem consilio . . . gerimus rem?* **mittimus,** 'discard'.

814. commodius . . . in omnis. The normal construction, *commodus* + dative, is found in Terence in *Hec.* 585.

815. hanc is identical with *illa* (813). **perliberalis,** *per-* as prefix intensifying adjectives and adverbs (also verbs, e.g. *percupio*), is commonest in colloquial speech; for Cicero cf. Laurand, *Etudes sur Cicéron* (1925), pp. 271 f., 389 f.

Exit Nausistrata into her own (Chremes') house.

816. quid istuc negotist? 'What's all this business/carry-on of yours?' Even though Demipho verifies that the door of Chremes' house is shut, Chremes is afraid of his news being overheard and refuses to explain till Demipho and he are indoors.

817. di nos respiciunt, 740n. **nuptam cum tuo filio,** *nubere* usually + dative, but *nuptus* always with *cum* + abl. in Terence.

818. tutus ad narrandum, '*ad* to indicate purpose . . . is common after Adjs. denoting fitness, etc.' (Allardice, pp. 102–3).

819. at tu. 'Well then'; *at* stresses the alternative to talking out in the open. **intro** into Demipho's house.

ACT V. SCENE 4

Antipho, returning from the direction of the forum after informing Phaedria that his thirty minae will be forthcoming, reflects on the misery of his own situation compared with that of Phaedria, all of whose difficulties have been solved by the provision of a small sum of money.

820. utut, 'no matter how', 'in spite of how'; cf. 468n. **fratri,** 'cousin' (as Gk. ἀδελφός), for *fratri patrueli* ('cousin on the father's side').

821. **scitum.** 'How wise . . . !'

822. **quas . . . mederi possis,** acc. instead of the usual dative after *mederi.*   **possis,** subjunctive in consecutive relative clause.   **quom . . . sient,** Subj. by attraction—particularly common when, as here, the affected clause stands inside (usually immediately after the conjunction or relative) the clause on which it depends; cf. 839, 1030.

823. **simul,** commonly = *simul ac* in Silver Latin, but is rare in early Latin and clearly originates in parataxis, i.e. *simul* (adverb) = 'at the same time' and *repperit* and *expediuit* are parallel main verbs.

825. **celetur . . . patefit.** The subjunctive indicates that the hope of concealment is remote, whereas the prospect of exposure is an open possibility.

827. As Antipho moves along the stage in search of Geta, he has his back to Phormio, who now enters from the forum.   **ubinam . . . possim.** The Subj. with a verb whose meaning already contains the potential idea is noteworthy.

ACT V. SCENE 5

Phormio enters from the direction of the forum and, without seeing Antipho, turns to the audience. He expresses his delight at having settled Phaedria's troubles. At the sound of his voice Antipho turns round. Phormio tells him that Phaedria and he are going to retire from view to have a few days' quiet revelling.

829. Phormio's delight is mirrored by the short clauses with asyndeton.

830. **propria,** abl.—the only example after *potiri* in Terence; 281n. **emissast manu,** often occurs in Plautus; it is also found in Livy and Tacitus. The classical phrase is *manu mittere.*

832. **aliquot hos dies,** 159n.   **sumam.** *Sumere* with an adverb + *diem* or *operam* = *consumere,* 'spend'; so *Ad.* 287, *hilare sumamus diem.* But when, as here, there is no adverb, *sumere* = 'take time off'.

833. **sed Phormiost.** *Sed* marks a light contrast with the speaker's previous intention or expectation, 'Oh! It's Phormio'; cf. *Merc.* 329–30, *nunc adeo ibo illuc* (sc. *ad portum*); *sed optume gnatum meum uideo eccum.* **quid ais?,** etc. 'Tell me', 'Yes?' 'What's Phaedria going to do now?' For *quid ais* introducing a further question, cf. 199n.

834. **satietatem amoris . . . absumere,** cf. *Amph.* 472, *satietatem dum capiet pater illius quam amat.* **absumere,** metaphorically with an abstract noun is rare: Virg. *Aen.* I. 555, *sin absumpta salus* is not exactly parallel in sense.

835. **partis tuas acturus est** refers to 216–18; *partis*, a metaphor from the stage, is already found in Plautus; cf. Ter. *Eun.* 151, *priores partis habere*, *Ad.* 880, *non posteriores* (sc. *partis*) *feram*.

836. **suas** (sc. *partis*) is emphatic by its position outside its clause (*ut ageres*); the reference is to 260 f., esp. 267, *tradunt operas mutuas.* **causam ut . . . diceres**, noun clause explanatory of *suas* ⟨*partis*⟩.

837. **apud me** = Fr. *chez moi*: cf. 926, 934. **Sunium**, town and promontory of S.E. Attica: it must be remembered that the *mise-en-scène* is Athens.

838. **ancillulam**, cf. 665. **emptum**, acc. supine (governing a direct object *ancillulam*) to express purpose after a verb of motion; cf., 462n. **dudum**, 'just now', cf. 786n.

839. **conficere**, here in the sense of *consumere, perdere*; cf. Cic. *pro Flacco* 90, *patrimonium . . . conficere.*

840. As the sound of Demipho's house-door being opened is heard, Antipho and Phormio withdraw to the back of the stage. **ostium concrepuit**, Plutarch (*Public.* 20) states that, unlike the contemporary door of real life, the stage door opened outwards and that people about to go out of the house knocked on their own doors from the inside to warn passers-by to stand clear. It is not easy to prove that stage doors never opened outwards, but Plutarch's assertion that people knock on their own doors on the inside to warn passers-by that they are coming out is certainly wrong; κόπτω and its Latin equivalent *pulto/pulso* are never used of people going out of doors. Moreover, ψοφῶ and Latin (*con-*)*crepo* are used of an indeterminate noise, never of a deliberate knock: *ostium . . . te* is therefore 'That sounded like your door'. As the door was not held on hinges, this probably refers to the squeak of the vertical pivot in its socket; for a detailed discussion of the problem, cf. W. Beare, *The Roman Stage*, pp. 277 f.

ACT V. SCENE 6

Geta rushes out of Demipho's house in great excitement without seeing Antipho and Phormio. It is clear from his remarks that he has some wonderful news for Antipho. As he moves off towards Dorio's house, where he hopes to find his master, he is called back by Antipho. For a short time he teases Antipho by refusing to divulge his good news, but, when Phormio abruptly bids him tell his tale, he relates how he has overheard the secret of Phanium's parentage—she is Chremes' daughter by his bigamous Lemnian wife. Geta has been instructed to find Antipho to tell him that his father now accepts his marriage with Phanium and to bring him home.

841. Geta, coming straight down stage from Demipho's house, does not see Antipho and Phormio, who are up stage, probably in front of Chremes' house.

The scene begins with the second *seruos currens* episode. In the first (177 f., see note ad loc.) Geta had brought bad news for Antipho (with Phaedria): here he brings good news for Antipho (with Phormio).

o Fortuna, o Fors Fortuna. *Fortuna* = Gk. τύχη, but the distinction between two deities *Fortuna* and *Fors Fortuna* is a Roman conception: the deities had separate temples, traditionally dating back to Servius Tullius.

841–2. **quantis commoditatibus . . . hunc onerastis diem,** cf. *Capt.* 774, *ita hic me amoenitate amoena amoenus onerauit dies.* For the plural *commoditatibus,* cf. *An.* 569, *quot commoditates uide.*

842–3. **onerastis . . . exonerastis** (and, in 844, *onero*).

843 f. The puzzled comments of Antipho and Phormio are delivered aside to each other.

843. **quidnam hic sibi uolt?** 'What on earth does he mean (is he driving at)?' The reflexive pronoun is idiomatic but untranslatable in this phrase.

844. **mihi,** dative of disadvantage, cf. Pl. *Epid,* 344, *mihi cesso quom sto.* **qui non . . . onero.** Trans. 'instead of'; causal relative clause with indicative as, e.g., *An.* 646, *heu me miserum qui tuom animum ex animo spectaui meo.* For the subjunctive in a similar clause, cf. 751n. **umerum . . . onero pallio,** cf. *Capt.* 778 f., *eodem pacto ut comici serui solent coniciam in collum pallium, primo ex med hanc rem ut audiat; Eun.* 769, *attolle pallium.* The *pallium* is the Greek ἱμάτιον, an outdoor cloak; lifting up the cloak (over the shoulder) gave greater freedom of action and might be used metaphorically to indicate an intention of using speed or strength.

845. **haec quae contigerint.** Subj. by attraction in rel. clause; one might have expected an Ind. Question (*quae contigerint* without *haec*).

847. **heus Geta.** Antipho calls to Geta and steps forward. **em tibi.** 'There you are!' 'There, what did I tell you!' *Tibi* refers to an indefinite you (? anyone who happens to be listening).

848. **num mirum aut nouomst.** 'Isn't it just like it to be called back?'

849. **pergit hercle.** 'He's still at it'. **odio tuo,** for *odium* as 'tedious

or objectionable behaviour', cf. the common *odio me enicas*. **non manes?** = *mane*, as *non taces?* (987) = *tace*.

850. **uapula,** for a similar exhibition of slave insolence cf. *Asin.* 477–8 *tun libero homini | male seruos loquere?* LE. *uapula.* ME. *id quidem tibi hercle fiet.* **id quidem,** -*ěm* by B-B. **nisi resistis.** 'The Pres. for Fut. in threats (sc. in the protasis of conditions) is noteworthy' (Allardice, p. 120). Cf. Pl. *Cas.* 729, *dabo tibi μέγα κακόν* ('a good hiding'), *nisi resistis*.

851. **minitatur malum** *malum*, as often (e.g. 555, 644), = 'punishment'; cf. *malum minari* in Cic. *pro Caec.* 27, Livy IV. 49. 16.

852. **ipsust** = *ipsus est*; for *ipsus*, cf. 178n. **congredere.** 'Come here!' Geta addresses Antipho, *not* ' "Up to him at once" Geta addresses himself' (Ashmore); cf. Pl. *Bacch.* 980. **actutum,** 'at once', only here and *Ad.* 634 in Terence: a favourite adverb of Plautus, usually with an imperative.

853. This is one of a number of cases where the phrase *quantum est*, with or without a partitive genitive, refers to a collection of persons. *Hominum* might be partitive genitive dependent on *quantum*, but in view of collocations such as *Ad.* 218 (*hominum homo stultissime*) it is perhaps best taken as dependent on the superlative *ornatissime* and having the adj. *omnium* agreeing with it. Translating *quantumst* (sc. *eorum*) *qui uiuont* as 'the multitude of men alive' (more literally 'however great the amount ⟨of those⟩ alive'), we get 'O man most fortunate of all the multitude of men alive'.

854. **ab dis solus diligere.** Cf. *An.* 973, *solus est quem diligant di*.

855. **qui,** 'how', 123n. **credam,** 'I am to believe', indirect deliberative subjunctive.

856. **te delibutum . . . reddo,** for *reddo* with predicative adj., cf. 559. **delibutum,** 'soaked'; the prefix *de-* = 'thoroughly', as often in colloquial Latin, cf. *deamare, demirari*.

857. Phormio steps forward and brusquely bids Geta come to the point.

858. 'You here too, Phormio?' 'Yes'; for the tense of *aderas*, cf. 1012n.

859. **ut . . . dedimus.** Temporal *ut*, usu. takes perf. indicative in Terence; cf. 617. **modo,** temporal, 'only just now'. **apud forum,** Terence never says *in foro* (which is common in Plautus). **recta,** sc. *uia*.

860. **interea** sometimes means 'presently', 'after a time', rather than 'meanwhile'. Demipho had sent Geta to Phanium (777) to tell her to expect a visit from Nausistrata.

861. **nihil ad hanc rem est.** *Est* has the same force as *attinet* in 481; cf., without any verb, *An.* 683, *nil ad te.*

862. **gynaeceum,** Gk. γυναικεῖον, 'women's quarters', which were at the back of a Greek house and were segregated from the men's. *Gynaeceum* has a short *ĕ* in *Most.* 759 and never certainly has *ē*: for Latin short vowel representing a Greek diphthong, cf. 215n.

864. **quam ob rem,** *quăm* by prosodic hiatus, *ŏb* by B-B. For *quam ob rem* introducing an Ind. Question, cf. Allardice, p. 131. **esse uetitum,** '(said) it was forbidden'; impersonal *uetitum est* is not found again until Sallust.

866. **eumque . . . esse.** The abrupt change from quoted words with *inquit* to O.O. co-ordinated by *-que* is remarkable, but it should be noted that the acc. + inf. is only a reversion to the construction of 864.

867. **suspenso gradu.** Phaedrus II. iv. 18 says of a cat's stealthy tread by night *euagata noctu suspenso pede.*

868. **animam compressi.** 'I held my breath'. **aurem admoui.** Note the singular; one listens best at a door by turning the head and using one ear.

869. **hoc modo,** accompanied by an appropriate gesture, e.g. cupping his hand to his ear. **modo,** *-dō,* cf. 181n. **captans,** intensive form of *capio* (cf. *iactare* from *iacio*), here with conative sense; cf. *Cas.* 444, *captandust horum clanculum sermo mihi*; Livy XXXVIII. 7. 8, *aure admota sonitum fodientium captabant.*

872. **uxori tuae,** dative of advantage or person concerned, where a genitive might have been expected; the present example is one of many 'in expressions which designate the relations of persons to each other' (Bennett II. 142).

874. Though Phormio can scarcely believe that his trumped-up tale of Phanium's kinship with Antipho can be the truth, the accuracy of Geta's words is proved by the instructions which he bears to bring Antipho indoors to rejoin his wife.

875. **causae,** partitive genitive depending on *aliquid.*

876. **intus,** placed emphatically at the beginning of its clause to stand as close as possible to *extra,* with which it is contrasted. **inter sese ipsi egerint.** Cf. *Hec.* 192. When *inter se* is intensified by *ipsi,* the normal order is *ipsi inter se*; but *Hec.* 511 has *inter se . . . ipsi.*

877. Antipho had presumably heard the tale from Phanium or her nurse Sophrona. By modern standards it seems lame that Antipho should recall this fact only when it is too late to help, but in Plautus' *Captiui* Tyndarus similarly recalls a vital clue only at the end of the play, when

the problem it could have solved has already been settled. **inaudiui,**
'I happened to hear': *inaudiui* here only in Terence. Plautus uses the
archaic form *indaudiui*. Only the perfect stem tenses are found. **immo
etiam,** *etiam* = 'still further'; trans. 'What's more . . .'

878. **quo mage credas,** *quo* introducing a final rel. clause in which
there is a comparative adverb (*mage*).

879. **patre,** sc. *tuo*. **denuo,** contracted from *de nouo*; it may be used
as a synonym for *iterum* or *rursus*.

880. **eius adhibendae.** The old men grant Antipho permission
to *take* Phanium as his wife, affecting to ignore that he has already done
so. The variant *habendae* gives the easier sense, 'permission to *keep* her
as his wife', but will scan only if altered to the archaic form *habendai* (*āī*-
as *Cliniāī* (*Ht.* 515)).

881. **em** (omitted by A) is common with imperatives (52n.), but
is not found elsewhere with *quin* + imperative.

882. **quin . . . rape,** 223n. **fecero. AN. heus,** hiatus at change of
speaker. For the future perfect expressing immediacy, cf. 516n. (*conduplicauerit*).

883. Exeunt Antipho and Geta to Demipho's house. Phormio remains
on the stage.

ACT V. SCENE 7

Phormio is quick to realize how knowledge of Chremes' secret can
be used to avoid repaying the thirty minae which have been spent on
Phaedria's music-girl.

884. **tantam fortunam . . . esse his datam,** acc. + infinitive
of exclamation.

885-6. **eludendi occasiost . . . et Phaedriae curam adimere,**
note the change of construction after *occasio* from genitive gerund to inf.
Both constructions, but not together, occur in Plautus.

886. **curam . . . argentariam,** cf. *Pseud.* 300, *pereo . . . inopia
argentaria.*

887. **quoiquam . . . supplex,** for dative after *supplex* cf. Allardice,
pp. 28–9.

888. **nam idem,** *năm* by prosodic hiatus.

888-9. Taking *ingratiis* ('against their will') with *ei datum erit*, trans.
'as surely as it has been handed over, it shall be his for keeps, whether
the old men like it or not'. With the punctuation *ita ut datumst ingratiis,*

trans. 'as surely as they were reluctant to part with the money, he shall have it'.

889. **hoc,** accusative. **qui,** 123n. **re ipsa,** cf. *Hec.* 778, *in re ipsa inuenimus,* 'in the event', 'as it happens'.

890. **gestus . . . uoltusque,** for *uoltus,* cf. 210: the metaphor here is from acting, 'I must play a new part.'

891. **angiportum.** Plautus and Terence use the second declension neuter form rather than the 4th declension masculine form in *-us* (exc. Plaut. *Cist.* 124, *angiportu,* abl. sing.). The *angiportum* is commonly supposed to be an alley or passage leading back from the street between two houses. This interpretation has been questioned, most recently by W. Beare (*The Roman Stage,* Appendix C, pp. 246–53), who maintains that *angiportum,* which may be used of the main street on which the houses on the stage front (Plaut. *Pseud.* 971), means the back lane behind the houses or the side entrances off the stage. Beare says, 'I now hold that there were no hiding-places on the stage' (249 note 1); 'it appears abundantly clear that the "alley" of which editors so often speak could have had neither place nor function on the Roman stage. The only means of entry and exit were the house-doors and the side entrances' (253). Beare discusses the present passage on pp. 252–3. It is clear from 898 to 899 that Phormio appears in a manner that is intended to make Demipho and Chremes believe that he has come (presumably from the forum) to find them: he can give such an impression only by entering by the R.H. (forum) side entrance. To enter from an alley between the houses could only make the old men suspicious.

893. refers to the intention announced in 837–8. **non eo,** for present tense cf. 1044n. Phormio draws aside into the *angiportum.*

ACT V. SCENE 8

Demipho and Chremes reappear from the house of the former, delighted with the apparently happy solution of Chremes' worries about his Lemnian daughter, and determined to recover the thirty minae from Phormio at once. Phormio, who has been standing in the *angiportum,* moves towards Demipho's house and, on being greeted by Demipho, professes his readiness to carry out his side of the bargain by marrying Phanium. When Demipho says that he has changed his mind and requests Phormio to return the thirty minae, Phormio becomes indignant and asserts that, if Demipho is not prepared to give him Phanium in marriage, he must at least be allowed to keep the thirty minae. As

Demipho's language becomes more threatening, Phormio lets it be known that he knows about Chremes' Lemnian marriage. The wind is completely taken out of Chremes' sails and he now begs Phormio to say no more about repaying the thirty minae. Demipho, however, is made of sterner stuff. Realizing that Chremes' secret cannot now be kept from Nausistrata, he recommends Chremes himself to tell what she will in any case hear from others; at the same time he is determined that Phormio shall not make capital out of the situation. Assisted by Chremes he seizes Phormio and is about to drag him off to the law-courts when Phormio shouts for Nausistrata to come out of her house.

894. **gratias habeo.** Usually the singular *gratiam* is used with *habere* and *referre*; the fact that the plural is always used in *gratias agere* may account for *gratias habeo* here. But *gratias habere* occasionally occurs independently in Plautus, e.g. *Poen.* 1274, *di deaeque omnes, uobis habeo merito magnas gratias.*

895. **quando** is regularly causal in Terence; Allardice, p. 113. **euenere . . . prospere.** Cf. Pl. *Pseud.* 574, *mihi . . . lepide omnia prospereque eueniunt.*

896. **quantum potest,** 'as quickly as possible'.

897. **prius quam dilapidat,** for present tense, cf. 719n. **dilapidat.** The metaphorical sense is common only in late Latin, the literal sense is almost unattested. If the basic sense is 'to scatter like stones', the metaphor is very close to our 'make ducks and drakes of' (literally of making flat stones skim along the surface of the water like ducks and drakes, metaphorically of 'throwing away', 'squandering'). **nostras triginta minas,** belongs equally to *dilapidat* and *ut auferamus.*

898. Phormio comes out of his hiding-place and marches up to Demipho's house, pretending not to see Demipho and Chremes, who are conversing at the front of the stage. At the sound of Phormio's voice Demipho turns round and moves to speak to him. **Demiphonem si domist,** for proleptic accusative, cf. 354n. **si domist uisam,** the *si* clause is virtually an Ind. Question, cf. 490n.

899. **ut quod . . .** The general sense of what is to be understood is clear from 906-7, e.g. *ut quod promisi (promiserim) id facere paratum me esse nuntiem.*

900. **ita hercle.** 'Yes, indeed.' **credidi,** sarcastically, as *credo* frequently.

901. **ridiculum,** trans. 'Don't be absurd!' Literally, 'It's absurd (to ask such a question)'. For 'omission' of *est* cf. 238n. **uerebamini,**

uerĕ- by B-B, though a 'vowel long by nature is rarely shortened' (Laidlaw, p. 22).

902. **recepissem,** in the sense of *suscipere,* 'undertake'; cf. *Ht.* 1056, *ad me recipio,* 'I take it on myself'.

903. Spoken with an air of injured innocence. **quanta quanta,** in the sense of the indefinite *quantacumque,* 'however great'; cf. *Ad.* 394, *quantus quantu's.*

905. This line is spoken sarcastically of Phormio, 'Isn't he, as I said, the perfect gentleman?' Many editors transpose it to before 894 or after 896 and refer it to Phanium.

906. **id,** direct object of *nuntiatum* (supine expressing purpose), merely anticipates the clause *paratum me esse,* and should be omitted in translation.

908. **posthabui,** not in Plautus nor elsewhere in Terence, but cf. *Hec.* 483, *quom te postputasse omnis res prae parente intellego.*

909. **postquam . . . animum aduorteram,** for the rare pluperfect after *postquam,* cf. *An.* 177, Allardice, p. 142.

910. Demipho's excuse for his surprising change of front is very weak.

911. **qui,** *quĭ* by prosodic haitus.

914. **coram,** adverb, as always in Pl. and Terence.

915. **inluditis me.** Terence has *aliquem inludere* (thrice), *in aliquem* and *in aliquo inludere* (once each), never *alicui inludere.* The construction *alicui inl.* later becomes fairly common, but never ousts *aliquem inludere.* Cicero in his speeches has *alicui rei inl.* but *aliquem inludere,* in his philosophical works *aliquid* and *aliquem inludere.*

921–2. The forum was the normal place of business of the banker (τραπεζίτης; *tarpezita, argentarius*). Demipho had paid Phormio in cash, but is willing to accept repayment by means of a credit entry at his banker's (cf. L & S, s.v. *rescribere,* I.B. 2).

923. **quodne,** *quod* is relative not interrogative; *-ne* is added to the rel. pronoun when there is an ellipse of the interrogative main clause, viz. *argentumne iubes rescribi quod ego discripsi porro?*

925. **sin est ut uelis.** 'If you really wish': cf. 270.

926. **hic,** sc. *apud me.* **maneat,** jussive subjunctive.

928–9. **quom . . . remiserim.** Whether *quom* is causal or concessive, the Subj. deserves note, as it is not obligatory in such clauses in Terence, cf. 23n., 202n. **alterae,** dat. fem. sing. for classical *alteri,* which Terence uses only as masc. dat. sing. (*An.* 427).

929. **dabat,** 'offered'.

930. **in' hinc malam rem,** Bentley, O.T. *In'* = *is-ne*; for absence

of preposition, cf. 368n. The MSS. have various readings, all introducing the preposition *in*. **cum istac magnificentia** (*cŭm ĭst-*, by prosodic hiatus and B–B), 'You and your . . .' For *cum* in imprecations, cf. 465n.

931. **fugitiue,** an intolerable insult to a freeman.

932. **irritor.** 'I'm being provoked'. 'You're provoking me'.

932–3. **duceres . . . daretur,** imperfect for pluperfect subjunctives, cf. 107–8n. **fac periclum,** 'Just try!' *Periclum* = 'trial'.

933–4. **ut filius . . . habitet,** noun clause explanatory of *hoc* (934). **uostrum,** not *tuum*.

935. **quaeso quid narras?** 645–6n.

936. **immo,** normally a spondee, here and in five other passages as first word of the line scans *ĭmmŏ*. The second syllable is short by B–B, but the initial short syllable has not been explained. **in ius ambula,** cf. 981, *in ius eamus*, 'go to court (to settle a matter in dispute)'.

938. **indotatis,** such as Phanium.

940. Chremes, for whom Phormio's words have a special meaning, addresses Phormio for the first time during the present scene. His initial indifference (*quid id nostra?*) soon gives way to alarm and utter despair. **quid id nostra,** sc. *refert*. **nihil,** sarcastically.

941. **hem,** 'What?' expressing uneasy surprise. **quid est?** addressed to Chremes, 'What's up?'; cf. 58n.

942. **nullus sum.** 'I'm done for'.

943. **sepultus sum,** metaphorically; (?) 'I'm a goner'.

944. **denarrabo,** 'tell (the whole tale)'; for the force of *de-*, cf. 856n. **obsecro,** cf. 742n. The initial position is less common than the parenthetical.

945. **oh tune is eras?** spoken with affected surprise; for the imperfect, where English uses the present, cf. 1012n. **ut ludos facit!** (*ut* = 'how'). The difference between the two brothers is clearly brought out here. Chremes will do anything to appease Phormio, if only his secret can be kept from Nausistrata: Demipho, realizing this to be impossible, is determined that Phormio shall not get away with the thirty minae that they have handed over to him.

946. **missum te facimus,** 'we let you off'.

947. **argentum . . . condonamus te,** for the two accusatives after *condonare*, cf. Allardice, p. 9; Afranius 173, *id aurum me condonat litteris*.

949. **sententia.** *Hec.* 312, *itidem illae mulieres sunt ferme ut pueri leui sententia*, suggests that *sententia* here means '(childish way of) changing your mind'.

951. **indictumst . . . inritumst,** for the prefix *in-* with negative force, cf. *Ad.* 507, *non me indicente haec fiunt.*

952. **unde,** 'from what source', virtually = *a quo.*

953. **nisi,** 'only', 'but'; 475n.

954. **monstri,** 'portent', 'miracle'.   **scrupulum,** lit. a small stone, which, when lodged in a shoe, proves an obstacle to walking.

956. **satius est** = *melius est.*

957. **animo . . . praesenti,** 'presence of mind', cf. *Eun.* 769, *fac animo haec praesenti dicas*; Cicero *pro Mil.* 62 has *praesentiam animi.*

958. Hiatus between *tuom* and *esse*; cf. Laidlaw, p. 92.

959. **id celare . . . uxorem.** Two accusatives are common with *celare.*

961. **placabilius** active, 'more likely to appease'; 226n.

962. **inpuratum** used as a noun, cf. 669n.

963. **ulcisci,** hiatus at change of speaker.

964. **gladiatorio animo,** a purely Roman allusion; trans. 'with a look of do or die'.

967. **quom . . . excessit.** The *quom* clause explains *hoc* in 966. **e medio,** 'out of the way', here a euphemism for 'dead'.

969. **ex re istius,** 'to his (Chremes') advantage'.

970. **ain tu?** is usually followed by another question. Here, as in *Asin.* 812, it expresses an indignant 'What!' and, as there, is followed by an indignant, repudiating subjunctive.

970 f. **lubitum fuerit . . . feceris . . . sis ueritus . . . uenias.** *Venias* is repudiating subjunctive, 'are you to come?', the three preceding verbs are subjunctive by attraction. For *lubitum fuerit* (instead of *lubitum sit*), cf. Allardice, p. 56: 'The Perf. Part. Pass. seems originally to have been a Verbal Adj. in *-tus* with no special past meaning . . . There is no great occasion for surprise, therefore, when we meet seemingly irregular combinations . . .'

971. The genitive *feminae* after *uereri* is apparently on the analogy of *pudet.*

972. **nouo,** 'unprecedented', 'unheard of'.   **faceres contumeliam.** The phrase, which occurs in both Plautus and Terence, is criticized by Cicero (*Phil.* III. 22) as non-classical in the mouth of M. Antonius.

973. **lautum,** supine expressing purpose after verb of motion.

975. **ut ne** is occasionally found in Plautus and Terence in a consecutive clause of 'willed result', where classical Latin would have *ne*; noun clauses after *facere* and *efficere* may similarly be negatived with *ne* or *ut ne* when stress is laid on 'the result aimed at', e.g. Cic. *Verr.* I. 25,

fecit animo libentissimo populus Romanus ut . . . ne eiusdem pecunia de honore deicerer. For *ut ne* in a negative final clause, cf. 168n. **exstillaueris**, 'dissolve in tears'; Don., *quasi totum in lacrimas conuerti.*

976. **malum quod isti di . . . duint.** The whole of this line is identical with Plaut. *Most.* 655; similar expressions occur in *Amph.* 563, *Pseud.* 1130. *Malum* might be taken as an independent imprecation and *quod* as connecting relative, 'Damnation! And may the gods visit it upon the fellow!' but more probably *quod* (= *aliquod*) is an indefinite pronominal adjective (cf. Kroll, *Glotta* III. 3 f.). **isti** (dative) refers to Phormio, but is addressed to Chremes.

977. **adfectum,** almost = *praeditum.* **quemquam . . . hominem.** *Quisquam* used adjectivally with *homo* is common in Plautus and Terence; it is also Ciceronian.

978. **scelus,** abstract for concrete in terms of abuse; 373n.

981. **huc,** to Chremes' house; Phormio is confident of winning his case before Nausistrata.

982. **adsequere, retine,** addressed to Chremes, while Demipho turns towards his own house to fetch reinforcements. **dum . . . euoco,** for the present tense = 'until' after *dum,* cf. 513n.

983. **enim,** as an affirmative conjunction **or** particle (113n.) may stand first in its sentence.

983–4. **una iniuriast tecum.** 'That's one action for assault against you'; Don. pro '*actio iniuriarum ex lege*'. Cf. Gk. αἰχίας δίχη. **tecum,** sc. Demipho, who comes up in answer to Chremes' call for help and lays hold of Phormio. **alterast tecum.** Emboldened by Demipho's action, Chremes too lays hold of Phormio.

986. **os opprime inpurum.** *Inpurus* elsewhere in Terence only of persons, but cf. Cic. *Phil.* V. 20, *orationem ex ore impurissimo euomuit.* An alternative punctuation, adopted by Dz-H. and Marouzeau, is to place a colon after *opprime*; *inpurum,* used substantivally, is then object of *uide*; for such proleptic accusatives, cf. 354n.

986–7. Demipho's attempt to stop Phormio from calling a second time on Nausistrata fails. **uide quantum ualet,** for the indicative, cf. 358n. **non taces?** = *tace*; cf. 849n.

988. **taceam?** repudiating subjunctive in sentence-echo. **pugnos . . . ingere,** cf. *Ad.* 171, *pugnus . . . in mala haereat.* Plautus has a rich variety of phrases including *pugnum in os inpinge* (*Rud.* 710) and *hisce ego iam sementem in ore faciam pugnosque obseram* (*Men.* 1012).

989. **uel,** 'if you like'; 143n. **exclude,** 'knock my eye out'.

est ubi, 'sometime', Gk. ἔστιν ὅτε, lit. 'there is a time when'; cf. *Pseud.* 1325, *erit ubi te ulciscar, si uiuo.*

ACT V. SCENE 9

As Nausistrata comes out to see what is the cause of the commotion, Demipho and Chremes shamefacedly let go of Phormio. Chremes is speechless with terror and unable to answer his wife's questions. Phormio then tells Nausistrata of the double life that Chremes has been leading. Nausistrata's rage bursts forth, but finally, after much pleading from Demipho, she begins to show signs of relenting. Before a reconciliation can be effected, Phormio tells Nausistrata that the thirty minae have been spent in purchasing Phaedria's music-girl. Chremes' protest against this misuse of the money is cut short by Nausistrata, who remarks that a man with two wives has little ground for criticizing his son for having one mistress. She announces her intention of waiting for Phaedria's opinion before deciding whether or not to forgive her husband. After expressing her indebtedness to Phormio, she invites him, at his suggestion, to dinner.

990. **qui,** pronoun; 129n.

993. **caue . . . creduas,** cf. 764. *Creduas* here only in Terence, common in Plautus; an alternative form for *credas* used at line-end *metri gratia,* as *perduint* for *perdant.*

994. **abi** here introduces a contemptuous challenge 'Go on! (Just) touch him!'

995. **quid istic narrat?** 'What does he mean?' *Istic* is spoken pointing to Phormio.

996-7. **quid . . . credam,** lit. 'with respect to what, pray, am I to believe him?' Trans. 'How can I believe him when (*qui*) he hasn't said a word?' or 'What is there to believe when . . .'

999. **recte sane,** sarcastically agrees with Chremes; trans. 'Of course not'. The O.T. wrongly prints a full stop after *times.*

1001. **narret,** repudiating subjunctive in sentence -echo. **tibi,** 'for you', i.e. 'at your command'. **sedulo,** sarcastically, 'You've done a fine job for your brother!'

1003. **huic.** Nausistrata.

1004. **clam te.** Terence uses *clam* both as an adverb and as a preposition with the accusative, mostly with the pronouns *me* and *te* (*Hec.* 396, *clam . . . patrem*). *Clam* as a preposition with the accusative is ante-classical (also in *Bell. Hispan.*); in classical Latin it is mostly an adverb, but is used as a preposition *with the ablative* in Lucr. I. 476, Cic. *ad Att.* X. 12a. 2 (?), Caes. *B. C.* II. 32. 8, *Bell. Afr.* 11. 4, Ovid *Am.* II. 13. 3. The article on *clam* in L & S is inaccurate.

1005. **mi homo.** Nausistrata, incredulously, to Phormio (she addresses her husband as *mi uir* (991, 1002)).

1006. **inde,** 'from/by her'.

1007. **dum tu dormis.** 'While you were asleep'; *dormire* may be used metaphorically of inaction or of being oblivious of something. Here both literal and metaphorical meanings are present.

1009. **hoc actumst.** Chremes has asked 'What's to be done?' Phormio replies that this business is already finished and done with. This interpretation seems better than taking *actumst* as merely a variant on *sic factumst* in 1006.

1010. **qui,** a connecting relative, whose antecedent (e.g. *em uiros,* 'that's men for you') must be supplied from the context, is best omitted in translation, 'It's only when they come to their wives that they turn old men!' For the thought, cf. Pl. *Asin.* 812. **mi,** ethical dative, here almost 'I tell you'.

1011. **distaedet.** The prefix *dis-* (a colloquialism) intensifies the force of the verb.

1012. **haecin erant.** The imperfect, like the Greek imperfect (esp. of εἰμί with ἄρα), expresses 'the surprise attendant upon disillusionment' (Denniston, *Greek Particles* 35-7; for Terence, cf. Allardice, p. 65), translatable 'So this then is what your frequent journeys and long stays at Lemnos meant?' **haecin,** *haec = tales.* **itiones, . . . mansiones,** for the abstract nouns, especially common in the comic dramatists, cf. 857 *pollicitationes* and lists in Draeger, *Hist. Syntax* I² 10 f. *Itiones* and *mansiones* occur first in Terence.

1012-3. **haecin erant . . . haecin erat,** anaphora; the rhetorical figure emphasizes Nausistrata's indignation. **fructus,** cf. 680, where the singular is used to indicate the profit from a single year.

1014. **esse . . . culpam meritum,** sc. *eum* (acc. subject).

1015. **qui** is the indefinite and enclitic adverb found in *atqui*; trans. 'perhaps'. **uerba fiunt mortuo** refers to the *laudatio funebris*; cf. *Poen.* 840. Here and in 1026-30 Phormio speaks for all to hear. The words are spoken sarcastically to indicate that Chremes is as good as dead.

1016. **tua . . . tuo,** possessive adjj. for objective genitive pronouns, cf. 469n.

1017. For a somewhat different account of the affair, cf. 873; perhaps

Demipho is deliberately trying to minimize the offence. **uinolentus,** cf. *Cist.* 158–9, *isque hic compressit uirginem, adulescentulus,* ⟨*ui,*⟩ *uinolentus, multa nocte, in uia.* **abhinc annos quindecim.** The acc. of duration is the usual construction after *abhinc* in Plautus and Terence. The ablative is found only at Pl. *Most.* 484. **mulierculam.** The diminutive helps to stress the insignificance of the affair.

1018. **attigit,** cf. *Hec.* 136 for the euphemism.

1021. **quid,** sc. *feram*; lit. 'What am I to bear calmly?' but English would rather say 'How am I to bear it calmly?' **defungier,** absolutely, 'to make an end of the matter', as in *Eun.* 15.

1022. **aetate,** causal, 'because of his age'. **porro,** temporal, 'in the future', 'as time goes on'.

1025. **exspectem aut sperem,** indirect deliberatives.

1026. **exsequias . . . ire,** either acc. of motion towards, as *domum ire* (this seems to be the explanation of *infitias ire*, 'to deny'), or internal acc. (cf. *iter ire*), 'go on a funeral journey or procession'.

1027. **sic dabo,** *dare* almost = *facere*, cf. Pl. *Poen.* 1286, *sic dedero*; *Pseud.* 155, *sic datur.* **lacessito.** The future force of the imperative in -*to* is clearly shown by the tense of *uolet.*

1028. **faxo,** for form and constructions, cf. 308n. **sum,** archaic form for *eum,* is restored from Donatus: MSS. read *sit mactatus* (ADL) or *eum* (others). **mactatum . . . infortunio,** here only in Terence, but quite common in Plautus.

1029. **sane,** contemptuously concessive, 'All right then!' **redeat . . . in gratiam.** Cf. Cic. *Phil.* VIII. 25, *in gratiam redeo*; more often *cum aliquo in gratiam redire,* e.g. *Phil.* II. 118, *redi cum re publica in gratiam.*

103. **dum uiuat,** *dum =* 'as long as'; Subj. by attraction (822n.); cf. *Ht.* 950–1, *adeo exornatum dabo, adeo depexum ut dum uiuat meminerit semper mei.* **usque,** 'continuously', to be taken with *ogganniat.* **ogganniat,** cf. *Asin.* 422, *centiens eadem imperem atque ogganniam.* *Gannire* literally of the cry (bark or yelp) of a dog or fox.

1031. **at meo merito credo,** sc. *factum* (*est*), sarcastically spoken. **quid ego nunc commemorem . . . ?** Nausistrata clearly intends to go on at some length, but is cut short by Demipho's *noui aeque omnia tecum* (= 'You don't need to tell me').

1032. **in hunc,** 'towards him'; cf. *Hec.* 471–2, *si nunc memorare hic uelim quam fideli animo et benigno in illam et clementi fui.*

1032–3. **aeque . . . tecum.** Cf. *Asin.* 332, *ut aeque mecum haec scias.*

1033. **mimime gentium,** *gentium* merely emphasizes the negative *minime,* 'No, not at all'; cf. *Ad.* 342, *ah minime gentium: non faciam.*

1034. **fieri infectum.** Cf. *Aul.* 741, *factumst illud: fieri infectum non potest; Truc.* 730, *stultus es qui facta infecta facere uerbis postules.*

1035. **purgat,** usu. transitive with acc. of person or offence, e.g. 186, *purgem me?* For the omission of the accusative, cf. *Aul.* 753, *non mi homines placent qui quando male fecerunt purigant.*

1036. Aside, to the audience. **priusquam . . . dat.** Contrast the fut. perfect tense in 1045; for the reason, cf. 719n. **mihi prospiciam,** dative as with *consulere.*

1040-1. **filius homo adulescens** = *filius, qui est homo adulescens.* **filius . . . unam amicam, tu uxores duas,** adversative asyndeton: *unam* contrast with *duas, amicam* with *uxores.*

1042. **nihil pudere!** exclamatory infinitive; cf. 233 *non pudere!*

1043. **immo,** rejects the appeal of *ignosce* (1035).

1044. **ignosco,** etc. For the present tenses in this line, cf. 388n.

1047-8. **immo . . . spem.** A strong case can be made out for giving these words to Chremes, as Bentley suggested. **discedo,** cf. 773; Pl. *Stich.* 395, *sane discessisti non bene.* **quid est** for indicative, cf. 358n.

1049. **amicus . . . summus,** 35n.

1050. **Phormio.** Nausistrata repeats the name as a gesture of friendliness. Donatus well compares *Ad.* 891 (Demea has just decided to treat everyone with exaggerated kindness). DE. *o qui uocare?* GE. *Geta.* DE. *Geta, hominem maxumi preti te esse hodie iudicaui animo meo.* **quod potero,** 'as far as I can'; rel. clause with restrictive force.

1051. **faciamque et dicam,** for -*que et,* cf. *Eun.* 876, *accipioque et uolo, Ad.* 64, *aequomque et bonum;* it is rare in prose. **benigne dicis.** In Pl. and Ter. *benigne* does not have the force it may have in classical Latin of polite refusal.

1052. **hodie,** here means 'today': contrast 377, *et saepe.*

1053. **me ad cenam uoca.** Only here and in 325-45 does Phormio show the parasite's normal interest in food; see Introduction, p. 20.

1055. **faxo aderit,** 308n. **CANTOR.** The final valediction in the plays of Terence and some plays of Plautus has prefixed a Greek ω (omega) as a *nota personae.* As Hor. *A.P.* 155 reads, *donec cantor 'uos plaudite' dicat,* ω (the last speaker) is generally held to signify *cantor.* Exeunt omnes— Nausistrata, Chremes and Demipho into Chremes' house, Phormio to fetch Phaedria. As Phormio has been continuously on the stage since line 829, the arrangement mentioned at 837 still stands, and Phaedria will probably be at Phormio's home.

Index to Commentary

Vocabulary

The symbol – indicates that a vowel is (or probably is) long; the symbol is not inserted over diphthongs, as all diphthongs are long. Hyphens are inserted only to facilitate abbreviation. Parts of speech are indicated only where confusion might arise. Nouns in *-us* are masculine, nouns in *-a* are feminine, unless otherwise stated. Small *u* and capital *V* are used for both vocalic and consonantal *u*.

The following points should be noted:

1. Where classical Latin has *-uus* and *-uum* in 2nd declension nouns and adjectives, Terence has *-uos* and *-uom*.
2. Terence tends to leave prefixes unassimilated, e.g. *ad-sequor, in-purus,* where classical Latin tends to assimilate (*assequor, impurus*).
3. Where the genitive singular of 4th declension nouns (mostly in *-i*) is found in Terence, it is quoted; an entry such as *conspectus,* 4th declension, indicates that those forms of the word that occur in Terence belong to the 4th declension, but that they do not include the genitive singular.
4. Verbs followed by the figure 1, 2, or 4 may be assumed to be conjugated regularly; where the perfect or supine of a 3rd conjugation verb is omitted in the vocabulary, it indicates that this part of the verb is not found in Terence.
5. An appropriate translation of interjections will vary according to time and place. An attempt is made to explain in the notes the significance of each interjection as it occurs. Here, as elsewhere, the student is advised to read the notes before having recourse to the vocabulary.

ā, ab, abs, *from, by, in* (340n.)

ab-dūcō, -dūxī, -ductum, 3, *lead off, take away*

ab-eō, -iī, -itum, -īre, *go away, go off*; abī, *go on! get away!*

abhinc, *ago*

ab-rādō, -rāsī, -rāsum, 3, *scrape off*

ab-ripiō, -ripuī, -reptum, 3, *snatch away*

absque, 188n.

ab-sum, āfuī, abesse, *am away, am absent*

ab-sūmō, -sūmpsī, -sūmptum, 3, *take (away), consume*

ab-undō, 1, *overflow*

ab-ūtor, -ūsus sum, 3, *misuse*

ac, *and, and moreover, as*

ac-cēdō, -cessī, -cessum, 3, *go towards, am added*

ac-cidō, -cidī, 3, *happen, befall*

ac-cingō, -cīnxī, -cīnctum, 3, *gird
up*; accingor, *I prepare myself*

ac-cipiō, -cēpī, -ceptum, 3, *receive,
accept*

accipiter, -tris, *m., hawk*

ac-currō, -currī, -cursum, 3, *run up*

ac-cūsō, 1, *accuse*

ācer, ācris, ācre, *keen, severe, sharp*

āctor, -ōris, *m. actor-manager*

āctūtum, *at once*

ad, *to*

ad-dō, didī, -ditum, 3, *add*

ad-dūcō, -dūxī, -ductum, 3, *bring
here, bring up*

ad-eō, -iī, -itum, -īre, *go up to,
approach*

adeō, *advb., to this point, so (much),
indeed, moreover*

ad-fectō, 1, *make (one's way)*

ad-ferō, -tulī, -lātum, -ferre, *bring
(here)*

ad-ficiō, -fēcī, -fectum, 3, *furnish
with, trouble*

adfīnis, -e, *(person) connected by
marriage*

ad-gredior, -gressus sum, 3, *attack*

ad-hibeō, 2, *call in, send for*

adhūc, *still, up to now*

ad-imō, -ēmī, emptum, 3, *take
away*

ad-ipiscor, -eptus sum, 3, *get,
obtain*

adiūmentum, -ī, *n., aid, help*

adiūtō, 1, *help*

ad-iuuō -iūuī, iūtum, 1, *help*

adiūtor, -ōris, *m., helper*

ad-loquor, -locūtus sum, 3, *speak
to*

ad-mittō, -mīsī, -missum, 3, *commit (a fault)*

admodum, *very, very much so,
quite, just so*

ad-moueō, -mōuī, -mōtum, 2,
move up, bring near

ad-orior, -ortus sum, -orīrī, 4,
attack

ad-portō, 1, *bring here, carry here,
carry up*

ad-probō, 1, *approve*

ad-sequor, -secūtus sum, 3, *follow
close*

ad-simulō, 1, *pretend*

ad-sum, -fuī, -esse, *am here, assist,
attend*

ad-ueniō, -uēnī, -uentum, 4, *arrive*

aduentus, -ī (4 *decl.*), *arrival*

ad-uigilō, 1, *keep awake*

adulēscēns, -ntis, *m., young man;
adj., young*

adulēscentia, -ae, *youth (-fulness)*

adulēscentulus, -ī, *young man*

ad-uocō, 1, *summon (to my aid)*

aduorsārius, -ī, *opponent*

ad-uorsor, 1, *oppose*

aduorsum *and* aduorsus, *prep.
against*

aduorsus, -a, -um, *meeting, un-
favourable*

ad-uortō, -uortī, uorsum, 3, *turn
to*; animum aduorto, *notice*

aedēs, -ium, *f., house*

aediculae, -ārum, *(little) house,
cottage*

aegrē, *sickly*; aegre est mihi, *feel
upset*

aegritūdō, -inis, *f.*, *sickness, illness, grief*

aequālis, -e, *of one's own age, contemporary*

aequanimitās, -ātis, *f.*, *fair-mindedness*

aequē, *equally, as much*

aequos, -a, -om, *fair, right*

aerumna, -ae, *trouble*

aes, aeris, *n.*, *money*

aetās, -ātis, *f.*, *age, life*

age, *interj.*, *come (now)!*

ager, -rī, *m.*, *land, farm*

agitō, 1, *stir up, turn over*

agō, ēgī, āctum, 3, *do, deal with, arrange, plead (a cause), play (a part), give (thanks)*

āh, *interj.*, *ah! (often implies mild reproof*, 193n.)

aiō (*defect. vb.*), *say (yes)*

alicunde, *advb.*, *from somewhere, from somebody*

aliēnus, -a, -um, *another's, strange*

aliquā, *somehow*

aliquantulum, *a small amount, trifle*

aliquī, -qua, -quod, *adj. some*

aliquis, -quid, *indef. pron.*, *some, someone*

aliquot (*indecl.*), *several*

aliter, *otherwise*

aliunde, *advb.*, *from some other source*

alius, -a, -ud, *any other, other*

alō, aluī, 3, *feed, support*

alter, -era, -erum, *second, other*

ambō, -ae, -ō, *both*

ambulō, 1, *walk, go*

amīca, -ae, *(girl) friend, mistress*

amīcitia, -ae, *friendship*

amīcus, -ī, *friend*

ā-mittō, -mīsī, -missum, 3, *send away, let go, let off, lose*

amō, 1, *love*; amō tē, *I thank you*

amor, -ōris, *m.*, *love*

ā-moueō, -mōuī, -mōtum, 2, (*trans.*) *move off*

amplius, *comp. advb.*, *longer, further*

an, *interrog. conj.*

ancilla, -ae, *serving maid*

ancillula, -ae, *serving maid*

angiportum, -ī, *n.*, *alley, lane*

angō, ānxī, *throttle, torture*

anguis, -is, *m.*, *snake*

anicula, -ae, *poor old woman*

anima, -ae, *breath, life*

animaduortō, *see* aduorto

animus, -ī, *mind*

annus, -ī, *year*

ante, *prep. and advb.*, *before*

ante-cēdō, -cessī, -cessum, 3, *arrive earlier*

antehāc, *advb.*, *before*

ante-pōnō, -posuī, -positum, 3, *prefer*

antīquos, -a, -om, *old, of long standing*

anus (4 *decl.*), *old woman*

apertē, *openly*

ap-parō, 1, *prepare*

appellō, 1, *call (on)*

ap-pōnō, -posuī, -positum, 3, *put on the table*

apud, *prep.*, *with, near, in the house of, in the hands of*; nōn sum apud mē, *I'm not myself*

arbitror, 1, *think*

ardeō, -ēre, *burn with love for*, 82n.

argentārius, -a, -um, *concerning money*

argentum, -ī, *n.*, *money, cash, silver*

ars, artis, *f.*, *skill, art*; ars musica, *poetry, drama*

artifex, -icis, *c.*, *craftsman, worker*

aspernor, 1, *despise*

as-portō, 1, *carry off, transport*

astō, astitī, 1, *stand near*

astū, *abl. sing. of* astus *used as advb.*, *cunningly*

astūtē, *advb.*, *cunningly*

asymbolus, *making no contribution*

at, *but* (*it may be said*)

atauos, -ī, *father of a great-great-grandfather*

āter, -ra, -rum, *black*

atque, *and* (*moreover*), *as*

atquī, *yet, for all that*

attāt, *interj.*, *used of momentary discomfiture* (? *drat!*), 600n.

attendō, -tendī, -tentum, 3, *apply*

attineō, 2, *concern*

at-tingō, -tigī, -tāctum, 3, *touch*

au, *interj.*, *used by women, please no! please, don't!*

auāritia, -ae, *greed*

auctor, -ōris, *m.*, *adviser*

audācia, -ae, *audacity, cheek*

audācissimē, *superl. of*

audācter, *boldly, audaciously*

audāx, -ācis, *bold, daring, impudent*

audeō, ausus sum, audēre, 2, *dare, am eager to*

audiō, 4, *hear, am spoken of*

auferō, abstulī, ablātum, auferre, 3, *carry off*; aufer, *away with!*

auos, -ī, *grandfather*

auris, -is, *f.*, *ear*

aurum, -ī, *n.*, *gold*

auscultō, 1, *listen* (*to*)

aut, *either, or*

autem, *but*; *also to emphasize surprise in a question*

auxilium, -lī, *n.*, *help*

balineae, -ārum, *baths*

beātus, -a, -um, *happy, blessed*

bēlua, -ae, *fool, idiot*, 601 n.

bene, *advb.*, *well*

benedictum, -ī, *n.*, *kind word*

beneficium, -cī, *n.*, *a good turn*

benīgnus, -a, -um, *kind*

beniuolus, -a, -um, *well-wishing*

bibō, bibī, 3, *drink*

bīnī, -ae, -a, *two* (*each*)

bis, *twice*

blandē, *in a flattering manner*

bona, -ōrum, *n.*, *goods, property*

bonitās, -ātis, *f.*, *goodness*

bonus, -a, -um, *good, useful*

brūma, -ae, *shortest day*

callidus, -a, -um, *skilful, cunning*

calx, calcis, *f.*, *heel*

canis, -is, *c.*, *dog, hound*

canō, cecinī, cantum, 3, *sing*

cantilēna, -ae, *old song, old tune*

capillus, -ī, *hair*

capiō, cēpī, captum, 3, *take, receive, seize, undertake*

captō, 1, *try to catch*

caput, -itis, *n.*, *head, person, life*

carcer, -eris, *m.*, *jail, jail-bird*

cārus, -a, -um, *dear*

casa, -ae, *hut, cottage*

caueō, cāuī, cautum, 2, *beware* (*of*)

causa, -ae, *cause, pretext*

causā, *for the sake* (*of*)

cautus, -a, -um, *cautious*

cedo, *give me, bring me, tell me*

celere, *advb.*, *quickly* (*classical*, ce-
eriter)
cēlō, 1, *hide*
cēna, -ae, *dinner*
cēnseō, cēnsuī, cēnsum, 2, *vote,
think* (*best*), *suggest*
certē, *surely, at least*
certō, *advb.*, *certainly, for sure*
certō, 1, *contend*
certum est (mihi), *I am resolved*
certus, -a, -um, *sure, decided, resolved*; certior, *informed*
cerua, -ae, *hind, deer*
cessō, 1, *delay, am slow, hesitate*
cēterī, -ae, -a, *the other*(*s*), *the rest*
cēterum, *but, however*
circum-eō, -iī, -itum, -īre, *cheat*
citharistria, -ae, *lyre-player*
cīuis, -is, *c.*, *citizen*
clam, *advb. secretly, and prep.* (*with
acc.*), *unknown to*
clāmō, 1, *cry out*
clanculum, *secretly*
coepī, coeperam, *begin*
coeptō, 1, *attempt*
cōgitō, 1, *think, wonder*
cōgnātus, -a, -um, *akin*; *kinsman,
kinswoman*
cō-gnōscō, -gnōuī, -gnitum, 3,
recognize
cōgō, coēgī, coāctum, 3, *force,
compel*
coitiō, -ōnis, *f.*, *encounter*
colō, coluī, cultum, 3, *till, cultivate*
columen, -inis, *n.*, *pillar, prop*
cōmiter, *obligingly*
com-meminī, -memineram, *remember well*
com-memorō, 1, *relate, state*
com-mendō, 1, *entrust*

com-mereō, 2, *deserve*
comminiscor, commentus sum, 3,
devise
commoditās, -ātis, *f.*, *advantage*
commodum, *advb.*, *just now*
commodus, -a, -um, *fitting, profitable, suitable*
com-moror, 1, *stay*
com-moueō, -mōuī, -mōtum, 2,
move, stir, affect
commūnis, -e, *common, shared by
many*
com-mūtō, 1, *exchange*
cōmoedia, -ae, *comedy*
com-parō, 1, *arrange*
com-periō, -perī, -pertum, 4, *find
out, ascertain*
compes, -edis, *f.*, *fetter*
complūrēs, -ia, *several, very many*
com-pōnō, -posuī, -positum, 3,
settle, arrange
compositō, *advb.*, *by arrangement,
on purpose*
com-primō, -pressī, -pressum, 3,
hold (*one's breath*), *seduce*
con-cēdō, -cessī, -cessum, 3, *grant,
yield, step aside*
con-clūdō, -sī, -sum, 3, *shut up,
cage*
concordō, 1, *agree with*
con-crepō, -crepuī, -crepitum, 1,
creak
condiciō, -iōnis, *f.*, *match, marriage*
con-dōnō, 1, *make a present of, forgive* (*a debt*)
con-duplicō, 1, *double*
cōn-ficiō, -fēcī, -fectum, 3, *complete, achieve, do, get together,
spend*
cōnfīdēns, -ntis, *impudent, brazen*

cōn-fingō, -fīnxi, -fictum, 3, *make up, invent*

cōn-fiteor, -fessus sum, 2, *confess*

cōnflictō, 1, *struggle, fight*

cōnfūtō, 1, *stop from boiling over, repress*

con-gredior, -gressus sum, 3, *meet, come together*

congruō, congruī, 3, *agree*

con-iciō, -iēcī, -iectum, 3, *compare*; se conicere, *take oneself off in a hurry*

con-locō, 1, *match, settle in marriage*

con-loquor, -locūtus sum, 3, *talk with*

con-mōnstrō, 1, *point out*

cōnor, 1, *try*

con-percō, -persī, 3, *spare*

con-rādō, -rāsī, -rāsum, 3, *scrape together*

cōnscius, -a, -um, *sharing (guilty) knowledge*

cōn-sequor, -secūtus sum, 3, *overtake*

cōnsilium, -lī, *n.*, *advice, plan*

cōnsōlor, 1, *comfort, console*

cōnspectus, 4 *decl.*, *sight, view*

cōn-stituō, -stituī, -stitūtum, 3, *arrange, agree*

cōn-suēscō, -suēuī, -suētum, 3, *associate with, have intercourse with*

cōnsuētūdō, -inis, *f.*, *association, familiarity, relationship*

cōn-sulō, -suluī, -sultum, 3, *decide, devise, take thought for, advise*

con-temnō, -tempsī, -temptum, 3, *slight, despise*

contemplor, 1, *gaze (at)*

con-terō, -trīuī, -trītum, 3, *spend, waste*

con-tineō, -tinuī, -tentum, 2, *keep*

contingō, -tigī, 3, *befall (usu. of good fortune)*

continuō, *at once*

contortor, -ōris, *m.*, *perverter*

contrā, *advb. and prep.*, *on the other hand, against*

contrōuorsia, -ae, *dispute*

contumēlia, -ae, *insult*

contumēliōsē, *insultingly*

conuāsō, 1, *pack up*

con-ueniō, -uēnī, -uentum, 4, *agree (with), meet, interview*

cōpia, -ae, *means, abundance, access to a person*

cor, cordis, *n.*, *heart, mind*; cordi (*predic. dat.*), *dear*

cōram, *face to face*

cotīdiānus, -a, -um, *daily*

crās, *tomorrow*

crēber, -bra, -brum, *frequent*

crēdō, crēdidī, crēditum, 3, *believe, entrust*

crēscō, crēuī, 3, *grow*

crīmen, -inis, *n.*, *charge, reproach, accusation*

crux, crucis, *f.*, *cross, crucifixion* (368n.)

culpa, -ae, *blame, fault*

cum, *with*

cupiditās, -ātis, *f.*, *desire*

cupidus, -a, -um, *eager*

cupiō, cupere, 3 & 4, *am eager for*

cūra, -ae, *anxiety, trouble*

cūrō, 1, *see to*

currō, cucurrī, cursum, 3, *run*

cursus, 4 *decl.*, *run, running*

custōs, -ōdis, *m.*, *guardian*

damnō, 1, *find guilty, convict*

damnum, -ī, *n., loss*

dē, *from, out of, in accordance with, concerning*

dea, -ae, *goddess*

dēbeō, 2, *owe*

decem, *ten*

dēcidō, dēcidī, 3, *fall, drop down*

dē-cipiō, -cēpī, -ceptum, 3, *deceive*

dē-cumbō, -cubuī, 3, *lie down, take a place at the dinner table*

dē-fendō, -fendī, -fēnsum, 3, *ward off, defend*

dē-ferō, -tulī, -lātum, -ferre, 3, *carry, take*

dēfetīgō, 1, *wear out*

dē-fetīscor, -fessus sum, 3, *grow weary*

dē-ficiō, -fēcī, -fectum, 3, *fall short, fail*

dē-fit, (*defect.*) *is lacking*

dē-frūdō, 1, *cheat*

dē-fungor, -fūnctus sum, 3, *make an end, have done with*

dēgō, 3, *pass (time), live*

de-hortor, 1, *dissuade*

dē-līberō, 1, *weigh, think over*

dēlibūtus, -a, -um, *smeared over, covered with*

dēlīrō, 1, *am mad, rave*

dēmēnsum, -ī, *n., allowance*

dē-mīror, 1, *wonder (greatly) at*

dē-mōnstrō, 1, *show*

dē-narrō, 1, *tell in full*

dēnique, *at last, lastly, next*

dēnuō, *advb., anew, afresh*

dē-pecīscor, -pāctus sum, 3, *make a bargain*

dē-pingō, -pinxī, -pictum, 3, *portray*

dē-prāuō, 1, *make worse*

dē-putō, 1, *reckon*

dē-rīuō, 1, *bring down a stream, divert*

dēsertus, -a, -um, *deserted, abandoned*

dē-sinō, -siī, -situm, 3, *cease*

dē-sistō, -stitī, 3, *cease*

dē-spondeō, -spondī, -spōnsum, 2, *pledge, betroth*

dē-sum, -fuī, -esse, *am lacking, fail*

dē-terreō, 2, *frighten off*

dē-tineō, -tinuī, -tentum, 2, *keep*

dē-uerberō, 1, *whip hard*

dē-uītō, 1, *avoid, shun*

dē-uortor, -uorsus sum, 3, *turn aside, go in*

deus, -ī, *god*

dica, -ae, *lawsuit, action*

dicō, 1, *set apart*

dicō, dīxī, dictum, 3, *say, plead (a cause)*

dictiō, -ōnis, *f., saying, giving (of evidence)*

dictitō, 1, *keep on saying*

dictum, -ī, *n., word, saying*

diēs, diēī, *c. (m. in plural), day*

dignus, -a, -um, *fit, worthy*

dī-gredior, gressus sum, 3, *depart from*

dī-lapidō, *make ducks and drakes of*

dī-ligō, -lēxī, -lēctum, 3, *love*

dīlūcidē, *clearly, distinctly*

dīmidius, -a, -um, *half*

dīs, dītis, *rich*

dis-cēdō, -cessī, -cessum, 3, *go away, get off*

dīscō, didicī, 3, *learn*

di-scrībō, -scrīpsī, -scrīptum, 3, *pay out*

dis-simulō, 1, *conceal*

dis-soluō, -soluī, -solūtum, 3, *pay off*

dis-taedet (*impersonal*), *it wearies, is distasteful*

dis-trahō, -trāxī, -tractum, 3, *drag apart*

diū, *for a long time, long*

dīues, *see* dīs

diūtinus, -a, -um, *long*

dō, dedī, datum, dare, *give, grant, produce, say, deal with*

doleō, 2, *feel pain*; dolet, *it causes pain*

dominus, ī, *master, owner*

domus, -ī, f., (4 decl.), *house, home*; domi, *at home* (*locative*)

dōnec, *until*

dormiō, 4, *sleep*

dōs, dōtis, f., *dowry*

dōtāta, *dowered, a wife with a dowry*

dubitō, 1, *doubt*

dubius, -a, -um, *doubtful*

dūcō, dūxī, ductum, 3, *lead, escort, take in, marry*

ductō, 1, *take off, elope with*

dūdum, *for some time past, some time ago, just now*

-dum, *emphasizing enclitic*

dum, *while, until, provided that*

duo, -ae, -o, *two*

duplex, -icis, *double*

dūrus, -a, -um, *hard, difficult*

ē, ex, *out of, from, in accordance with*

ecastor, *interj. used by women, lit.* (*by*) *Castor! Heavens! Indeed! On my word!*, 574n.

ecce, *interj., see!*

eccerē, *interj., see there!*

eccum (ecce + hum), *here he is!*

ecferō, extulī, ēlātum, ecferre, 3, *carry out, publish*

ecquis, ecquid, *is there any?*

edāx, edācis, *gluttonous*

edepol, *interj. lit.* (*by*) *Pollux! meanings as* ecastor (*q.v.*), *but used by both sexes*

ē-doceō, -docuī, -doctum, 2, *explain, instruct*

ē-ducō, 1, *bring up*

ef-ficiō, -fēcī, -fectum, 3, *accomplish*

ef-futtiō, 4, *blab* (*out*)

egeō, 2, *am in poverty*

egestās, -ātis, f., *poverty, want*

ego, *I*

egomet, *emphatic form of* ego

ē-gredior, -gressus sum, 3, *go out, come out*

ēgregius, -a, -um, *exceptional, outstanding*

ehem, *interj., what!*, 52n.

eho, *interj., What? Here! Look here!* 259n.

ēi, *interj., alas*; ei mihi, *dear me!*

ē-iciō, -iēcī, -iectum, 3, *cast out, turn out*

ēloquentia, -ae, *eloquence*

ē-loquor, -locūtus sum, 3, *speak out*

ē-lūdō, -lūsī, -lūsum, 3, *cheat*

em, *interj., take it, there you are*

ē-mittō, -mīsī, -missum, 3, *send out*; emitto manu, *set free*

emō, ēmī, emptum, 3, *buy*

ē-morior, -mortuus sum, -mori and -morīrī, 3 & 4, *die at once*

ē-mungo, -mūnxī, -mūnctum, 3, clean out of, cheat of

ē-nicō, -nicuī, 1, kill, plague to death

enim, indeed, for (?)

enimuērō, indeed, to be sure

ē-nītor, -nīsus or -nīxus sum, 3, strive

ēnumquam, emphatic interrogative form of numquam

eō, advb., to that place, to that point, to such an extent

eō, iī, itum, īre, go

epistula, -ae, letter

equidem, strengthened form of quidem

era, ae, lady of the house, mistress

ergō, therefore, then, that is why

erīlis, -e, of a master or mistress

ē-ripiō, -ripuī, -reptum, 3, rescue

errō, 1, make a mistake

ē-rumpō, -rūpī, -ruptum, 3, break out, end in

erus, ī, master (of the house)

est ut, it is a fact that

et, and

etiam, also, even, still, as well, yes

etsī, although

eu, interj., bravo!

ē-uādō, -uāsī, -uāsum, 3, go to a point

ē-ueniō, -uēnī, -uentum, 4, happen

ē-uocō, 1, summon, call forth

ē-uoluō, -uoluī, -uolūtum, 3, extricate

ex, see ē

exaduorsum, advb., opposite

ex-animō, 1, deprive of life or spirit, alarm

ex-cēdō, -cessī, -cessum, 3, go out, depart

ex-cerpō, -cerpsī, -cerptum, 3, cut out, omit

ex-clāmō, 1, cry out

ex-clūdō, -clūsī, -clūsum, 3, knock out

ex-cruciō, 1, torture (severely)

ex-cutiō, -cussī, -cussum, 3, shake out

ex-edō, -ēdī, -essum, 3, eat up

exemplum, ī, n., pattern, model, form of punishment

ex-eō, -iī, -itum, -īre, go out, come out

exīstumō, 1, reckon, think

exitium, -tī, n., destruction, disaster

ex-onerō, 1, unburden

ex-ōrō, 1, win by entreaty

ex-pediō, 4, disentangle, explain

expedit, it is profitable

ex-perior, -pertus sum, 4, try

ex-petō, -petīuī, -petītum, 3, try hard to get, seek (after)

expiscor, 1, try to fish out

ex-plānō, 1, make clear, explain

ex-plōrō, 1, think out, investigate

exsequiae, -ārum, funeral (service)

exsilium, -lī, n., exile

ex-spectō, 1, look for, wait for, await

ex-stillō, 1, trickle away, dissolve

ex-timēscō, -timuī, 3, greatly dread

exs-tinguō, -tīnxī, -tīnctum, 3, quench

extortor, -ōris, m., robber, 'fraudulent converter'

extrā, prep. except, outside

ex-trahō, -trāxī, -tractum, 3, rescue

extrārius, -a, -um, stranger, outsider

ex-trūdō, -trūsī, -trūsum, 3, *thrust out, turn out*

fābula, -ae, *play, (idle) story*
fābulor, 1, *talk*
facessō, 3, *go away*
faciēs, *f.*, *face, beauty*
facilis, -e, *easy*
facinus, -oris, *n.*, *deed, fact*
faciō, fēcī, factum, 3, *make, do compose, give*; factum, *yes, quite so*
fallācia, -ae, *trickery*
fallō, fefellī, falsum, 3, *deceive*; me fallit, *I am mistaken*
falsus, -a, -um, *untrue*
fāma, -ae, *reputation, report*
famēs, -is, *f.*, *hunger, starvation*
familia, -ae, *f.*, *household, family*
familiāris, -e, *of the household or family, closely related*
familiāritās, -ātis, *f.*, *intimacy*
fateor, fassus sum, 2, *admit*
faxim, *(archaic)* subjunctive of faciō
faxō, *(archaic)* future of faciō
fēneror, 1, *lend at interest*; feneratus, *lent at interest*
fēnus, -oris, *n.*, *interest*
ferē, *mostly*
feriō (percussī, percussum), 4, *hit*
fermē, *almost, nearly*
ferō, tulī, lātum, ferre, 3, *bear, bring, get*
fidēlis, -e, *faithful, trustworthy*
fidēs, -ēī and -ē, *f.*, *trust(worthiness), confidence, honour, promise*
fidicina, -ae, *lyre-player*
fīlia, -ae, *daughter*
fīlius, -lī, *son*
fīnis, -is, *m.*, *end*

fīō, factus sum, fierī, *become*; *used as passive of* facio
flāgitium, -tī, *n.*, *misdeed, wickedness*
fleō, flēvi, flētum, 2, *weep*
forās, *advb.* (*to the*), *outside, out*
forīs, *advb.* (*at rest*) *outside*
foris, -is, *f.*, *door*
forma, -ae, *shape, beauty*
fors, fortis, *f.*, *chance*; Fors, *Chance*; Fors Fortuna, *Luck*
fors sit an, *it may be that, perhaps*
fortasse, *perhaps*
forte, *advb. by chance*
fortis, -e, *strong, stalwart*
fortitūdō, -inis, *f.*, *bravery, hardihood*
fortūna, -ae, *luck, fortune; see also* Fors
fortūnātus, -a, -um, *lucky*
forum, -ī, *n.*, *market, market-place*
frāter, -tris, *brother, sts., first cousin*
frētus, -a, -um, *relying on* + *abl.*
frigeō, 2, *am cold*
frūctus, -ī (4 decl.), *profit, return*
fruor, frūctus sum, 3, *enjoy*
frūstrā, *in vain, to no purpose*
fuga, -ae, *flight*
fugiō, fūgī, fugitum, 3, *flee, run away*
fugitāns (*nom. only in Terence*), *inclined to avoid*
fugitīuos, -ī, *(a) runaway*
fugitō, 1, *avoid, flee from*
fungor, fūnctus sum, 3, *perform*
fūnus, -eris, *n.*, *funeral*
furtum, -ī, *n.*, *theft*

gallīna, -ae, *hen*
garriō, 4, *talk nonsense*

gaudeō, gāuīsus sum, 2, *am glad, rejoice*

gaudium, -dī, *n., joy*

genius, -ī, 44n., '*inner man*'

gēns, gentis, *f., tribe, people;* minime gentium, *never in this world*

genus, -eris, *n., birth, kin, kinship*

gerō, gessī, gestum, 3, *carry on, transact*

gestiō, 4, *am eager*

gestus, (-ūs), *bearing, attitude*

gladiātōrius, *suiting a gladiator, desperate*

gnātus, ī, *son*

gradus, (-ūs), *step*

Graecē, *in Greek*, 26n.

grandis, -e, *big;* grandior, *advanced in years*

grātia, -ae, *favour, gratitude;* gratiae (*pl.*), *thanks*

grātiīs, *without cost*

grauis, -e, *heavy, serious*

grex, gregis, *m., company (of actors)*

gynaeceum, -ī, *n., women's quarters*

habeō, 2, *have, feel, consider, wear, marry*

habitō, 1, *dwell, live*

haereō, haesi, 2, *stick, am in a difficulty*

haesitō, 1, *stick*

hahahae, *interj. (sardonic laughter), ha! ha!*, 411n.

hariolor, 1, *am a soothsayer, have second sight*, 492n.

hariolus, -ī, *soothsayer, diviner*

haruspex, -icis, *soothsayer, diviner*

hau, haud, *not*

heia, *interj., Come! Come now!*, 508n.

hem, *interj., What? What's that?*, 52n.

hercle, *interj., lit., (by) Hercules! Heavens! Indeed! (used mostly by men)*, 574n.

herī, *yesterday*

heu, *alas*

heus, *interj., drawing attention, Ho there! Look here! Look (out)!*, 398n.

hic, haec, hoc, *this, the former, the next*

hīc, *here, hereupon*

hinc, *from here, hence*

hoc, *advb., to this place, hither (= class.* huc)

hodiē, *today; often merely an emphasizing particle*, 377n.

homō, hominis, *man, fellow, human being*

honestē, *creditably, honourably*

honōs, -ōris, *m., good name*

hōra, -ae, *hour*

horridus, -a, -um, *rough, unkempt*

hospes, -itis, *c., stranger, friend (from) abroad*

hūc, *to this place, hither*

hūī, *interj., expressing disgust or disapproval, Phew!*, 302n.

huius modī, *of this kind*

iam, *by now, at once, soon, already, any longer*

iamdūdum, *for some time past*

ibi, *there, thereupon*

īdem, eadem, idem, *the same*

idōneus, -a, -um, *fit, suitable*

igitur, *therefore*

īgnōbilis, -e, *low-born*

īgnōrō, 1, *am ignorant of, ignore, disown*

īgnōscō, īgnōuī, īgnōtum, 3, *forgive, pardon*

īgnōtus, -a, -um, *unknown*

īlicet, *it's all up*

īlicō, *directly, immediately*

ille, illa, illud, *that, the other, the former*

illī *and* illīc, *there, in that matter*

illic (= ille + ce)

illūc, *to that place, thither*

immō, *on the contrary, no (indeed)*

im-mūtō, 1, *change*

imperium, -rī, *n., (supreme) command*

imperō, 1, *(give the) order*

im-petrō, 1, *gain by asking*

in, *in, into, for*

inaudīuī, *(only in perfect) have heard mention of*

in-cendō, -dī, -sum, 3, *set on fire, inflame*

in-ceptō, 1, *start, undertake*

incertus, -a, -um, *doubtful*

in-cidō, -cidī, 3, *fall into*

in-cipiō, -cēpī, -ceptum, 3, *undertake*

incōgitāns, -antis, *thoughtless*

incommodum, -ī, *n., disadvantage, unpleasantness*

incrēdibilis, -e, *incredible*

in-cūsō, 1, *accuse*

inde, *thence, from that place or person*

indicō, 1, *disclose*

indictus, -a, -um, *unsaid*

indīgnus, -a, -um, *unworthy, monstrous*

indīligenter, *carelessly*

indōtāta, *fem. adj., undowered, without a dowry*

in-eō, -iī, -itum, -īre, *enter, go into*

ineptiae, -ārum, *fooleries, absurdities*

ineptiō, 4, *(pres. only) talk foolishly*

ineptus, a, -um, *foolish*

inexōrābilis, -e, *stubborn, deaf to entreaty*

īnfectus, -a, -um, *undone*

īnfēlīx, -īcis, *unlucky*

īnferus, -a, -um, *of the lower world*

īnfirmus, -a, -um, *unstable, temporary*

īnfortūnium, -nī, *n., misfortune*

ingenium, -nī, *n., nature, character, bent*

ingenuos, -a, -om, *free-born, gentlemanly*

in-gerō, -gessī, -gestum, 3, *pile on*

ingrātiīs, *advb., against one's will*

inhūmānus, -a, -um, *inhuman*

in-iciō, -iēcī, -iectum, 3, *throw into, put into*

inimīcitiae, -ārum, *enmity*

inīquos, -a, -om, *unfair*

initiō, 1, *initiate*

iniūria, -ae, *wrong, assault, action for assault*

iniussū, *without orders*

inlīberāliter, *in an ungentlemanly way*

in-lūdō, -lūsī, -lūsum, 3, *make fun of*

inmeritō, *undeservedly*

immortālis, -e, *immortal*

in-mūtō, 1, *change*

inopia, -ae, *lack of means*

inops, inopis, *without means*

inparātus, -a, -um, *unready, unprepared*

in-pediō, 4, *entangle*

in-pellō, -pulī, -pulsum, 3, *drive on, drive into*

in-pendeō, -pendī, -pēnsum, 2, *overhang, impend*

in-pingō, -pēgī, -pāctum, 3, *hurl against*

inpluuium, -uī, *n., impluvium, central well*

in-pōnō, -posuī, -positum, 3, *put upon*

improuīsus, -a, -um, *unforeseen*; dē inprouīso, *unexpectedly*

inprūdēns, -dentis, *careless, unwitting(ly)*

inpudēns, -tis, *shameless*

inpūrātus, -a, -um, *foul, unclean*

inpūrus, -a, -um, *foul*

inquam, inquit (*defective*), *I say, he says*

in-rīdeō, -rīsī, -rīsum, 2, *laugh at*

inritus, -a, -um, *unratified, retracted*

īn-sāniō, 4, *am mad, behave like a mad man*

īnsānus, -a, -um, *mad*

īnsciens, -ntis, *ignorant, foolish*

īnscītia, -ae, *foolishness, folly*

īnsidiae, -ārum, *ambush*

in-simulō, 1, *accuse*

īn-sistō, -stitī, 3, *set about, begin*

īnstīgo, 1, *goad on*

īn-stituō, -uī, -ūtum, 3, *set in place, set in order*

īn-stō, -stitī, *am pressing*

īn-struō, struxī, -structum, 3, *draw up*

īn-sum, *am in*

integer, -gra, -grum, *undamaged*; dē integrō, *afresh*; in integrum, *to the original position*

intel-legō, -lēxī, -lēctum, 3, *understand*

inter-cēdō, -cessī, -cessum, 3, *pass between, exist between*

inter-dīcō, -dīxī, -dictum, 3, *forbid*

intereā, *meantime, after a time*

in-terō, -trīuī, -trītum, 3, *mix, pound*

inter-ueniō, -uēnī, -uentum, 4, *come in upon*

intrō, *to the inside, indoors* (*motion*)

intrō-dūcō, -dūxī, -ductum, 3, *introduce*

intus, *inside, indoors* (*without motion*)

in-ueniō, -uēnī, -uentum, 4, *light upon, find*

in-uestīgō, 1, *track down*

inuidia, -ae, *envy, jealousy*

inuītus, -a, -um, *unwilling*

ioculāris, -e, *laughable*

ipse *and* ipsus, -a, -um, *-self*

īrācundia, -ae, *wrath*

īrāscor, īrātus sum, 3, *become angry*

irrītō, 1, *provoke*

is, ea, id, *that; also he, she, it*

iste, ista, istud, *that* (*of yours*)

istic, istaec, istuc, (= iste + ce), *emphatic form of iste, etc.*

istōrsum, *in that direction*

ita, *so, thus, as follows, on this condition, yes*

item, *also*

iter, itineris, *n., way, journey*

iterum, *again, a second time*

itidem, *in the same way, similarly*

itiō, -ōnis, *f., going, visit*

iubeō, iūssī, iūssum, 2, *order, bid, request*

iūdex, -icis, *c.* (*usu. m.*), *judge*
iūdicium, -cī, *n.*, *judgement*
iūrgium, -gī, *n.*, *quarrel*
iūs, iūris, *n.*, *right, justice, law, law-court*
iūstus, -a, -um, *just, fair, right*

labor, -ōris, *m.*, *work, toil*
lacessō, -ī, -ītum, 3, *provoke*
lacruma, -ae, *tear*
lacrumō, 1, *weep*
laedō, -sī, -sum, 3, (*try to*) *hurt*
laetus, -a, -um, *glad, merry*
lāmentor, 1, *lament, bewail*
later, -eris, *m.*, *brick*
Latīnē, *in Latin*, 26n.
laudō, 1, *praise*; laudō, *splendid! bravo!*
lauō, lāuī, lautum, 1, *wash, bathe*
legō, lēgī, lēctum, 3, *pick*
lēnis, -e, *mild, easy-going*
lēnō, -ōnis, *m.*, *slave-dealer, pander*
lepidus, -a, -um, *charming, delightful*
leuis, -e, *light, trifling*
lēx, lēgis, *f.*, *law, rule, condition*
līber, -era, -erum, *free*
līberālis, -e, *of a gentleman or gentlewoman, well-bred, decent*
libet, *see* lubet
licet, licitum est *and* licuit, 2, *it is permitted, it is lawful*
lītes, -ium, *f.*, *law-suit, row*
locō, 1, *settle in marriage*
locus, -ī, *place, state, condition, stage* (32), *time*
logī, *acc. pl.*, logōs, *m.*, (λόγοι) *empty words*
longus, -a, -um, *long*
loquor, locūtus sum, 3, *speak*
lubēns, -ntis, *glad*

lubet (libet), lubuit (libuit), lubitum est, 2, *it pleases*
lubīdō, -inis, *f.*, *inclination*
lucrum, -ī, *n.*, *gain*
lūdificor, 1, *make sport of*
lūdō, -sī, -sum, 3, *play, mock, fool*
lūdus, -ī, *game, music-school, entertainment*
lupus, -ī, *wolf*
lutum, -ī, *n.*, *mud*

mactō, 1, *afflict, ruin*
magis *and* mage, *advb.*, *more*
magister, -trī, *m.*, *master, person in charge*
magistrātus (4 *decl.*), *magistrate, official*
magnificentia, -ae, *boasting, bragging*
māgnus, -a, -um, *great*
māior, -ōris (*gen.*), *elder*
male, *badly*
maledīcere, *abuse*
maledictum, -ī, *n.*, *abuse*
male-faciō, -fēcī, -factum, 3, *do harm, do wrong*
maleficium, -cī, *n.*, *wrong-doing, 'bad turn'*
malitia, -ae, *spite, ill-will*
mālō, māluī, mālle, *irreg.*, *prefer*
malum, -ī, *n.*, *misfortune, punishment, flogging*; malum, *as interjection*, 723n., *the devil!*; malam rem, 930n.
malus, -a, -um, *bad*
mandō, 1, *entrust*
māne, *advb.*, *in the morning*
maneō, mānsī, mānsum, 2, *remain, wait* (*for*)
mānsiō, -ōnis, *f.*, *stay*

manus (4 decl.), f., hand
māter, -tris, mother
mātūrō, 1, hurry
māxumē, advb., most of all, to the
   greatest extent, certainly; quom
   māxumē, especially
medeor, 2, heal
meditor, 1, rehearse, practise
medius, -a, -um, middle; in mediō,
   open to all; ē mediō abīre,
   depart from our midst, die
meminī, meminisse, remember
memoria, -ae, memory
memoriter, advb., word for word
mēns, mentis, f., mind
mēnsis, -is, m., month
mercātus, acc., mercātum, market
mercēs, -ēdis, f., pay, reward
mereor, 2, deserve
meretrīx, -īcis, f., courtesan, harlot
meritō, deservedly
meritum, -ī, n., desert
merus, -a, -um, unmixed, pure
-met, see ego, nos
metuō, -uī, 3, fear
metus, -ūs and -uis, m., fear
meus, -a, -um, my, mine
mīles, -itis, soldier
mīliēns, a thousand times
mīluos, -ī, m., kite, bird of prey
mina, -ae, (Gk. μνᾶ) mina; for its
   value, see 410n., 557n.
minimē, advb., least of all, not at all
minitor, 1, threaten
minuō, -uī, -ūtum, 3, lessen,
   diminish
minus, advb. less; sts. almost = not
mīrificus, -a, -um, astonishing
mīror, 1, wonder (at)
mīrus, -a, -um, wonderful

miser, -era, -erum, wretched
miserandus, -a, -um, pitiable
miseret, miseritum est, 2, it causes
   pity
misericordia, -ae, pity, compassion
mittō, mīsī, missum, 3, send, dismiss, drop, give, pass over; missum faciō, dismiss
modestē, with moderation
modo, advb., just now, only, just,
   provided that; modo non,
   almost
modus, -ī, manner
molestus, -a, -um, troublesome
molliō, 4, soften, appease
molō, 3, grind
moneō, 2, advise
monitor, -ōris, m., instructor
mōns, montis, m., mountain
mōnstrum, -ī, n., portent, prodigy
morbus, -ī, illness, disease
morior, mortuos sum, 3, die
moror, 1, delay
mors, mortis, f., death
mōs, mōris, m., custom, way;
   mōrēs, morals
moueō, mōuī, mōtum, 2, move
mox, later on, soon; quam mox,
   how soon, how long it will be
   before
mulier, -eris, woman
muliercula, -ae, (wretched) woman
multimodīs, advb., very (much)
multō, advb., by far
multus, -a, -um, much, many
mūnus, -eris, n., gift
mūsicus, adj., see ars
mūtō, 1, change, break
mūtuos, -a, -om, mutual

nam, *enclitic and proclitic particle,*
    indeed
nam, *for*
namque, *for indeed*
nancīscor, nactus sum, 3, *light on,*
    find
narrō, 1, *tell, relate*
nāscor, nātus sum, 3, *am born*
nātālis, -e, *of birth*
nauta, -ae, *m., sailor*
-ne, *interrog. enclitic particle, often*
    shortened to -n
nē, *advb., not; conj., lest*
necesse *and* necessum, *neut. adj.,*
    inevitable, necessary
neglegentia, -ae, *negligence*
neglegō, -ēxi, -ēctum, 3, *neglect*
negō, 1, *deny, say no*
negōtium, -tī, *n., business, affair*
nēmō, *acc.* nēminem (*gen.,* nullius,
    abl., nullō), *no one, no man, no*
    (*adj.*)
nempe, *advb., of course, I presume,*
    you mean
neque, *neither, nor, and not*
nequeō, nequīre, *irreg., am unable*
neruos, -ī, *fetter, prison*
nesciō, 4, *do not know*
nescioquī, -quae, -quod, *some or*
    other
nēue, neu, *neither, nor* (*in final*
    clauses and prohibitions)
nex, necis, *f., violent death*
nī, *see* nisi; quidnī, *why not? of*
    course
nihil, nīl, *gen.* nihilī, *nothing, no use*
nimium, *too much*
nisi, nī, *if not, unless; only, but,*
    475n.
nōlō, nōluī, nōlle, *irreg., am un-*

willing; noli, nolite + *inf.* =
    do not
nōmen, -inis, *n., name*
nōminō, 1, *name*
nōn, *not*
nōndum, *not yet*
nōnne, *interrog., particle, surely* . . .?
nōsmet, *emphatic form of* nos, *we, us*
noster, -tra, -trum, *our, ours*
nostrapte, *emphatic form of* nostra
nōtus, -a, -um, *known*
nōuī, nōueram *and* nōram, nōuisse,
    know
nouos, -a, -om, *new*
noxa, -ae, *fault, blame*
nūbō, nūpsi, nūptum, 3, *am mar-*
    ried (*of the woman*)
nūdus, -a, -um, *bare, naked*
nūllus, -a, -um, *no, none;* nullus
    sum, *I'm done for*
num, *interrog., particle, surely not*
    . . .?
numerus, -ī, *number, amount*
nummus, -ī, *small coin, drachma* (?)
numquam, *never*
nunc, *now, as it is*
nūntiō, 1, *announce, bring news of*
nūntius, -tī, *messenger, message*
nūptiae, -ārum, *marriage*
nusquam, *nowhere*
nūtrīx, -īcis, *f., nurse*

ob, *prep., on account of, for,*
    meeting
ob-eō, -iī, -itum, -īre, *die*
ob-iciō, -iēcī, -iectum, 3, *throw in*
    the way
ob-iūrgō, 1, *scold, rebuke*
ob-lectō, 1, *charm, delight*
ob-secrō, 1, *entreat, pray*

ob-sequor, -secūtus sum, 3, *comply with, gratify*

ob-stipēscō, -stipuī, 3, *become dumb*

ob-stupefaciō, -fēcī, -factum, 3, *strike dumb*

obuiam, *advb.*, *to meet*

occāsiō, -ōnis, *f.*, *opportunity*

oc-cidō, -cidī, 3, *die*

oc-cīdō, -cīdī, -cīsum, 3, *kill*

oc-cipiō, -cēpī, -ceptum, 3, *begin*

occupō, 1, *preoccupy*

ōcius, *compar. advb.*, *quickly*

oculus, -ī, *eye*

odiōsus, -a, -um, *boring, irksome, troublesome*

odium, -dī, *n.*, *dislike, annoyance*

of-fendō, -fendī, -fēnsum, 3, *find, come upon*

officium, -cī, *n.*, *duty*

og-ganniō, 4, *growl at, snarl*

ōh, *interj.*, *Oh!*, 51n.

ohe, *interj.*, *Hold hard!*, 418n.

oiei, *interj.* (*trisyllabic*), *Oh no!*, 663n.

ōlim, *at that time, at the time, some time ago*

o-mittō, -mīsī, -missum, 3, *let go*

omnis, -e, *all, every, every kind of*

onerō, 1, *load, burden*

onus, -eris, *n.*, *load, burden*

opem (*acc.*), opis, *f.*, *help*

opera, -ae, *work, effort, aid, attention*

operiō, -ruī, -rtum, 4, *shut*

opēs, -um, *f.*, *means*

opīnor, 1, *think, take it that*

opitulor, 1, *give help*

oportet, oportuit, *it befits*

op-perior, -pertus sum, 4, *wait for*

oppidō, *advb.*, *just so, very*

op-pōnō, -posuī, -positum, 3, *pledge, mortgage*

opportūnē, *opportunely, at the right moment*

op-primō, -pressī, -pressum, 3, *gag, stop, shut*

op-tingō, -tigī, 3, *befall*

optō, 1, *desire, long for*

optumē, *excellently*

op-tundō, 3, *deafen*

opus, -eris, *n.*, *need; work, farm-work*

ōrātiō, -ōnis, *f.*, *speech, style*

orbus, -a, -um, *fatherless, orphan-(-ed)*

ordō, -inis, *m.*, *order*; ordine, *from beginning to end*

ornātus, -a, -um, *well-supplied*

ōrō, 1, *pray, plead* (*a cause*)

ōs, ōris, *n.*, *mouth, face, voice*

ostendō, -dī, -tum, 3, *show*

ostium, -tī, *n.*, *door*

ōtiōsus, -a, -um, *unoccupied, free*

ōtium, -tī, *n.*, *leisure, rest*

pactum, -tī, *n.*, *way, manner*

paedagōgus, -ī, *attendant* (*slave in charge of children*)

paene, *almost*

paenitet, *it causes regret, dissatis-faction*

palaestra, -ae, *wrestling-school, gym-nasium*

palam, *openly*

pallium, -lī, *n.*, *cloak*

palma, -ae, *palm, prize*

pār, paris, *equal, right, reasonable*

parasītus, -ī, *parasite, sponger, hanger-on*

parcō, pepercī *and* parsī, 3, *spare,
am sparing*

parēns, -ntis, *c., parent*

pariō, peperī, partum, 3, *bear (a
child), get;* parta, *savings*

pariter, *equally*

parō, *make ready, try*

pars, partis, *f., part, portion;* partes,
role, part in a play

parum, *too little, very little*

parumper, *for a short time*

paruos, -a, -om, *little, small*

pāscō, pāuī, 3, *feed*

passus, *perf. participle of* pandere, *to
spread*

patefīt, *used as passive of* patefacio,
to make open, reveal

pater, -tris, *father*

paternus, -a, -um, *of a father,
fatherly*

patior, passus sum, patī, 3, *suffer,
put up with, endure*

patrōcinor, 1, *champion, defend*

patrōnus, -ī, *champion*

patruos, -ī, *uncle, father's brother*

paucī, -ae, -a, *few*

paueō, pāuī, 2, *quake with fear*

paullulum, -ī, *n., a very little*

paullum, *advb.,* and paullum, -i,
noun, a little

pauper, *not well-off, poor*

paupertās, -ātis, *f., (comparative)
poverty*

pauxillulum, -ī, *n., a very, very
little*

peccātum, -ī, *n., fault, slip*

peccō, 1, *commit an offence, am at
fault*

pecūnia, -ae, *money*

pedetemptim, *slowly, step by step*

pel-liciō, -lexī, -lectum, 3, *allure,
entice*

Penātēs, -ium, *m., household gods*

pendeo, 2, *hang*

per, *through, by means of, because of,
in, in the name of*

percārus, -a, -um, *very dear*

per-contor, 1, *question (thoroughly)*

perditē, *desperately, to distraction*

per-dō, -didī, -ditum, 3, *ruin,
destroy, forget; its passive is* per-
eō, *die, am ruined*

per-ficiō, -fēcī, -fectum, 3, *complete, accomplish*

pergō, perrexī, perrectum, 3, *go,
go on, persist in*

perīclum, -ī, *n., peril, danger, trial*

perinde, *advb., in like manner*

perlīberālis, -e, *very decent (lady-
like)*

per-mittō, -mīsī, -missum, 3,
entrust

perperam, *falsely, wrongly*

per-sequor, -secūtus sum, 3, *follow
after*

per-spiciō, -spexī, -spectum, 3, *see
clearly, observe closely*

per-suādeō, -suāsī, suāsum, 2, *persuade*

per-timēscō, -timuī, 3, *fear greatly*

per-ueniō, -uēnī, -uentum, 4,
arrive

pēs, pedis, *m., foot*

pessum, *advb., to ruin*

petō, peti(u)ī, petītum, 3, *seek,
look for, try to get, ask*

phalerātus, -a, -um, *with fine
trappings*

piget, *it sickens, causes regret*

pignus, -oris, *n., pledge*

pistrīnum, -ī, *n.*, *mill*

plācābilis, -e, *making for peace*

placeō, 2, *please*; placet, *good!*

placidē, *calmly, quietly, gently*

plācō, 1, *appease*

plāga, -ae, *stripe, blow*

plānē, *clearly, plainly*

platea, -ae, *street*

plaudō, 3, *clap hands*

plector, 3, *am beaten, punished*

plērīque, -aeque, -aque, *very many, most*

plērumque, *mostly*

plōrō, 1, *wail, lament*

plūrimum, *mostly*

plūs, *pron. and advb.*, *more*

poēta, -ae, *m.*, *poet*

pol, *interj.*, *lit.* (*by*) *Pollux!*, 574n.

polliceor, 2, *promise*

pollicitātiō, -ōnis, *f.*, *promise*

pollicitor, 1, *promise*

pōne, *advb.*, *back*

pōnō, posuī, positum, 3, *place, suppose*

populāris, -is, *m.*, *fellow country-man or townsman*, 35n.

populus, -ī, *people*

porrō, *advb.*, *further, still, thereupon, henceforth*

portitor, -ōris, *m.*, *custom-house official*

portō, 1, *bring, carry*

portus (4 *decl.*), *harbour*

possum, potuī, posse, *am able, can*; potest (*impers.*), *it is possible*

post, *advb.*, *after*(*wards*)

post-habeō, 2, *value less, postpone*

posthāc, *after this time*

postillā, *after that time*

postquam, *conj.*, *after, because*

postrēmō, *finally, last*

postrēmus, -a, -um, *last*

postrīdiē, *on the next day*

postulō, 1, *demand*

potestās, -ātis, *f.*, *legal authority, permission, means, opportunity*

potior, potītus sum, potīrī, 3 & 4, *get possession of, meet with*

potior, *comp. adj.*, *preferable*

potis, *also* pote, *indecl. adj.*, *able, possible*

potissimum, *soonest, preferably*

potius, *preferably* (*of two*)

pōtō, 1, *drink, tope, tipple*

prae, *ahead, forward*

prae-beō, 2, *supply, afford, play*

praeceps, -ipitis, *headlong*

praedicō, 1, *assert*

prae-dīcō, -dīxī, -dictum, 3, *foretell*

praedium, -dī, *n.*, *farm, estate*

praemium, -mī, *n.*, *prize, reward*

praesēns, -ntis, *present, resolute*; in praesentia, *for the present*

praesertim, *especially*

prae-stituō, -uī, -ūtum, 3, *fix beforehand*

prae-stō, -stitī, 1, *am better, excel*

praestō, *advb.*, *at hand, present, ready*

praeter, *past, beyond, except*

praftereā, *besides*

praeter-eō, -iī, -itum, -īre, *go by, pass*

praeterhāc, *besides*

prāuos, -a, -om, *bad*

precātor, -ōris, *m.*, *intercessor*

precem (*acc.*), precis, *f.*, *prayer*

precor, 1, *pray, entreat*

prendō, -dī, -sum, 3, *seize, catch hold of*

prīdem, *advb.*, *some time since*

prīmārius, -a, -um, *of the highest rank or character*

prīmo, *at first*

prīmum, *advb.*, *first, in the first place*

prīmus, -a, -um, *first, leading*

principium, -pī, *n.*, *beginning*

prior, prius, *earlier, first (of two), preferred*

prīuō, 1, *deprive, rob of*

priusquam, *conj.*, *before*

prō, *prep.*, *on behalf of, in place of, in accordance with*

prō, *exclamatory interjection*, 351n.

probē, *well, honestly, excellently*

probrum, -ī, *disgrace*

probus, -a, -um, *good, honest, excellent*

prō-cūrō, 1, *take care of, manage*

prōd-eō, -iī, -itum, īre, *come or go forward, come or go out*

prō-ferō, -tulī, -lātum, -ferre, 3, *bring out*

proficīscor, profectus sum, 3, *start, set out*

prōgeniēs (5 *decl.*), *f.*, *family*

prōgnātus, -a, -um, *born*

pro-hibeō, 2, *prevent, forbid*

proinde, *advb.*, *just*

prōlogus, -i, (Gk. πρόλογος) *prologue*

prō-loquor, -locūtus sum, 3, *speak out*

prō-mereor, 2, *deserve*

prō-mittō, -mīsī, -missum, 3, *promise*

propemodum, *nearly*

properō, 1, *hasten*

propior, -ius, *nearer*

propitius, -a, -um, *favourable*

proprius, -a, -um, *of one's own*

propter, *because of*

prōrsum, *absolutely*

prosperē, *successfully*

prō-spiciō, -spexī, -spectum, 3, *see (ahead), watch out*

prōtēlō, 1, *rout*, 213n.

protinam, *at once, forthwith*

prō-uideō, -uīdī, -uīsum, 2, *foresee, provide for*

prōuincia, -ae, *sphere of duty, office*

proxumus, -a, -um, *nearest, next, next of kin*

-pte, *enclitic attached to noster, etc.*

pūblicitus, *advb.*, *at the state's expense*

pūblicus, -a, -um, *public, common*

pudet, puduit, 2, *it causes shame*

pudor, -ōris, *m.*, *shame, modesty*

puellula, -ae, *young girl*

puer, -erī, *boy, slave*

puerilis, -e, *childish*

pūgnus, -ī, *fist*

pulcher, -chra, -chrum, *fine, beautiful*

pulchrē, *well, excellently, finely*

pulchritūdō, -inis, *f.*, *beauty*

punctum, -ī, *n.*, *moment*

pūrgō, 1, *clear, justify (oneself)*

putō, 1, *think, consider*

quaerō, quaesīuī, quaesītum, 3, *look for, ask for, inquire about*

quaesō, 3, *pray, please!*

quālis, -e, *of what sort, of which sort*

quam, *how, how much, than*; quam prīmum, *as soon as possible, at once*

quandō, *when? since*

quandoquidem, *since, because*

quantum potest, *as soon as possible*

quantus, -a, -um, *how big? how much? as big as, as much as*

quantus quantus, *however great*

quasi, *as if, as it were*

queō, quīuī (*irreg., and defect.*), *am able*

quī, quae, quod, *rel. pron. and interrog. adj., who, which*

quī, *indecl. abl., how, in what way,* 123n.

quia, *because*

quid, *why?*

quīdam, quaedam, quoddam, *a (certain)*

quidem, *indeed, for sure*

quiēscō, -ēuī, -ētum, 3, *become quiet*

quiētus, -a, -um, *calm, quiet*

quīn, *who not, which not, why not*

quindecim, *fifteen*

quinque, *five*

quippe, *for*

quis, quae, quid, *who? what?*

quisquam, quicquam, *any, anyone; usu in neg. sentences*

quisque, quaeque, *each*

quisquis, quicquid *and* quidquid, *whoever*

quīuīs, quaeuīs quid- *or* quod -uīs, *any you like*

quō, *interrog. and rel. advb., to which place, to which point*

quō, *conj.* + *comp., in order that*

quoad, *when, until, when?*

quod (*esp. with si*), *but*

quoi, quoius, *dat. and gen. sing. of the relative, for classical* cui, cuius

quom, *when, although, whereas*

quoque, *also*

quōquō, *to whatever place*

quōr, *why?*

quot, *how many? as many as*

rap-iō, -uī, -tum, 3, *seize, carry off*

ratiō, -ōnis, *f., reckoning, account*

ratiuncula, -ae, *small account*

ratus, -a, -um, *ratified*

re-cipiō, -cēpī, -ceptum, 3, *take back, undertake;* se recipere, *return*

rēcta, sc. uiā, *directly, straight*

rēctē, *rightly, all right*

rēctus, -a, -um, *straight*

red-dō, -didī, -ditum, 3, *pay back, restore, grant, answer, bring in*

red-dūcō, -dūxī, -ductum, 3, *lead back*

red-eō, -iī, -itum, īre, *go back, come back, return, come to a state, come to a point*

red-igō, -ēgī, -āctum, 3, *bring back, restore, reduce*

re-fellō, -fellī, 3, *refute*

re-ferō, rettulī, rellātum, referre, 3, *repay, refer*

rēfert, *it concerns*

rēgnō, 1, *am king*

re-iciō, -iēcī, -iectum, 3, *throw (back), reject, refuse*

relicuos, -a, -om, *remaining, left over*

re-linquō, -līquī, -lictum, 3, *leave*

remedium, -dī, *n., cure, remedy*

re-mittō, -mīsī, -missum, 3, *send back*

re-nūntio, 1, *send (back) word of*

reor, ratus sum, 2, *think, reckon*

re-periō, repperī, repertum, 3, *find (out)*

re-petō, -peti(u)ī, -petītum, 3, *(try to) recover*

re-prendō, -dī, -sum, 3, *hold (back)*

repudium, -dī, *n.*, *renouncement of marriage contract*

re-quīro, -quīsīuī, -quīsītum, 3, *look for*

rēs, reī, *f.*, *matter, property, interest, affair, business*

re-scindō, -scidī, -scissum, 3, *rescind, annul*

re-scīscō, -sci(u)ī, scītum, 3, *get to know*

re-scrībō, -scrīpsī, -scrīptum, 3, *pay back*

re-sistō, -stitī, 3, *intr.*, *stop*

re-spiciō, -spexī, -spectum, 3, *look back (at), consider, regard*

re-spondeō, -spondī, -spōnsum, 2, *answer*

respōnsum, -ī, *n.*, *answer, reply*

re-stinguō, -stīnxī, -stīnctum, 3, *quench*

restis, *acc.* -im, *f.*, *rope, halter*

re-stituō, -uī, -ūtum, 3, *restore*

restō, restitī, 1, *remain, am left over*

re-supīnō, 1, *bring back*

rēte, -is, *n.*, *net*

re-tineō, -tinuī, -tentum, 2, *keep, hold back*

re-trahō, -trāxī, -tractum, 3, *drag back*

re-uereor, 2, *respect*

re-uocō, 1, *call back*

rēx, rēgis, *m.*, *king, patron*

rīdeō, rīsī, rīsum, 2, *laugh*

rīdiculus, -a, -um, *laughable, absurd*

ringor, rictus sum, 3, *bare the teeth*

rogitō, 1, *ask*

rogō, 1, *ask*

rūfus, -a, -um, *red, red-headed*

rūmor, -ōris, *m.*, *talk*

rūrsum, *advb.*, *back, in turn*

rūs, rūris, *n.*, *the country*

sacruficō, 1, *sacrifice*

saepe, *often*

saeuidicus, -a, -um, *furious*

saeuos, -a, -om, *fierce, grim*

saltem, *at least*

salueō, 2, *used in salutations*; salue, saluete, *greetings!*

saluos, -a, -om, *safe (and sound)*

salūtō, 1, *greet*

sānē, *very, to be sure*

sānus, -a, -um, *sane*

sapiēns, -ntis, *wise*

sapientia, -ae, *wisdom*

sapiō, 3, *am wise*

sat, satis, *quite, enough*

satietās, -ātis, *f.*, *one's fill*

satin, = *satisne*

satius, *comp. advb.*, *better*

scapulae, -ārum, *shoulder-blades*

scelus, -eris, *n.*, *sin, wickedness, crime, rascal*

sciēns, -entis, *knowing, skilful*

scīlicet, *advb.*, *for certain, surely, of course*

sciō, 4, *know, know how, can*

scītus, -a, -um, *sensible, reasonable, good-looking*

scopulus, -ī, *rock*

scrībo, scrīpsī, scrīptum, 3, *write, compose, bring (an action)*

scrīptūra, -ae, *composition, style*

scrūpulus, -ī, *lit.*, *a small stone; cause for doubt, 'spoke in the wheel', 'fly in the ointment'*

sē, *third person reflexive pronoun*

sector, 1, *follow, pursue*

secundus, -a, -um, *favourable*

secus, *otherwise*

sed, *but*

sedeō, sēdī, 2, *sit*

sēdulō, *diligently, zealously*

semel, *once*

semper, *always*

senectūs, -ūtis, *f.*, *old age*

senex, senis, *old man*

sententia, -ae, *opinion, judgement; ex sententiā, satisfactor(il)y*

sentiō, sēnsī, sēnsum, 4, *feel, realize, am aware of, know about it*

sepeliō, sepultum, 4, *bury*

sequor, secūtus sum, 3, *follow, go with, attend*

sermō, -ōnis, *m.*, *conversation*

seruiō, 4, *am a slave*

seruitūs, -ūtis, *f.*, *slavery*

seruō, 1, *keep, save*

seruos, -ī, *slave*

sescentī, -ae, -a, *six hundred, hundreds of*, 668n.

sī, *if*

sīc, *so, as follows, thus*

silentium, -tī, *n.*, *silence*

sileō, 2, *am silent*

similis, -e, *like*

simul, *at once*

simultās, -ātis, *f.*, *anger, hostility*

sīn, *but if*

sine, *prep.*, *without*

singulātim, *advb.*, *one by one*

sinō, sīuī, situm, 3, *place, leave, allow, let be*

siquidem, *if indeed*

sīs = si uis, *if you please*

sobrīnus, -i, *cousin on the mother's side*

sōdēs = si audes, *(if you) please*

soleō, solitus sum, 2, *am accustomed to*

sollicitūdō, -inis, *f.*, *anxiety*

soluō, soluī, solūtum, 3, *pay*

sōlus, -a, -um, *alone, only*

somnium, -nī, *n.*, *dream, moonshine*

spatium, -tī, *space, room, time*

spernō, sprēuī, sprētum, 3, *scorn, fall out with*

spērō, 1, *hope*

spēs, speī, *f.*, *hope, expectation*

spondeō, spopondī, spōnsum, 2, *betroth*

st! *interj.*, *calling for silence*, 743n.

statim, *regularly*

sterculīnum, -ī, *n.*, *muck-heap*

stimulus, -ī, *goad*

stō, stetī, 1, *stand, succeed, support*

strēnuos, -a, -om, *active, diligent*

studeō, 2, *am eager*

studium, -dī, *n.*, *calling, profession, zeal*

stultitia, -ae, *folly, foolishness*

stultus, -a, -um, *foolish*

suādeō, suāsī, suāsum, 2, *urge*

suāsus (4 *decl.*), *persuasion*

suāuis, -e, *sweet, pleasant*

sub-iciō, -iēcī, -iectum, 3, *whisper, prompt*

subitō, *suddenly*

subitus, -a, -um, *sudden*, 200n.

sub-olet, 2, *there is an inkling*

sub-ueniō, -uēnī, -uentum, 4, *help*

suc-centuriātus, -ī, *soldier in reserve*

sūdō, 1, *sweat*

sum, *archaic form of* eum (*is*),
 1028n.
summa, -ae, *sum total*
summus, -a, -um, *highest, greatest,
 very great*
sūmō, sumpsī, sumptum, 3, *take,
 borrow*
sumptus (4 *decl.*), *cost, expense*
suō, 3, *sew, devise*
suos, -a, -om, (*his, her, its, their*)
 own
supellex, supellectilis, *f.*, *furniture*
superbē, *haughtily, arrogantly*
super-sum, -fuī, -esse, *am over,
 superfluous*
superus, -a, -um, *above*
supplex, -icis, *suppliant*
supplicium, -cī, *n.*, *punishment*
suscēnseō, 2, *am angry*
sus-cipiō, -cēpī, -ceptum, 3, *undertake, take up, acknowledge· as
 one's own child*
sus-pendō, -dī, -sum, 3, *hang up;*
 suspēnsō gradū, *on tip-toe*
sus-tineō, -tinuī, -tentum, 2, *support*
suus, *see* suos

taceō, 2, *hold my tongue, am silent*
tacitus, -a, -um, *silent, in silence*
taedet, 2, *it bores, sickens*
talentum (*Gk.* τάλαντον), -ī, *n.*,
 talent (= 60 *minae*)
tam, *as much, so much, so, as well*
tamen, *nevertheless, yet*
tametsī, *although*
tandem, *at length; also used in indignant questions,* 231n.
tangō, tetigī, tāctum, 3, *touch*
tantō opere, *so much*

tantummodo, *only*
tantundem, *just so much*
tantus, -a, -um, *so much, so great,
 as much, as great*
tēgulae, -ārum, *tiles*
temerē, *rashly, without cause, by
 chance*
temperāns, -antis, *heedful*
temptō, I, *test*
tempus, -oris, *n.*, *time, fitting time,
 opportunity*
tendō, 3, *stretch, set*
teneō, 2, *hold, understand*
tennitur, *archaic form of* tenditur
tenuis, -e, *thin, poor*
tenuiter, *poorly*
terra, -ae, *land*
testimōnium, -nī, *n.*, *evidence*
testis, -is, *c.*, *witness*
timeō, 2, *fear*
timidus, -a, -um, *fearful*
timor, -ōris, *m.*, *fear*
tolerō, I, *bear, put up with*
tōnstrīna, -ae, *barber's shop*
tot, *so many*
tōtus, -a, -um, *whole*
tractō, I, *handle*
trā-dō, -didī, -ditum, 3, *hand over,
 transfer*
tranquillus, -a, -um, *calm*
trānsdere, 3 (*see* trādere)
trāns-eō, -iī, -itum, -īre, *cross*
trāns-igō, -ēgī, -āctum, 3, *transact,
 complete*
trēs, tria, *three*
trīduom, -ī, *n.*, (*space of*) *three days*
trīgintā, *thirty*
tristis, -e, *out of sorts, glum*
triumphō, I, (*win a*) *triumph*
tū, *you* (*sing.*)

tum, *then, moreover*

tumultus, -ī (4 *decl.*), *uproar, disturbance*

tuos, -a, -om, *your, yours*

turba, -ae, *trouble, disturbance, uproar*

turpis, -e, *shameful, disgraceful*

tūte, *emphatic form of* tu

tūtor, 1, *guard, protect, look after*

tūtus, -a, -um, *safe*

ualeō, 2, *am in health*; uale, ualete, *good-bye*

uānitās, -ātis, *f.*, *fickleness, unreliability*

uāpulō, 1, *get a thrashing*

ubi, *where, wherein, with whom*

uehō, uexī, uectum, 3, *carry, bring*

uel, *either, or, if you like*

uendō, -didī, -ditum, 3, *sell*

uenia, -ae, *leave, permission*

ueniō, uēnī, uentum, 4, *come*

uenter, -tris, *m.*, *belly*

uerberō, -ōnis, *m.*, *rogue, rascal (one who deserves a whipping)*

uerbum, -ī, *n.*, *word*; uerba do, *cheat*

uerēcundus, -a, -um, *bashful, modest*

uereor, 2, *fear*

uērum, *but*; uērum tamen, *nevertheless*

uērus, -a, -um, *true*

uestītus (4 *decl.*), *clothing*

uetō, uetuī, uetitum, 1, *forbid*

uetus, -eris, *old*

uia, -ae, *way*

uīcīnia, -ae, *neighbourhood*

uicissim, *in turn*

uideō, uīdī, uīsum, 2, *see, consider, look to*

uideor, uīsus sum, 2, *seem*; uidētur, *it seems good*

uīlis, -e, *cheap*

uīlitās, -ātis, *f.*, *cheapness*

uīn = uisne

uincibilis, -e, *likely to win*

uincō, uīcī, uictum, 3, *overcome, win, prove*

uīnolentus, -a, -um, *drunk*

uiolenter, *violently*

uir, uirī, *man, husband*

uirgō, -inis, *maiden, girl*

uirīlis, -e, *manly*

uirtūs, -ūtis, *f.*, *manliness, valour, virtue*

uīs, acc. uim, *f.*, *violence, quantity*

uīsō, uīsī, uīsum, 3, *go to see*

uīta, -ae, *life, way of life, livelihood*

uituperō, 1, *blame, censure*

uīuō, uīxī, uīctum, 3, *live*

uīuos, -a, -om, *alive, living*

uix, *barely, scarcely, hardly*

uixdum, *scarcely yet*

ulcīscor, ultus sum, 3, *avenge, punish*

ulcus, -eris, *n.*, *sore*

ulterior, -ius, *further, beyond*

ultimus, -a, -um, *furthest, last, end of*

ultrō, *actually*

umerus, -ī, *shoulder*

umquam, *ever*

ūnā, *advb.*, *together*

unciātim, *ounce by ounce*

unde, *whence, from whom, from which*

unguō, ūnxī, ūnctum, 3, *anoint*

ūnicus, -a, -um, *only*

ūniuorsus, -a, -um, *whole, all together*

ūnus, -a, -um, *one, sole*

uocō, 1, *call, invite*

uolō, uoluī, uelle, *irreg., am ready, am willing*

uoltus (4 *decl.*), *face*

uoluntās, -ātis, *f., will, good-will*

uolup, *archaic neut. adj., pleasing, pleasurable*

uorsūra, -ae, *money borrowed to pay a debt*

uortō, uortī, uorsum, 3, (*make to*) *turn*

uoster, -tra, -trum, *your, yours*

uōx, uōcis, *f., voice*

usque, *perpetually, continuously, all the way*

ūsus (4 *decl.*), *need, experience*

ut, *how, when, as, that, in order that, on condition that*

uterque, utraque, utrumque, *each of two, both*

uti, = ut

ūtibilis, -e, *useful*

utinam, *particle of wishing, would that!*

ūtor, ūsus sum, 3, *use, make use of, experience*

utut, *conj., however*

uxor, -ōris, *f., wife*